Outstanding Dissertations in

ECONOMICS

A Continuing Garland Research Series

The Labor Market Experience of Workers Displaced and Relocated by Plant Shutdowns:

The General Foods Case

David Bruce Lipsky

Garland Publishing, Inc.
New York & London, 1979

Library of Congress Cataloging in Publication Data

Lipsky, David B 1939–
The labor market experience of workers displaced and relocated by plant shutdowns.

(Outstanding dissertations in economics)
Originally presented as the author's thesis, Massachusetts Institute of Technology, 1967.
Bibliography: p.
1. Food industry and trade—United States—Employees—Case studies. 2. Plant shutdowns—United States—Case studies. 3. Employees, Relocation of—United States—Case studies. 4. General Foods Corporation. I. Title. II. Series.
HD5718.F72U54 1979 331.1'3786-400973
78-75062
ISBN 0-8240-4140-2

All volumes in this series are printed on acid-free, 250-year-life paper.

Printed in the United States of America.

Preface

The Labor Market Experience of Workers Displaced and Relocated by Plant Shutdowns: The General Foods Experience

David B. Lipsky
Professor
New York State School of
Industrial & Labor Relations
Cornell University

June 1979

In 1964 a vice president of the General Foods Corporation came to Harvard University to make a presentation in a Wednesday afternoon seminar series run by that eminence grise of industrial relations, John Dunlop. The vice president discussed the impending shutdown and relocation of four venerable plants in General Foods' Jell-O Division, focusing particularly on the rather extraordinary policies the corporation was implementing to facilitate the adjustment of the 1800 employees who would be displaced by the shutdowns.

Professor Dunlop, intrigued by the implications of the corporation's innovative policies, concluded that the General Foods experience would be an excellent graduate student thesis topic. Dunlop did not, at that time, have a graduate student prepared to undertake such a study. (Two of his students, Peter Doeringer and Michael Piore, were already planning to do dissertations that eventually would result in their well-known book on "dual labor markets.") Not wishing to let a golden opportunity escape the grasp of an aspiring student, Professor Dunlop contacted Professor Charles Myers of M.I.T. and asked Professor Myers whether he had a graduate student who might be interested in studying the General Foods experience. At that moment I was considering potential thesis topics, hoping to identify a project that I might launch in the fall of 1964. When Professor Myers approached me about the possibility of studying the General Foods case, I knew at once that I had found my topic. I had not been at the Harvard seminar, but the description that Myers, and later Dunlop, gave me of the unfolding General Foods story convinced me of the potential value of studying this particular case.

Research on plant shutdowns and worker displacement has a long and fruitful history in labor economics. Indeed, Professor Myers himself, in collaboration with George Shultz, had done an important study of workers displaced by plant shutdowns in the late 1940s.[1] But almost all of these previous studies had been of plant closures that did not involve any particular effort by employers (or, indeed, unions) to cushion the effect of the closure on the affected workers. The General Foods case was unique in that the corporation guaranteed all of its displaced employees a job at a new production facility being constructed in Dover, Delaware. The corporation not only guaranteed a job, but also offered to pay for all the costs connected with its employees' relocation, including the costs of moving household furnishings, closing and brokerage fees on the sale and purchase of homes, expenses incurred by the employee and his family during the trip to their new home, interim wages during the move, the lease cancellation costs incurred by employees who rented apartments and homes, and so on. The corporation even offered free trips to employees who wished to explore the Dover community and search for new living quarters prior to moving.

In sum, the corporation attempted to reduce the monetary costs of employee relocation to zero. For employees who elected to terminate and remain behind, the corporation offered generous severance allowances and some job counselling.

Why did General Foods adopt this elaborate set of policies? Essentially, there were two reasons: First, the corporation worried about its ability to recruit a large work force in the small community of Dover, particularly about the availability of workers with the skills and training necessary to the new plant's production process. To the extent that the corporation could persuade the workers in the old plants to transfer to the new Dover location, it could save the costs associated with recruiting, selecting, placing, and training a new work force. Moreover, if General Foods did not bring a large complement of workers into Dover, it would need to compete with employers already in the area for workers, and this competition would put upward pressure on the Dover wage structure.

Second, General Foods was sensitive to its image as an employer and fearful that a series of plant shutdowns that left the displaced employees without protection would result in bad publicity, particularly in the affected communities, and generate adverse feelings about its many consumer products. Thus, the corporation's generous policies were not entirely the product of altruism; they were based on a rational calculation of costs and benefits.

The better part of the first half of my thesis chronicles the development of the personnel policies used by General Foods in the shutdown and relocation of its production facilities, analyzes the rationale for the corporation's policies, and attempts to place the selection of these policies in the context of the range of choices open to companies (and unions) that face the impending displacement of a large number of workers. I was concerned with the logic of such policy choices, particularly from a company's standpoint, and sought to demonstrate that seemingly generous policies could represent a rational choice for a company interested in cost minimization. I hasten to add that I never could prove that General Foods' policies constituted the most economical or efficient means of achieving its objectives, since so many of the relevant variables (such as company "good will" and hypothetical savings in recruitment costs) were virtually unquantifiable.

The second half of the thesis analyzes the experience of samples of workers who elected either to relocate with the corporation or to terminate and remain in their home community. Of the 1800 employees at the four old plants, 423 (23.5 percent) transferred to Dover; but only 179 (14.2 percent) of the hourly employees compared to 253 (42.3 percent) of all salaried workers transferred. Other factors that were discovered to be related to an employee electing the transfer option were age, sex, marital status, number of dependents, education, years of seniority, years of residence in the old area, and home ownership. Employees who transferred tended to be younger, male, married with several dependents, more educated, more senior workers, who had been residents of their communities for shorter periods of time. Surprisingly, those who transferred also tended to be home owners. In sum, although less than a quarter of the workers relocated to Dover, those who did were the "cream" of the corporation's workers -- precisely the kind of worker the corporation thought it would have difficulty recruiting in the Dover area. General Foods had hoped that a larger number would elect transfer. (As I noted in the thesis, one assistant personnel manager told me he expected 90 percent of the workers to transfer!) On balance, however, the corporation's policies worked in the desired direction, easing some of the company's initial problems at a large, new production facility.

The workers who stayed behind tended to have a difficult time finding new jobs. The terminated workers averaged 18.6 weeks of unemployment in a period when the national average was about 14 weeks. About 60 percent of the terminated workers were unemployed for a period in excess of 16 weeks. The thesis provides a detailed analysis of the experience of the terminated workers, using a regression model to explain weeks of unemployment. This analysis shows that the workers who experienced the most difficulty gaining reemployment were those who were older, less educated, less skilled, female, and single.

All the implications of these findings were regrettably not apparent to me when I wrote my thesis. It was only later -- when I came to write an article based on the thesis -- that I realized the full significance of my empirical findings, for a comparison of the workers who relocated with the terminated workers who suffered the most protracted periods of unemployment described two different sets of workers with nearly (but not completely) opposite characteristics. On this basis I could conclude that workers most likely to benefit from the protection of the interplant-transfer system were least likely to exercise the option of relocation and that workers who least needed the protection were most likely to move.[2] Note that this conclusion is based solely on the criterion of expected weeks of unemployment after termination. In other words, if the workers who elected relocation had, instead, chosen termination, their unemployment experience would have been significantly better than that of the workers who actually did terminate.

This conclusion can be demonstrated by means of an exercise I did not perform in the thesis. By plugging the mean values of the characteristics of the relocated workers into the regressions run on the experience of the sample of terminated workers, the expected duration of unemployment for the relocated workers can be estimated. (This exercise assumes, of course, that the structural relationship between the dependent variable, weeks of unemployment, and the independent variables, represented by the regression coefficients of these variables, can be applied to the sample of relocated workers.) The results of performing this exercise indicate that the expected duration of unemployment for the sample of relocated workers was between 13 and 16 weeks, depending on the exact specification of the regression used to make the calculation. This can be compared to the mean of 18.6 weeks actually experienced by the terminated sample.

In a "comment" on my article, Thomas Kochan argued that it was enough to know that salaried employees tended to relocate and that hourly employees tended to terminate to conclude that the relocated workers would have had a better labor market experience than the terminated workers.[3] In fact, however, differences in the occupational status of the two samples account for very little of the estimated difference in the samples' actual and expected unemployment duration. It would be closer to the truth to argue that it was sufficient to know the difference in the age distributions of the two samples to conclude that their unemployment experience would be significantly different. Age was one of the most important determinants of relocation and it was clearly the most significant variable explaining the terminated workers' length of unemployment: younger workers tended to relocate, older workers tended to have a very difficult time gaining reemployment. In fact, however, it is the combination of factors (such as age, sex, and occupational status) differentiating one group from the other that fully explains the differences in their actual and expected unemployment experience.

It follows that if the General Foods experience is any guide, the use of an interplant transfer system can serve only as a limited way of avoiding the hardship of worker displacement after plant shutdown. It would be better from the viewpoint of the workers affected by plant shutdowns to offer them greater protection for the period following their displacement, rather than to devote corporate resources to the enhancement of relocation opportunities. In particular, the older worker suffers particularly when he (or she) is displaced and would benefit greatly from company and union efforts designed to provide protection following termination. For example, higher severance benefits, intensive job counselling, retraining programs, and maintenance of health insurance and retirement programs beyond termination would be especially valuable forms of protection for the older worker.

But if this conclusion is valid, then employers who seek to develop rational policies to handle plant shutdowns and relocations face an essential dilemma. If the employer is constructing a new facility in a small and distant labor market, it may be in his best interest to induce as many of his employees to transfer as he possibly can. On the other hand, it is in the interest of the displaced employees to be provided with as much protection as possible against the hardships of termination. If such protection is offered by the employer, however, he makes the termination option that much more attractive to his employees and further reduces the probability of inducing a large number to transfer. As a generalization, then, in a situation of the General Foods type, the more attractive the relocation opportunity is compared to the termination option, the more the system tends to benefit the employer. Conversely, the more attractive the termination option is compared to the relocation opportunity, the more the system tends to protect the terminated employees and defeat the employer's objective.

Of course, employers in the United States are under no obligation to provide either relocation opportunities or protection for terminated employees, and it is safe to say that most do not. Furthermore, there are no comprehensive statistics on exactly how many plants shut down each year, let alone how many of these shutdowns constitute a transfer of operations from one area to another. There is, in fact, considerable debate about the seriousness of the plant relocation problem. In one study, it was estimated that a mere 1.5 percent of employment losses in the northern states for the period 1969-72 were the result of the "out-migration" of businesses and plants. The author of this study concluded that any attempt to regulate "runaway plants" would be "a solution to a nonexistent problem."[4] Many plant shutdowns occur because of the total cessation of an owner's business operations. Others occur because of the transfer of capital from the United States to a foreign country. Under such circumstances any consideration of relocating the affected workers becomes impractical, to say the least.

On the other hand, many plant relocations are accompanied by a legal change in the name of the firm, and only careful investigation can reveal whether the closing of an old plant is linked to the construction or expansion of a plant in another region of the country. One such detailed study concluded that plant relocations in Michigan accounted for a loss of 30,000 jobs in that state between 1970 and 1974.[5]

Whether the problem of plant shutdowns and relocations is serious or not, it is clear that currently there exists more concern about the phenomenon than ever before. When I did my thesis research in the mid 1960s, the spectre of automation and technological change made the topic of worker displacement a ripe and voguish one. But in succeeding years, a robust economy fueled by the Vietnam War and the press of other social problems eclipsed the concern for workers displaced by plant closures. Now a combination of circumstances has caused a resurgence of interest in the subject.

Clearly one reason for the revival of interest is the concern for the movement of industry out of the north and midwest and into the "sunbelt." This movement has been occurring over a long period of time, and I did not fully realize the extent to which the General Foods movement from Massachusetts and New York to a border state was a perfect exemplar of a much larger, ongoing experience.

Another growing concern is the effect of foreign competition on the life and death of our industrial establishments. This concern was in part manifested in the Trade Act of 1974, which provides liberal allowances, a full range of employment assistance services, training, and job search and relocation allowances to workers displaced because of increased foreign imports. In the first three years of the Trade Act's existance nearly 300,000 workers received benefits.[6]

A third reason for renewed interest is the belief that the growing concentration of American industry, particularly the rise of multinational and conglomerate corporations, has made it possible for major employers to change the geographic location of their plants with greater ease and perhaps greater frequency. General Foods, for example, is a major multibillion dollar multinational, and the closing of four plants and investment of $50 million in a new facility represented hardly more than a ripple in the tide of the corporation's affairs.

A fourth factor is the realization that, with the baby boom generation now in its thirties, we can look forward to a protracted "graying" of the labor force. An older labor force is a less mobile, less flexible labor force -- a fact that I hope my thesis helped to substantiate. Displacements caused by plant shutdowns clearly cause a greater problem for older than younger workers. Also, the growing number of females in the labor force and the concomitant increase in two-earner households serve to reduce the potential geographic mobility of the work force, making worker adjustment to plant shutdowns all the more difficult.

In sum, changes in the structure of both the demand for and the supply of labor have focused new attention on the problems caused by plant shutdowns and relocations. This renewed concern helps to explain why Congress in recent years has sought to provide protection for workers displaced by shutdowns, particularly when those shutdowns are the result of federal statutes and regulations. In addition to the Trade Act of 1974, Congress has provided protection of various forms (which may include, but is not limited to, severance benefits, supplementary unemployment benefits, relocation allowances, and training and placement assistance) to the following groups of workers:[7]

- railroad workers displaced by the consolidation of the northeast rail system into Conrail.
- airline workers displaced by the increase in competition brought about by the deregulation of the airlines.

- health care employees displaced by federal promotion of noninstitutional forms of treatment of both mentally ill and disabled people.
- defense workers displaced by military base closures or cutbacks and terminations in defense contracts.
- lumber workers displaced as a result of the expansion of the Redwood National Park authorized by Congress in 1968.

Legislation protecting the redwood workers, which was passed by Congress in 1978, is interesting because it provides more generous benefits to the affected workers than any other measure to date. Covered workers are provided with supplemental unemployment benefits equal to the level of their earnings prior to the expansion of the Redwood National Park. They are also permitted to maintain their fringe benefits, including health insurance and pension rights; they are provided with retraining, job-search allowances, and relocation allowances; and they are given preferential hiring rights to all jobs that become available in the expanded park. These benefits are available, on the basis of seniority, to covered workers for up to six years. Only 1200 workers are covered by the 1978 legislation; however, Congress may find it difficult in the future to be less generous with other groups of workers displaced by similar federal government actions.

Congress is in the process of considering other legislation that would protect diverse groups of displaced workers. One bill introduced in a recent session is particularly worth mentioning. The National Employment Priorities Act, first introduced in Congress in 1977, would establish a National Employment Relocation Administration (NERA) within the Department of Labor. Under this act, companies would be required to file notices with NERA of their intent to to close or transfer operations one year in advance of such action. Workers displaced because of plant shutdown or relocation would be eligible for income maintenance benefits, maintenance of health and pension benefits, relocation allowances, retraining, and early retirement benefits. In the event of a plant relocation, displaced employees would have the right to continue in their jobs at the new location. In a word, the National Employment Priorities Act, if passed by Congress, would require all relocating employers to provide their employees with an array of benefits and protections even more extensive than those provided by General Foods in the mid 1960s.

If the National Employment Priorities Act is to be given serious consideration, then the lessons of the General Foods experience (and similar experiences) must be weighed carefully. There are critical issues of efficiency and equity entangled in all such policy proposals. It may be a laudable objective to provide, through public means, protections and benefits for displaced workers, but we should certainly not be blind to the implications of such policies.

A final note: When asked to consent to the publication of my thesis, I frankly had mixed feelings. It is a sobering experience to read again one's Ph.D. thesis twelve years after its completion. I see now flaws and limitations I did not see then. "Vanity," according to Joseph Conrad, "plays lurid tricks with our memory." Properly chastened, I no longer can regard my work as the paragon of research I once thought it to be. I make no apology, however, and ask the reader's indulgence. However imperfect the researcher, there remain, nevertheless, important lessons in his research.

FOOTNOTES

1. Charles A. Myers and George P. Shultz, The Dynamics of a Labor Market (New York: Prentice-Hall, 1951).

2. David B. Lipsky, "Interplant Transfer and Terminated Workers: A Case Study," Industrial and Labor Relations Review, Vol. 23, No. 2, January 1970, pp. 191-206.

3. Thomas A. Kochan, "Interplant Transfer and Terminated Workers: A Case Study - Comment," Industrial and Labor Relations Review, Vol. 24, No. 3, April 1971, pp. 442-446.

4. Richard McKenzie, Restrictions on Business Mobility (Washington, D.C.: The American Enterprise Institute, 1979).

5. This study is discussed in Robert Howard, "Runaway Plants," The New Republic, May 26, 1979, pp. 16-19.

6. U.S. Department of Labor, Office of the Assistant Secretary for Policy, Evaluation and Research, "Public Policy and Economic Dislocation of Employees," October 1978, unpublished paper.

7. For a detailed discussion of all the policies discussed here, see "Public Policy and Economic Dislocation of Employees," op. cit.

THE LABOR MARKET EXPERIENCE OF WORKERS DISPLACED AND RELOCATED BY PLANT SHUTDOWNS: THE GENERAL FOODS CASE

by

DAVID BRUCE LIPSKY

B.S., Cornell University
(1961)

SUBMITTED IN PARTIAL FULFILLMENT
OF THE REQUIREMENTS FOR THE
DEGREE OF DOCTOR OF
PHILOSOPHY

at the

MASSACHUSETTS INSTITUTE OF TECHNOLOGY

May, 1967

Signature of Author ....
Department of Economics, May 22, 1967

Certified by ....
Thesis Supervisor

Accepted by ....
Chairman, Departmental Committee on Graduate Students

ABSTRACT

"The Labor Market Experience of Workers Displaced
and Relocated by Plant Shutdowns:
The General Foods Case"

by

David B. Lipsky

Submitted to the Department of Economics on May 12, 1967, in partial fulfillment of the requirements for the degree of Doctor of Philosophy in Economics.

This study enalyzes the experience of workers affected by the shutdown and relocation of four General Foods plants over the period 1962-65. The General Foods case was selected for detailed examination because of the rather unique set of personnel policies used by the company to cushion the impact of the shutdowns on the affected workers.

Chapter I examines the implications of the General Foods case in the context of recent policy developments in the private and public spheres designed to facilitate the labor market adjustment of workers affected by plant shutdowns.

Chapter II presents the methodological considerations underlying this case study, including the selection of the samples to be interviewed, the construction of the questionnaires, and the actual process of interviewing.

Chapter III provides some background information on the corporation's shutdown and consolidation decision. The nature and characteristics of the corporation, the plants, and the communities affected by the decision are discussed.

In Chapter IV the personnel policies used by General Foods to provide relocation opportunities and severance benefits to affected workers are examined in detail. In essence, every worker at the shutdown plants was guaranteed a job at the new facility with virtually all the expenses of relocating reimbursed by the company. Alternatively, the worker could elect to terminate and receive a severance allowance based on age and seniority. A classification of personnel policies for plant shutdowns is developed in order to provide a more general framework for the understanding of such policies.

In Chapter V the personnel policies and problems of starting the new Dover plant, including placement, wages, seniority, and union relations, are discussed. Nearly 30 per cent of the affected employees were able to remain with the corporation despite the plant shutdowns. However, only about 15 per cent of the 1,200 hourly employees relocated to Dover. Nevertheless, the proportion of General Foods employees electing transfer were comparable to, if not a bit higher than, the proportions transferring in other reported cases of plant shutdowns.

In Chapter VI an attempt is made to delineate the determinants of worker relocation by comparing the characteristics of the General Foods relocated workers to those of the displaced workers and to migrants in general. Younger, higher skilled male workers were most likely to relocate. However, the transfers differed in several important respects from migrants in general. For example, a greater proportion of blue-collar workers relocated than one might expect, given the migration pattern for the population as a whole. Other factors, such as education, income, past mobility, seniority and home ownership were also considered.

In Chapter VII the impact of the move on the relocated workers is examined. The workers' evaluation of certain company policies, such as advance notice and the provision of moving expenses, was favorable. About 30 per cent of the relocated workers had sought alternative employment before moving to Dover. In addition, the relocation triggered a good deal of movement into and out of the labor force by the wives of the transferred workers. The workers expressed general but not complete satisfaction with their new jobs, the new plants, and the new community.

In Chapter VIII the experience of the displaced employees is analyzed. Particular attention is devoted to an assessment of those factors important to the re-employment of the displaced workers. Age, sex, and occupational status were most strongly related to length of unemployment. Number of dependents and alternative sources of income were also significantly related. Other factors, such as seniority, education and severance pay were only weakly related to duration of unemployment.

Finally, some conceptual and administrative problems of interplant transfer systems are discussed in the concluding chapter.

Thesis Supervisor: Charles A. Myers
Title: Professor of Industrial Relations
Massachusetts Institute of Technology

ACKNOWLEDGMENTS

I wish to acknowledge a special debt of gratitude to Professor Charles A. Myers, chairman of my thesis committee, not only for his helpful criticism and guidance on the preparation of this thesis, but also for his support and encouragement through the four years of my graduate education. To the other members of my committee, Professors Douglass V. Brown and Abraham J. Siegel, I acknowledge my appreciation for their cooperation and helpful suggestions.

I should also like to thank Professor John T. Dunlop of the Department of Economics at Harvard University, who initially suggested the topic as a worthwhile subject for study, and provided needed assistance in my research. I extend thanks also to Professor Robert Evans, Jr., now of Brandeis University, for his useful suggestions.

This thesis would not have been possible without the cooperation of literally scores of General Foods employees, past and present, too numerous to name individually. However, I should be remiss if I did not extend special thanks to Mr. Harry Chandler, former Personnel Manager of the Jell-O Division, and currently Personnel Manager of the Maxwell House Division of the General Foods

Corporation, whose thoughtful interest and continuing support were essential to the completion of this project.

I wish to acknowledge my appreciation to the Industrial Relations Section and the Alfred P. Sloan School of Management at M.I.T., and to the National Science Foundation, for their financial support of the dissertation research.

The form and presentation of the manuscript have been improved by the excellent typing of Miss Beatrice Rogers.

To my wife, Sandy, I owe a debt which will take more than a lifetime to repay. Not only did she type the earlier drafts of this manuscript and bear more than her share of the rigors of graduate student life, but she provided the love, understanding and encouragement which enabled me to continue with the project to the end.

TABLE OF CONTENTS

CHAPTER PAGE

CHAPTER	PAGE

LIST OF TABLES

TABLE		PAGE

CHAPTER V

CHAPTER VI

TABLE		PAGE

TABLE | PAGE

TABLE | PAGE

TABLE | PAGE

CHAPTER I

INTRODUCTION: THE SIGNIFICANCE OF THE GENERAL FOODS EXPERIENCE

The major purpose of this study is to provide an economic and sociological analysis of the experience of displaced and relocated workers. The occasion for the study is the shutdown and consolidation of four Eastern plants in the Jell-O Division of the General Foods Corporation into a new facility located in Dover, Delaware. The four old plants were: (1) The Walter Baker Chocolate Company in Dorchester, Massachusetts; (2) The Franklin Baker Cocoanut Company in Hoboken, New Jersey; (3) The Minute Tapioca and Rice plant in Orange, Massachusetts; and (4) The Jell-O Gelatin dessert plant in LeRoy, New York.

Chapters III, IV, and V include a discussion of the development and implementation of management policies, particularly with regard to personnel, to handle the transition from the old plants to the new facility. In this section, and in succeeding sections as well, some attempt will be made to gauge the effectiveness of these policies and to assess their influence on the decisions and experiences of the employees. Chapters VI and VII are given over to an analysis of those workers who chose to move with the company to the new production facility. Our concern in this section is to specify the determinants of relocation, and to analyze the process of, and adjustment to, relocation of those workers who elected to move with the company. To carry out these objectives, a sample of transferred employees was interviewed in Dover, Delaware.

In Chapter VIII the task of analyzing the unemployment experience and job-finding capabilities of those General Foods workers who elected to terminate their employment is undertaken. The analysis is based on a sample of displaced workers interviewed in the Boston area.

In an age of constant technological and industrial change, continuing research on all aspects of worker adjustments necessitated by such changes is of paramount importance. Further expansion of our knowledge leading to a deeper understanding of the problems connected with periods of transition in the lives of members of the working force is fundamental to the avoidance of unnecessary hardships connected with such periods, and to the intelligent development of management, union and government policies intended to ameliorate the process of labor-force adjustment to change.

In the specific research area of worker displacement, not to mention the more general area of labor mobility, the amount of research conducted has been overwhelming.[1] Less is known about that special category of the geographically mobile worker -- the transferred employee.[2] Still less is known about the development of a management policy to facilitate employee transfers and terminations necessitated by the geographical shift of production facilities.[3]

---

[1]In the area of worker displacement, see the summary study by William Haber, et al., The Impact of Technological Change (Kalamazoo, Mich.: The W. E. Upjohn Institute for Employment Research, 1963), 62 pp. Two significant studies not summarized by Haber, et al., are Richard C. Wilcock and Walter H. Franke, Unwanted Workers (Glencoe, Ill.: The Free Press, 1963), 340 pp., and Irvin Sobel and Hugh Folk, "Labor Market Adjustment by Unemployed Older Workers," Employment Policy and the Labor Market (Berkeley and Los Angeles: University of California Press, 1965), Arthur M. Ross, ed., pp. 333-357. For a summary of the important work done in the general area of labor mobility, see Herbert S. Parnes, Research on Labor Mobility (New York: Social Science Research Council, Bulletin 65, 1954), 205 pp.

[2]See Norman M. Bradburn, Inter-Plant Transfer: the Sioux City Experience (Chicago: National Opinion Research Center, University of Chicago, May, 1964), 60 pp. On geographic mobility in general, see John B. Lansing, et al., The Geographic Mobility of Labor: A First Report (Ann Arbor, Mich.: Survey Research Center, 1963), 315 pp.

[3]Arnold R. Weber, "The Interplant Transfer of Displaced Employees," Adjusting to Technological Change (New York: Harper and Row, 1963), Gerald G. Somers, et al., eds., pp. 95-143; Arnold R. Weber and David P. Taylor, "Procedures for Employee Displacement: Advance Notice of Plant Shutdown," Journal of Business, Vol. 36, No. 3, July, 1963, pp. 302-315; George P. Shultz and Arnold R. Weber, Strategies for the Displaced Worker (New York: Harper and Row, 1966); and U. S. Department of Labor, Bureau of Employment Security, Work Force Adjustments to Technological Change: Selected Employer Procedures (Bulletin No. E-215, January, 1963).

This thesis attempts to fill some of the gaps in our knowledge and understanding of these areas by a detailed examination of one specific case involving plant shutdowns and the transfer of production operations.

While it is recognized that the General Foods experience is in many ways unique, the lessons of this case may have wider applicability. The General Foods case is representative of a new direction in the treatment of workers threatened with unemployment. It is unique in that it involved an extraordinary attempt by management to soften the period of transition for workers affected by the transfer of production facilities. But more particularly, it was unique in that management's major emphasis was an effort to persuade and encourage workers -- <u>both</u> blue collar and white collar -- to transfer to the corporation's new production site at company expense. This effort to induce the relocation of a large number of workers represents a relatively new departure in American employee relations.[4]

The history of managerial policy designed to facilitate worker adjustment to impending displacement is mostly one of blank pages

---

[4]Philip Taft, "Organized Labor and Technical Change: A Backward Look," Somers, <u>et al.</u>, <u>op. cit.</u>, p. 39. The terms "severance pay," "dismissal compensation" and "termination allowance" will be used interchangeably in this study.

prior to the rise of collective bargaining. In the 1920's, following the example set by Hart, Schaffner, and Marx and the Amalgamated Clothing Workers, adoption of a policy of severance pay for displaced employees became a common practice in American industry. Little was added to the arsenal of weapons to deal with worker displacement until the United Automobile Workers pioneered the use of supplementary unemployment benefits to handle worker lay-offs in the automobile industry. Over the last decade, growing concern with technological change has brought forth a spate of schemes to mitigate the impact of impending worker displacement. Most notable among these efforts was the attempt by the Armour Company and its unions to retrain workers displaced by plant shutdowns.[5] The general orientation of almost all policies -- whether private or public -- intended to enhance the worker's adaptive capacity to change is an attempt to furnish the worker with some means of adjusting to displacement _within a given labor market_. Policies designed to provide the worker with a financial buffer, to equip him with a new set of skills, to provide him with employment counseling, to induce industry to move into distressed areas, to promote community develop-

---

[5]See Weber, _op. cit._; Shultz and Weber, _op. cit._; Edwin Young, "The Armour Experience: A Case Study in Plant Shutdown," Somers, _et al._, _op. cit._, pp. 144-158; and James J. Healy, ed., _Creative Collective Bargaining_ (Englewood Cliffs, N. J.: Prentice-Hall, 1965), pp. 137-165.

ment efforts -- the list could be extended -- all rest on the premise that labor is fundamentally immobile, and that adjustment to change must be a strictly localized process. Only recently have attempts been made to develop policy on the basis of a slightly altered premise -- that labor is not necessarily immobile, and that adjustment to change need not be a burden carried only by the area affected. The attempt by General Foods to relocate an entire work force to a new area is an effort based on the alternative premise.

In the face of the continuous movement of production facilities and the threat of job elimination because of technological change, is the geographical relocation of workers a feasible and efficacious policy to use? Should we try to move the worker to the work?

As a part of public policy, such an approach has been used with some success by several European countries -- most notably Sweden, West Germany, Great Britain, Belgium, Holland and France.[6]

---

[6]For a full description of public relocation assistance programs in Western Europe, see Margaret S. Gordon, Retraining and Labor Market Adjustment in Western Europe (Washington: U. S. Department of Labor, Manpower Administration, Monograph No. 4, August, 1965), pp. 155-170 and U. S. Congress, Joint Economic Committee, Programs for Relocating Workers Used by Governments of Selected Countries (Economic Policies and Practices, Paper No. 8, 1966), 89th Congress, 2nd Session, 76 pp. Note that Italy is the only Western European country which does not use some form of relocation assistance as a part of public policy. See also Bertil Olsson, "Policy Implications of Technological Change in

(Footnote continued)

The most far-reaching policy is employed by Sweden. Rehn and Lundberg provide a brief description of Swedish policy:

> Geographical mobility from surplus areas to areas with excess demand for labor is encouraged through various grants and allowances. The employment office can in such cases pay travel expenses for a recruitment visit, for the actual move, and for monthly visits to the worker's home in case the family cannot follow the breadwinner immediately. Family allowances may also be granted for maintaining the extra household for nine months, with gradual reductions in the allowance. In addition, the moving worker can get "starting help" of 300 Sw. Kr. on condition that he stays in the new place for a minimum of three months. . . .[7]

Sweden, in contrast to other European countries, will move a worker when it is only likely that he will become unemployed. It is not necessary for him to be actually unemployed.[8]

However, it is clear that the relocation policies of Sweden and other European countries have not shaped vitally the mobility patterns of these countries, and that the massive immigration over the past decade of workers into the north and west of Europe from Turkey, Italy, Africa, and Greece has not been in response to such

---

(Footnote continued)

Western Europe," Somers, *et al.*, *op. cit.*, pp. 190-205, and "Obstacles to Labour Mobility and Social Problems of Resettlement: A Survey by the European Coal and Steel Community," *International Labour Review*, Vol. 76, No. 1, July, 1957, pp. 72-83.

[7]Gosta Rehn and Erik Lundberg, "Employment and Welfare: Some Swedish Issues," *Industrial Relations*, Vol. 2, No. 2, February, 1963, p. 8. Note that one American dollar equals about 5 Sw. Kr.

[8]Gordon, *op. cit.*, p. 156.

policies. As Gordon concludes, " . . . much more research is needed before their impact can be evaluated."[9]

In the United States the development of systems of interplant transfer of employees is now progressing apace in several important collective bargaining relationships -- most notably between the Steelworkers and the steel industry, International Harvester and the United Automobile Workers, and Ford, Chrysler, and General Motors and the UAW.[10] In a recent statement, the Automobile Manufacturers Association outlines the industry's policy on plant closings and transfers of major operations:

> Whenever management decides to close a plant or to transfer major operations, the union is informed in advance and a memorandum is negotiated regarding the rights of employees affected. The protective programs can be and are as varied as the needs of the employees involved. . . Employees who wish to continue their careers with the company and accept transfer to the new location retain full seniority and full rights under all benefit plans. To further encourage employee mobility, the transferred employees may be eligible for a moving allowance of up to $580.[11]

---

[9] *Ibid.*, p. 200.

[10] Weber, *op. cit.*, pp. 95-143; Richard A. Beaumont and Roy B. Helfgott, *Management, Automation and People* (New York: Industrial Relations Counselors, 1964), pp. 66-81.

[11] Automobile Manufacturers Association, "Technological Change and Employment in the Automotive Industry," a statement to the National Commission on Technology, Automation and Economic Progress, p. 5.

The 1962 agreement between the United States Steel Corporation and the USW contained significant provisions on the interplant transfer rights of steel workers. These rights were reaffirmed in the 1965 pact. Briefly, under the negotiated agreement, a steel employee, who meets the qualifications, shall be given "priority . . . over other applicants . . . for job vacancies . . . at other steel plants of the company located within a limited agreed-upon geographical region," provided that he file a written request with the company. Should he be assigned a job, the employee becomes eligible to receive a relocation allowance according to an agreed schedule which contains graduated amounts based on the geographical distance involved in the transfer.[12] The transfer rights of employees now in force in the automobile and steel industries are of a limited and elementary nature. Nevertheless, they signify the recognition by two major industries of the utility of lessening the barriers to geographical mobility by the provision to workers of the opportunity to relocate under certain prescribed conditions. As is made explicitly clear in Chapter IV, the transfer rights established for General Foods employees are much broader than those currently in effect in either the automobile or steel industries.

---

[12]Steelworkers of America, United, AFL-CIO, and United States Steel Corporation, Agreement between, September 1, 1965, Section 13M, but also see Section 13N.

In the area of public provision of relocation assistance to workers, the United States lags far behind most Western European nations. However, under the 1963 amendments to the Manpower Development and Training Act, a hesitant start has been made. The amendments authorize the Secretary of Labor to institute a program of "labor mobility demonstration projects" in order to assess the effectiveness of providing loans or grants (or both) to unemployed individuals to induce an increase in their geographical mobility. The program, extended to June 30, 1967, by the 1965 amendments to the MDTA, is only now past the gestation stage; apparently sixteen such "demonstration projects" have been conducted, and the results have not yet been analyzed.[13]

It appears, then, that we are moving strongly in the direction of encouraging, through public and private measures, the geographic relocation of workers in order to facilitate the dynamic adjustment of the labor market to continual change and flux. Recommendations are heard from many quarters that we should continue in this direction. For example, Beaumont and Helfgott write:

> What may be needed . . . are broad-based informational programs to acquaint members of the labor force with available work in other occupations and industries,

---

[13] U. S. Congress, Joint Economic Committee, *op. cit.*, pp. 42-54.

> as well as other localities. Beyond this, there may be need to consider means to finance relocation including workers' moving expenses and possibly buying out the equity in a home for those who are willing to relocate for new job opportunities. Schemes for increasing labor mobility are worth consideration. They contribute, if only in a minor way, to the solution of the problems of structural labor adjustment; more significantly, they help the worker to move to accept a job elsewhere -- a cheaper solution than bearing the continuing cost of supporting him as unemployed.[14]

Bakke states that it should be the objective of public policy to "provide the conditions in the labor market which make possible a truly free choice of jobs and workers."[15] Among the conditions he lists is:

> the reduction of restrictive costs of movement for individuals and their families so that movement otherwise desirable and acceptable to workers or employers is not hampered. There is no freedom to choose a job to which one cannot afford to move. . .[16]

However, it is not absolutely certain that the implications of a movement in the direction of encouraging the geographical mobility of labor are wholly beneficial. Before we decide that shaping public policy in this area on the Swedish model is desirable -- and before we decide that it is worth while encouraging employers

---

[14]Beaumont and Helfgott, op. cit., p. 323..

[15]E. Wight Bakke, A Positive Labor Market Policy (Columbus, Ohio: Charles E. Merrill, 1963), p. 63.

[16]Ibid., p. 65.

to assume more of the cost of worker relocation, either unilaterally or through collective bargaining arrangements -- it is vitally necessary that the answers to certain crucial questions be found.

Surprisingly, after years of research, there are still some fundamental questions about mobility that remain unanswered, and many specific questions about geographic mobility that remain unasked. For example: What is the optimum level of mobility for our economy? If we restrict our concern to geographic mobility, what level of movement is optimal from the viewpoint of our stated policy objectives of maximizing employment, economic growth and price stability? Is it better to encourage labor mobility, or the mobility of other factors of production, such as capital? What mix of movement by the factors is optimal? How should the costs of movement be allocated among the individual worker, the employer, and society? Are the benefits of induced geographic mobility greater or less than the costs, both monetary and otherwise? Of course, the answers to most of these questions would depend upon one's perspective. The answer might be quite different, depending on whether the worker's, the employer's, or society's welfare is considered.

Unfortunately, the nature of this study prevents us from attempting to answer most of these important questions. However, an attempt is made to present some evidence on the relative costs and benefits of geographic mobility for the worker and for the employer. Certainly, encouraging employers to adopt liberal policies of interplant transfer would be senseless if it were shown that these policies had proved to be ineffective and unnecessarily costly; and persuading workers to transfer to a new and strange area would be perilous if it were known that other workers following a similar course had not been able to make a successful adjustment. The General Foods experience provides an opportunity to investigate the feasibility and effectiveness of a liberal interplant transfer system from the viewpoint of the worker and the employer -- and indirectly of society.

CHAPTER II

THE DESIGN AND METHOD OF THE STUDY

A study of this nature presents numerous problems of methodology. It is not claimed that all of them have been solved; it is hoped that most of them have been recognized.

Design of the Research

Basically, this thesis is a case study. It is a case study in the sense that only the policies and personnel of one company are examined. Secondly, the thesis involves the use of survey techniques, including the selection of appropriate samples and the administration of both "structured" and "semi-structured" interviews.[1]

The case study is a time-honored method in the area of labor market research. Nevertheless, it can be argued that the case approach to the study of such problems has serious drawbacks. It is recognized that the minutiae of an isolated case are of interest, if at all, only to those directly involved in the case. However, the counter-argument can be made that only through knowledge of a specific case can understanding of the more general problem be obtained. Indeed, replication of such case studies is the social scientist's equivalent of

---

[1]Bernard Berelson and Gary A. Steiner, Human Behavior: An Inventory of Scientific Findings (New York: Harcourt, Brace and World, 1964), pp. 31-32.

the repeated laboratory experiment. Each "experiment" (*i.e.*, case) adds to our knowledge of the process involved and enhances our ability to isolate the "universals."

In addition, the study of a particular experience, such as that of General Foods, is the only way in which certain problems can be approached. On a more aggregated level the unique problems of the individual case often tend to disappear. For example, in this study there is an extensive analysis of the unemployment experience of the displaced worker. Yet on a more aggregated level -- even on the corporate level -- there was no net loss of employment. In fact, for General Foods the transfer of production facilities meant a net increase in job opportunities. Still, the shutdown caused many individual families to undergo the very real problem of an extended period of joblessness.

Finally, we know that other case studies have provided valuable guidelines for policymakers in government, industry and the union movement. During the 1930's studies carried on under the auspices of the Works Progress Administration[2] helped to focus attention on the prob-

---

[2]See, for example, Daniel Creamer and Charles W. Coulter, *Labor and the Shutdown of the Amoskeag Textile Mills*, U. S. Works Progress Administration, Report No. L-5 (Philadelphia: Works Progress Administration, November, 1939), 342 pp; Daniel Creamer and Gladys V. Swackhamer, *Cigar Makers -- After the Lay-Off*, U. S. Works Progress Administration, Report No. L-1 (Philadelphia: Works Progress Administration, December,

(Footnote continued)

lems encountered by the unemployed worker. These studies and others provided a starting point for the establishment of a sound unemployment compensation system. More recently, the study of the experience of the Armour Company in its attempts to provide displaced employees with job retraining gave our lawmakers practical lessons to heed in the establishment of a nationwide system of retraining through the Manpower Development and Retraining Act of 1962.[3]

As Selltiz and associates have pointed out, ". . . every investigator, in his selection of a topic for research . . . is expressing his judgment or feeling about what is important to study. . ."[4] The study of the General Foods experience was undertaken because the opportunity for a thorough study was there, but also because it was deemed important to add to our knowledge of the behavior of workers under the impact of industrial and technological change.

(Footnote continued)

1937), 93 pp.; and Gladys Palmer and Constance Williams, Reemployment of Philadelphia Hosiery Workers after Shut-downs, U. S. Works Progress Administration, Report No. P-6 (Philadelphia: Works Progress Administration, January, 1939), 100 pp.

[3]Armour Automation Fund Committee, Progress Report, Chicago, June 19, 1961; George P. Shultz and Arnold R. Weber, Strategies for the Displaced Worker (New York: Harper and Row, 1966); Edwin Young, "The Armour Experience: A Case Study in Plant Shutdowns," Adjusting to Technological Change (New York: Harper and Row, 1963), Gerald Somers et al., eds., pp. 144-158; James J. Healy, ed., Creative Collective Bargaining (Englewood Cliffs, N. J.: Prentice-Hall, 1965), pp. 137-165.

[4]Claire Selltiz et al., Research Methods in Social Relations (New York: Holt, Rinehart and Winston, 1962), p. 29.

In initially designing the study, it was felt that the major area of concentration would be the study of the workers displaced by the plant shutdowns. Soon, however, emphasis was also placed on the development of management policies and on the experience of relocated workers. After a complete examination of the relevant literature, it was found that particularly in the latter two areas our knowledge is far from complete. It became necessary, then, to develop a tentative outline of the project including a reasonable estimate of the objectives of the study together with a group of working hypotheses.

A study of the operations of a large corporation would not be possible without the complete cooperation of responsible individuals in the organization. The author was fortunate to receive complete cooperation from General Foods officials, past and present, whose donation of time and effort was generous and unstinting. Interviews were held with several officials responsible for the transfer of operations. Furthermore, all company documents bearing on the relocation were made available for examination.

While interviews with responsible company officials and examination of company documents furnished much valuable information, the major portion of this thesis rests on evidence gathered from interviews with samples of employees who were either terminated from their jobs or who chose transfer to the new production facility.

The difficult problems of methodology, then, revolved around (1) the choosing of samples to be interviewed, (2) the construction of appropriate interview forms to be used with the samples, (3) obtaining the interviews, and (4) the choice of the best methods of analysis of the interview returns.

Choosing the Samples

The drawing of samples to be interviewed presented particularly thorny problems. In a case study such as this, a complete polling of all the individuals involved might be considered ideal; in fact, however, in this case (as in most others) it was not possible. With regard to those General Foods employees electing termination it was not possible because, very simply, the interviewing process was begun and ended before the final shutdown of the plants. Therefore, a significant number were still employed at the old plants and fell outside the design of the study. The same consideration made choosing a random sample of all who would be terminated an impossibility. Furthermore, cost and time factors dictated a narrowing of the study to only one of the affected plants -- the Walter Baker plant in Boston, Massachusetts.[5]

---

[5]Plans were also made to interview displaced workers from the Jell-O plant in LeRoy, New York. Those interviews were never completed.

At the time this study was begun -- September, 1964 -- the Walter Baker plant was employing 304 workers. The plant had achieved peak employment of 875 in the previous September. A good number (at least 50) were temporary employees not eligible for relocation allowances. The approximate deployment of Walter Baker employees between 9/1/63 (peak employment) and 9/11/64 (commencement of study) was as follows:

Still employed	304
Transferred to Dover	150
Eligible for transfer but terminated	230
Retired, quit, discharged, deceased, terminated because of temporary employee status, transferred to the other GF facilities, or unaccounted for	190

That is, there were 230 terminated Walter Baker employees as of September, 1964, who had been eligible to transfer to Dover, but who had elected to stay in the Boston area. Of the 230, 60 had been salaried personnel, and 170 were hourly rated. It was decided to attempt to interview as many of the 230 as possible. Of the 304 still employed, another 230 were to be terminated over the next eight months. Therefore, the number of terminations as of September, 1964, represented only one-half the number who eventually were to be terminated at Walter Baker. It was fully realized at the start that concentrating on the first 230 terminees might bias the results in the sense that the experience of this group might not represent the experience of the entire group of Walter Baker terminations. Under the cirsumstances there was no recourse but to go ahead with the interviewing, and hope for the best.

However, even the hope of interviewing all of the first group of 230 terminated employees was not to be realized. The major constraining factor here was time: there simply was not enough time for one interviewer to reach all 230 individuals. The time factor aside, it still would have been impossible to reach all 230, as anyone familiar with interviewing in the field will instantly recognize. Terminations had begun at Walter Baker as early as October, 1963. Most of those contacted for interviews had been gone from Walter Baker for six months or more. In that period of time, a good number had moved out of the area, leaving no forwarding address and/or becoming too costly to contact. A few former Baker employees lived as far away as Hyannis, Massachusetts, and Nashua, New Hampshire; they also were too costly to contact. Still others, when contacted, simply refused to consent to an interview. Several granted interviews but, for one reason or another, were excluded from the final analysis. In the end, usable, completed interviews were obtained from 116 former Walter Baker employees.

The following is a brief description of the interviewing procedure used with the terminated employees. Those chosen to be interviewed were first sent a letter, printed on stationery with a Massachusetts Institute of Technology letterhead.[6] The letter explained briefly the objectives of the study and informed the recipients that the sender would contact them "in a few days" to "arrange for an interview." The letter stressed the brevity of the time required of them and assured them that "all answers . . . are strictly CONFIDENTIAL." It emphasized also the independent nature of the study, pointing out that "the Walter Baker Company has absolutely nothing to do with this survey." The letter was sent to the address listed for the former employee in the company records (often, as it turned out, an incorrect address; in fact, for three persons the address turned out to be fictitious!).

Within a few days of sending the letter, the interviewer would arrive at the address of the former employee. In some cases, several trips to the address would be necessary before finding the interviewee at home. Whenever possible an attempt would be made to gain an interview immediately. Barring that, an appointment would be made for a later time. The interview itself averaged 45 minutes to one hour in length; but the interview represented only the top of the iceberg of time spent on each individual. The interviewing in the field con-

[6]A copy of the letter is contained in the Appendix.

tinued, with interruptions of varying intervals, from October, 1964, to March, 1965.

Fortunately, complete access to company personnel records allowed a check to be made on (1) the validity and reliability of the responses of the 116 persons interviewed; and (2) the representativeness of the sample, i.e., whether the 116 in the sample were representative of the 460 total terminations at Walter Baker.

Company records contained the following information about each employee:

1. Date of birth
2. Years of seniority and/or date of hiring
3. Weekly wage or salary
4. Amount of severance pay
5. Years of school

The records indicated also the employee's marital status and number of dependents, but in many cases this information was badly out of date. The information gathered in the interviews was cross-checked on the five items listed above with company records. It was difficult to reconcile salary and wage figures reported in the interviews with the figures listed in the company records because the company records did not include payments made under the Bedaux incentive plan[7] used for production employees. Many of the Baker employees considered the bonuses received under the Bedaux Plan a

---

[7]A description of the Bedaux Plan is contained in David W. Belcher, Wage and Salary Administration, 2nd ed. (Englewood Cliffs, N. J.: Prentice-Hall, 1964), pp. 397-399.

stable and permanent part of their weekly income. (As it happened, the Bedaux Plan was dropped at the new plant in Dover.) Quite frankly, a judgment had to be made on whether the respondent's reported weekly income was "reasonable" in light of his listed base income and his responses to the four other items contained in the company files.

The overwhelming majority of those interviewed supplied information that checked remarkably well with company records. The deviation on any given item was extraordinarily slight. Strangely, the strongest tendency exhibited was a predilection on the part of a few individuals to overstate the number of years they had spent in school.[8] The net aggregate error on this item, however, was estimated to be no greater than plus 5 per cent. All in all, the correspondence between reported items and those in company records was high enough to lend a comfortable degree of confidence to the responses to questions for which no check was possible.

The information contained in the company files also permitted a comparison of the sample of 116 terminated employees against all 460 former Baker employees. Tables 2.1 through 2.6 compare the sample

[8]It has been suggested that this tendency might have resulted from the fact of the interviewer's close identification with M.I.T.

COMPARISONS OF SAMPLE INTERVIEWED
AT WALTER BAKER AGAINST ALL TERMINATIONS
(Sample = 116)

Table 2.1
Comparison of Means

	Sample (116)	All Terminations at Walter Baker (460)
Age	46.7	47.2
Seniority	13.3 years	15.6 years
Weekly Wage	$100.	$104.
Severance Pay	$1,511.	$1,898.

Table 2.2
Comparison of Sex Distributions

	Sample		All Terminations	
	No.	%	No.	%
Male	85	73.3	341	74.1
Female	31	26.7	119	25.9

Table 2.3
Comparison of Age Distributions

	Sample		All Terminations	
	No.	%	No.	%
Under 24	2	1.7	6	1.3
25-34	22	19.0	79	17.2
35-44	24	20.7	98	21.3
45-54	29	25.0	134	29.1
55-65	39	33.6	143	31.1

Table 2.4

Comparison of Weekly Wage Distributions

Weekly Wage	Sample No.	Sample %	All Terminations No.	All Terminations %
Under $70	1	.9	1	.2
$ 70-79	3	2.6	5	1.1
80-89	24	20.7	83	18.0
90-99	36	31.0	149	32.4
100-109	29	25.0	116	25.2
110-119	12	10.3	55	12.0
120-129	5	4.3	15	3.3
130-139	2	1.7	8	1.7
140-149	1	.9	6	1.3
Over $150	3	2.6	22	4.8

Table 2.5

Comparison of Seniority Distributions

Years	Sample No.	Sample %	All Terminations No.	All Terminations %
0-4	5	4.3	17	3.7
5-9	48	41.4	144	31.3
10-14	27	23.3	86	18.7
15-19	11	9.5	63	13.7
20-24	8	6.9	66	14.3
25-29	10	8.6	45	9.8
30-34	4	3.5	23	5.0
35-39	1	.9	9	2.0
40 and over	2	1.7	7	1.5

Table 2.6

Comparison of Severance Pay Distributions

Severance Pay	Sample		All Terminations	
	No.	%	No.	%
$ 0-100	2	1.7	5	1.1
101-250	8	6.9	25	5.4
251-500	27	23.3	74	16.1
501-750	11	9.5	38	8.3
751-1000	9	7.7	34	7.4
1001-1500	16	13.8	62	13.5
1501-2000	12	10.3	61	13.2
2001-3000	15	12.9	75	16.3
3001-4000	8	6.9	30	6.5
4001-5000	4	3.5	24	5.2
5001-7500	3	2.6	27	5.9
7500+	1	.9	5	1.1

against all terminations on five variables: sex, age, seniority, weekly wage (or salary), and amount of severance pay. All things considered, the sample does seem to be a good representation of the "population." Table 2.1 shows that, on the average, the sample was very slightly younger, had about two years less seniority, and made about $4.00 a week less than the average of all terminations. None of these differences are statistically significant. However, the difference of $387 between the average severance pay (or "termination allowance") of the sample and that of all terminations is significant. There is a simple explanation for this size difference. Each General Foods employee's termination allowance was determined by the product of his average weekly wage and a certain predetermined number of weeks -- where the precise number of weeks used as a multiplier depended on <u>both</u> the employee's age and seniority. That is, an employee's termination allowance was based on three variables: (1) weekly wage, (2) age, and (3) seniority. Therefore, the effect of the small differences between the sample and all terminations on each of the three variables (wage, seniority, and age) combined to produce a large difference in the amount of severance pay granted.

A comparison of sex, age, wage, seniority, and severance pay distributions between the sample and all terminations reveals that the "match," for the most part, is very close. The most obvious differences occur (1) in the comparison of seniority distributions: Table 2.5 shows that there is a heavier concentration in the 5 to 9-year category for the sample (41.4 per cent) than for all terminations (31.3 per cent) -- still, the 5 to 9-year category is the modal category for both the sample and all terminations; and (2) in the comparison of severance pay distributions: Table 2.6 shows that almost one-quarter of the sample received from $251 to $500 in severance pay, whereas only about 16 per cent of all terminations did receive this. Here, however, whereas the $251--500 category is clearly the mode for the sample, it is not so for all terminations. On the other hand, the median amount of severance pay for both the sample and all terminations is approximately $1,300. In summary, while there are some obvious differences between the sample of terminations interviewed and the total number of terminations, the differences are not considered serious, and the sample is judged to be sufficiently representative of the total.

The workers relocated in Dover constituted the second group to be interviewed. In terms of the physical effort required, obtaining interviews with this group was much easier than with the group of displaced workers. General Foods consented to permit interviewing to be carried on during working time and on company premises. While this decision greatly expedited the interviewing process, allowing a large number of workers to be interviewed in a short period of time, it must be considered that the time and place of the interviews may have seriously biased the results.

In deciding to interview on company premises, decisions had to be made on at least two methodological questions. Would interviews obtained within the confines of the plant inhibit the free response of the worker? Would the difference in social environment cause an incompatibility between the responses of the relocated workers and those of the displaced workers? After much thought and consultation, it was decided that the gains possible from some alternative procedure would not compensate the additional costs. Since at the same time, it was decided to use a primarily fixed-choice, confidential questionnaire which the respondent would fill in himself, it was judged that the relative anonymity of this kind of interviewing form would help to promote free and unbiased responses.[9] The first page of the questionnaire informed the worker that

> . . . General Foods has had no role in initiating or conducting this project. We asked General Foods to cooperate, and we have kindly been granted permission to use General Foods' premises to conduct this survey. However, no one from General Foods will ever see any of the questionnaires. Furthermore, the questionnaire is anonymous -- nowhere are you asked to give your name. When the final report is written no one will be able to identify any participant in the survey or his individual responses.[10]

---

[9]Selltiz et al., op. cit., p. 240.

[10]A copy of the questionnaire used with relocated workers is contained in the Appendix.

The workers were asked to read the first page of instructions, and the majority were observed to have read these instructions very carefully. In addition, the instructions were paraphrased verbally for most of the respondents.

Most workers were interviewed in a small conference room adjacent to the personnel office in the Dover plant. The interview form took an average of twenty minutes to complete. Up to eight workers were administered the questionnaire form at the same time. Scheduling the interviews was difficult, since it required pulling the workers off their jobs or catching them coming on or going off their shifts. Nevertheless, interviewing was completed within the space of one week, June 21 to June 25.

In choosing the group to be interviewed in the Dover plant, a number of optional methods presented themselves. Since interviews had been obtained with displaced Walter Baker employees previously, in order to assure comparability of data it was decided to give first interviewing priority to relocated Walter Baker workers. The Jell-O LeRoy workers were assigned second priority for two reasons: (1) it was hoped that additional interviews could be obtained with a sample of <u>displaced</u> LeRoy workers[11] -- hence allowing

---

[11]As pointed out above, those interviews were never obtained.

direct contrasts to be made between relocated and displaced LeRoy workers and (2) it was supposed that of the three remaining areas the experiences of the relocated LeRoy workers would probably be most distinguishable from the experiences of the relocated Walter Baker workers -- this supposition being made primarily because of the marked contrasts between the two old communities -- one a small, rural community, the other a major metropolitan area. It was decided to give less emphasis to interviewing relocated Orange, Massachusetts, and Hoboken, New Jersey, employees.

In retrospect, it appears that an attempt at a complete survey of all relocated workers certainly would have been feasible. However, it is not clear that any additional information of value would have been obtained. Table 2.7 shows the distribution of the sample of relocated workers interviewed by the area from which transfer took place.

In all, 215 relocated workers were interviewed, representing 50.8 per cent of all relocated General Foods employees. However, since the sample was chosen on a quota basis, with the objective of interviewing as many former Walter Baker and Jell-O-LeRoy workers as possible, the distribution of the sample indicates the relative exclusion of workers from the Franklin Baker plant, particularly. It is assumed, rightly or wrongly, throughout this thesis that the ex-

TABLE 2.7

SAMPLE OF RELOCATED WORKERS BY AREA FROM WHICH TRANSFER TOOK PLACE

	(1) Total Number of Transfers	(2) Total Number Interviewed	(3) Per Cent Interviewed (2) ÷ (1)
Walter Baker, Boston Massachusetts	187	137	73.3
Jell-O, LeRoy, New York	88	63	71.6
Minute, Orange, Massachusetts	34	13	38.2
Franklin Baker, Hoboken, New Jersey	114	2	1.8
Total	423	215	50.8

perience of the Franklin Baker transfers is not markedly different from that of the sample interviewed. It was not possible to interview 100 per cent of the transferred Walter Baker and Jell-O-LeRoy workers. Some workers were away from their jobs during the week when interviewing took place, because of illness, vacation or temporary assignment outside the plant. A small number refused to be interviewed. A few simply could not be released from their jobs (a decision made by their supervisor).

Construction of the Interview Forms

The final methodological consideration which needs discussion in this chapter is the construction of the interview forms used with the samples. This task was extremely difficult and important to the thesis; indeed, the entire success of the research rests on whether the "right" questions were used in the interview forms. As Morgenstern says:

> The difficulties of preparing good questionnaires and using them properly are, indeed, formidable but not appreciated by the public. The simple fact is that it is not easy to ask good questions and to insure that intelligent, reliable, and honest answers will be given. Science is, after all, nothing but a continuing effort to find the right questions, followed by the search for answers. It is not different in drawing up questionnaires for economic matters. Progress in science has often been blocked by having asked the wrong question. When a field such as economics depends so largely on asking humans rather than inanimate nature, the problem of the right question assumes new importance.[12]

Two separate questionnaire forms needed to be devised: one for the displaced Walter Baker employees, a second for the relocated workers in Dover.[13] Berelson and Steiner list five types of "verbal reports:"[14]

---

[12]Oskar Morgenstern, On the Accuracy of Economic Observations (Princeton, N. J.: Princeton University Press, 1963), pp. 29-30.

[13]A copy of the questionnaire form used with displaced workers is also contained in the Appendix.

[14]Berelson and Steiner, op. cit., p. 30, and discussion, pp. 29-33.

1. Free association
2. Unstructured or depth interview
3. Semistructured interview
4. Structured interview
5. Formal tests

The interview form used with the displaced worker group is primarily of the "semistructured" type. That is, it consists of several open-ended type questions. The interviewer exercised less control than under the wholly structured form of interview and the ordering of questions, as given on the interview form, was open to some manipulation by the interviewer. On the other hand, the interview form does contain a good number of pre-coded, fixed-choice questions, similar or identical to those contained in the form used with relocated workers.

The questionnaire used with relocated workers falls primarily in the "structured" interview category. Unlike the displaced worker form, it was not administered verbally, but was given to the respondent to be filled in, with the interviewer merely in attendance to answer questions of interpretation and lend general assistance. The questionnaire requires the respondent to provide 117 different items of information. All but nineteen of the items are provided through the device of the multiple choice or fixed-choice type question. Of the nineteen other items, only three are broadly open-ended questions

(Nos. 5, 19b and 54) and the remainder are questions of a type requiring a number, date, or one-word answer (e.g., age, date of move, former location).

The structured questionnaire was ideally suited to the purposes of this study. In addition to being a less costly procedure than other types of interviews, relatively impersonal, and suitable for use with a rather large number of individuals, the structured form had the great advantage of being highly standardized, therefore allowing for standardized responses and uniformity of measurement.[15] Ideally, the structured, "check-list" form would have been the preferable device for use with the sample of the displaced workers. However, in addition to the desire to obtain certain kinds of information not readily elicited through fixed-choice questions, the fact that it was necessary to interview displaced workers individually, in their homes and under widely varying conditions, made the less structured, wholly verbal form of interview an eminently more suitable form for use with the displaced worker group. In terms of fulfilling the purposes of this study, the use of the less structured interview form with displaced workers entailed the following disadvantages:

1. It took a great deal of time to complete and provided relative less relevant and useful information than the form used with relocated workers.

---

[15]Selltiz, et al., op. cit., pp. 238-241.

2. It decreased the degree of intra-sample standardization desired.
3. It was less impersonal, and required the interjection of the interviewer to an extent not required by the design of the research.
4. It caused a diminution in the degree of comparability between the displaced worker and the relocated worker samples.[16]

Needless to say, the use of a fixed-choice questionnaire presents its own set of problems. However, there were no problems not of a general nature, well known and well discussed in the literature.[17] Among the many pitfalls of fixed-choice questionnaires is the problem of providing an insufficient number of alternatives to the question asked and thereby inducing a response which would not otherwise be given. Every effort was made to avoid this source of bias. For example, where suitable, the option of "no opinion" or "don't know" was furnished. Great care was taken in the wording of every question so as to limit the degree of ambiguity or misinterpretation of meaning intended. Of course it cannot be claimed that every question

---

[16]Morgenstern, _op. cit._, pp. 28-29.

[17]For example, see Selltiz, _et al._, _op. cit._, pp. 235-278; and Morgenstern, _op. cit._, pp. 28-33.

is faultless, but the reader's attention will be drawn to every case in which the possibility of misinterpretation appears relatively high.

The design and purpose of the research itself provided the guidelines for the construction of the questions. At the same time, it was considered helpful to cull freely questionnaire forms used in other surveys for questions considered suitable to this piece of research. In this connection, various survey forms used by researchers at M.I.T., and also forms used in other studies similar to the present one, were examined. This practice of "plagiarizing" other questionnaire forms is certainly not uncommon in social science research and, indeed, has several advantages. One, it provides questions that are already, in a sense, pre-tested; two, it allows direct comparison of results to be made with other parallel studies.

Many of the questions used with relocated workers were identical to questions used by the University of Michigan Survey Research Center in its recently published study on the geographic mobility of labor.[18] The research design for this study anticipated that comparisons between the group of relocated workers interviewed for this study and the migrants interviewed by the SRC would provide a needed dimension on the

---

[18] John B. Lansing, *et al.*, *The Geographic Mobility of Labor: A First Report* (Ann Arbor, *Mich.*: *Survey Research Center, 1963)*, 315 pp. The questionnaire is reprinted on pp. 272-303.

determinants of relocation of the General Foods workers. Explicit comparisons between migrants in the SRC survey and relocated General Foods workers are carried out most extensively in Chapter VI.

Finally, it is hardly necessary to discuss the methods of analysis of the collected data. Suffice it to say, standard methods of data processing, statistical testing, and general evaluation were employed. The appropriateness of the analytical tools employed is implicit in the results reported in the succeeding chapters.

In summary, some procedures and methods used in this study have been discussed. The major part of the thesis rests on results obtained by interviewing two separate samples of workers. As Morgenstern says,

> The process of asking questions and getting answers is a delicate psychological one. Apart from lying and refusal to give information, there is forgetfulness, prompting by the questioner with its own consequent bias, lack of comprehension of the question, etc.[19]

But interviewing, fraught with danger though it may be, is still one of social sciences' best means of adding to our knowledge about man and his world. As Allport says,

> If we want to know how people feel: what they experience and what they remember, what their emotions and motives are like, and the reasons for acting as they do -- why not ask them?[20]

---

[19]Morgenstern, <u>op. cit.</u>, p. 29.

CHAPTER III

THE CORPORATION, THE PLANTS, AND THE SHUTDOWN DECISION

This chapter serves the function of providing some of the necessary background information on the decision to shut down and consolidate four General Foods plants. The plants affected by the decision were among the oldest in the General Foods organization. Each had been long-established in its community. It is clear from interviews that to many employees the thought of closing such venerable installations permanently was a disquieting, if not shocking, idea. Indeed, the fact that these plants were so firmly rooted in their communities is at least a partial explanation why General Foods was so long in making a determination on their future, and, once having decided to examine the question, was so surprised at the indicated savings to be obtained from their shutdown. In the end, economic imperatives were stronger than tradition, and a decision to shut down and consolidate the four old plants was made.

The Corporation[1]

The General Foods Corporation is the nation's largest food processor after the National Dairy Products Company. In fiscal 1965

---

[1]Unless otherwise footnoted, information on the General Foods Corporation has been obtained from the following sources:

(Footnote continued)

(April 1, 1964, to March 31, 1965) General Foods had gross sales of $1,478 billion and net profits after taxes of $86 million. Table 3.1 shows that growth in sales and net income has been consistent over an extended period.

The food products industry is a fiercely competitive industry, consisting of literally thousands of producing firms. In 1965 Americans spent $85.5 billion on food. Nevertheless, General Foods has been able to forge a place for itself as one of the industry's giants --

---

(Footnote continued)

Company records and talks with various company officials;
General Foods Corporation, <u>Annual Report</u>, various years, 1960 to 1965;
Moody's <u>Industrial Manual</u> and Moody's <u>Manual of Investments</u>, various years;
Standard and Poor's <u>Industry Surveys</u>, 1964, 1965;
"General Foods is Five Billion Particulars," <u>Fortune</u>, Vol. 69, March, 1964, pp. 114-117, pp. 158-165;
"Ready for Instant Growth," <u>Business Week</u>, April 24, 1965, pp. 69-74;
"General Foods: High Profits in a Low Profit Industry," <u>Forbes</u>, Vol. 90, August 1, 1962, pp. 20-24;
"Billions in the Pantry," <u>Time</u>, Vol. 71, June 9, 1958, pp. 86-88;
"Just Heat and Serve," <u>Time</u>, Vol. 74, December 7, 1959, pp. 92-96;
Robert E. Bedingfield, "Personality: Soap Flakes to a Mixed Fare," <u>New York Times</u>, March 7, 1965, Sec. 3, p. 3;
Jerry Allan, "A Shimmering $67 Million from $450 Outlay in Jell-O," <u>Buffalo Evening News</u>, March 14, 1962, p. 27;
Dean Richmond, "Lawless Container Buys Former Jell-O Factory in LeRoy," <u>Buffalo Evening News</u>, May 4, 1966, p. 18;
Nettie Leitch Major, <u>C. W. Post: The Man and the Hour</u> (Judd and Detweiler, Washington, D. C., 1963).

TABLE 3.1

GROSS SALES AND NET INCOME OF THE GENERAL FOODS CORPORATION, 1958-1965

Fiscal Year	Gross Sales (000,000)	Net Income before Income Taxes (000,000)	Net Income to Surplus (after Taxes) (000,000)
1965	$1,478	$177	$86
1964	1,338	179	84
1963	1,216	170	79
1962	1,189	156	72
1961	1,160	138	67
1960	1,087	130	61
1959	1,052	115	54
1958	1,008	105	48

Source: Moody's *Industrial Manual*, 1965, p. 2492.

indeed, as one of America's corporate giants. Only thirty to thirty-five companies in the United States do more business, in terms of net annual sales, and few exceed General Foods in net average annual return on invested capital, estimated to be 17.1 per cent over the period 1957 through 1962.[2] As *Fortune* has stated:

---

[2] *Fortune*, *op. cit.*, p. 115.

> . . . there is a case to be made for the proposition that over the past several years it was no aerospace or electronics prodigy but General Foods that has been the must successful billion-dollar company in the United States.[3]

While the food industry is allegedly a low-profit industry, General Foods -- and its chief competitors, Standard Brands, Corn Products, Kellogg, etc. -- have generally prospered in the affluent sixties.

General Foods is far and away the leader in several important food product areas: coffee (Maxwell House), pet food (Gaines), frozen food (Bird's Eye), and pre-packaged desserts (Jell-O). Its Post cereals run a distant second to Kellogg's. In addition, it also packages food products under such well-known brand names as Sanka and Yuban Coffee, Minute Rice and Tapioca, Franklin Baker Coconut, Walter Baker Chocolate, Calumet Baking Powder, Log Cabin Syrup, Kool-Aid, and Swan's Down Flour and Cake Mixes. As of March, 1964, it operated 63 processing plants: 42 in the United States, 3 in Canada, and 18 in other countries. It employed about 30,000 people and had a total wage and salary figure of approximately $195 million.

---

[3] Ibid., p. 115.

The General Foods Corporation has grown by merger and acquisition. Its nucleus was the Postum Cereal Company, founded in 1895 by C. W. Post. Its first product was Postum, a coffee substitute; but soon the company was producing a line of cereals, the leading seller being Grape-Nuts. C. W. Post died in 1914, but his company continued to prosper. Beginning in 1925, Postum began a program of product diversification through the acquisition of established, well-known companies. It first purchased the Jell-O Company of LeRoy, New York. In 1926, Postum added Igleheart Brothers and Company, maker of Swan's Down Cake Flour. Also in 1926 Minute Tapioca was added, and the following year the Walter Baker Chocolate Company and the Franklin Baker Company, maker of coconut products. Of the first five properties acquired by the Postum Company, four were to be affected by the shutdown decision of 1962.

In 1929 the title "General Foods" was adopted for the growing corporation. Below is a selected list of some of the additional acquisitions made by the corporation over the years:

Cheek-Neal Company (Maxwell House Coffee), 1928
Frosted Foods (Bird's Eye), 1929
Sanka Coffee, 1932
Arbuckle Brothers (coffee), 1937
Gaines Food Company (pet food), 1943
Paton Corporation (Yuban Coffee), 1944
Perkins Products Company (Kool-Aid), 1953
Four Seasons, Inc. (salad dressing), 1954
S.O.S. (scouring pads), 1957[4]

[4]The Federal Trade Commission has ordered General Foods to divest its S.O.S. scouring pad operations on anti-trust grounds. The Company intends to appeal the ruling. See "Mortimer Tells FTC Big Marketer's Woes," Advertising Age, Vol. 35, June 29, 1964, p. 3.

The Plants and the Communities

Table 3.2 shows the date of founding of the original company, the date of incorporation, and the date of purchase by General Foods -- or, more accurately, Postum -- of the four plants involved in this study.

In 1897 Mr. and Mrs. Pearl B. Wait of LeRoy, New York devised a dessert called Jell-O, made from a combination of pectin, gelatin, fruit flavoring and sugar. They sold the rights to the dessert to Orator Woodward for $450 in 1899. Twenty-six years later the Woodward family sold the Jell-O Company to Postum for an estimated $67 million.[5]

TABLE 3.2

DATE OF FOUNDING, INCORPORATION, AND ACQUISITION OF FOUR GENERAL FOODS PLANTS

	Date of Founding of Original Company	First Date of Incorporation	Date of Acquisition by General Foods (Postum)
Walter Baker, Dorchester, Mass.	1765	1898	1927
Franklin Baker, Hoboken, N. J.	1899	1923	1927
Jell-O LeRoy, N. Y.	1897	1923	1925
Minute, Orange, Mass.	1894	1894	1926

[5]The exact terms of the transaction are as follows: Postum acquired the entire outstanding stock of Jell-O, consisting of 50,000 shares of common stock and $1.5 million of preferred in exchange for 570,000 shares of Postum. In 1925 the market value on Postum stock went as high as 121. See Poor's Industrials, 1926 and 1927.

The town of LeRoy, situated between Rochester and Buffalo in upstate New York, had a population in 1962 of about 4,800. The Jell-O Company was one of the town's major employers. The company employed about 365 workers, representing about 25 per cent of the town's total industrial employment. The plant had never been unionized. The Lapp Insulator Company was also located in LeRoy, and a Sylvania Electric plant was in nearby Batavia. It is also possible for LeRoy citizens to commute to work in Rochester. The buildings of the Jell-O plant occupied six acres of land, and the company contributed three per cent to the town's total tax revenues.

Obviously the Jell-O plant was closely linked with LeRoy's history. As the plant's operation manager wrote:

> The Jell-O plant in LeRoy has been in existence since 1897. It is the oldest active industry in the area. Jell-O *is* General Foods, as far as the local community is concerned. Jell-O is considered the leading industry and the most desirable place to work. . .
>
> The Jell-O plant has been, and still is, a vital part of the total community. It is the parent plant of Jell-O. Its original owners built their fortunes in the Jell-O business and left their impact on the economic, social, educational, and spiritual life of the community through personal leadership and liberal philanthropies. General Foods continues to lead in its support of community activities. . .[6]

---

[6]Quoted in Edmund S. Whitman and W. James Schmidt, *Plant Relocation: A Case History of a Move* (New York: American Management Association, 1966), p. 21.

John Whitman of Orange, Massachusetts, founded the Minute Tapioca Company in 1894. He had acquired the rights to a process for removing lumps from tapioca. Tapioca flour, a product of the cassava plant, was always difficult to convert into a commercially salable item. Whitman's process allowed him to market a product which enabled the homemaker to prepare a smooth-textured pudding -- if not precisely in a minute, in a relatively short time.

Orange is located in the north central section of Massachusetts. In 1962 the town had fewer than 6,000 people. General Foods was the town's third largest employer (96 employees), after the Rodney Hunt Machine Company (340 employees) and the Farrington Needle Company (125 employees). Five miles west, in the town of Athol, the L. S. Starrett Company employed about 1,200 persons and the Union Twist Drill Company employed over 800. Like the LeRoy plant, Minute had never been organized.

The origins of the Walter Baker Chocolate Company go back to pre-Revolutionary America. The site of the old Walter Baker Company, on the Neponset River, the border between Dorchester and Milton, Massachusetts, saw manufacturing activity as early as 1634, when settlers ground the first corn meal and flour in New England. In 1665 the country's first powder mill was located on the site; later, the country's first iron-slitting mill occupied the same site. In

1765 Dr. James Baker, a Harvard College graduate, and John Hannon, an early immigrant from Ireland, began to grind the first chocolate made in North America on the Neponset River Mill site. In 1780 Dr. Baker acquired full ownership of the chocolate business, and made the first chocolate branded "Baker's." The business was to stay in the Baker family for another 104 years. The first Walter Baker, the grandson of the founder, ran the business from 1824 to his death in 1852. But it was under Henry L. Pierce, to whom the trustees of the Walter Baker estate leased the business, that the small mill thrived, grew fourfold, and became internationally known. Pierce ran the business from 1854 to 1896, assuming full ownership in 1884. In addition to his business activities, Pierce led an active public life. He was both mayor of Boston and a member of Congress. When he died in 1896, the plant employed 400 workers.[7]

Postum acquired Walter Baker in August, 1927, for 82,928 shares of Postum stock worth about $10 million. By 1962 the Walter Baker plant employed more than 800 workers and consisted of more than thirty antiquated buildings spread over twenty-two acres of land. The Walter Baker employees had been represented since World War II by the Food Packers Union Local 451, Amalgamated Meat Cutters

---

[7]This brief account of the history of the Walter Baker Company is based primarily on a 65-page company publication entitled "A Calendar of Walter Baker and Company, Inc., and Its Times," produced for the company's 175th anniversary in 1940.

and Butchers Workmen of North America, AFL-CIO. There had been one strike by Baker employees in the mid-1950's. The existing labor contract was due to expire in the summer of 1963.

The Franklin Baker Company did not have the illustrious history of its sister company; nor were its roots as embedded in the life of the community: it had moved to Hoboken in 1924 from Brooklyn. Franklin Baker (no relation to Walter Baker) founded the coconut processing business in 1894 in Philadelphia. He quickly established the concern as the leader in the consumer and industrial coconut market. Two months after Postum purchased Walter Baker, the acquisitive cereal company purchased the well-known coconut producer for more than $5 million. In 1962 the company employed more than 500 workers. Franklin Baker production and maintenance employees were represented by the Butcher Workmen, while the warehouse employees were members of the International Brotherhood of Teamsters. Although there had never been a strike at Franklin Baker, at the time when the shutdown decision was made, General Foods was in the process of negotiating a new labor agreement with the unions at Franklin Baker. In deciding on the timing of the shutdown announcement, General Foods had to take into account the effect of such an announcement on the negotiations at Franklin Baker.

In contrast to the Jell-O and Minute plants, the two Baker plants were located in large industrialized, urban areas. General Foods executives anticipated that the shutdowns would have dire consequences for employees at the two Baker plants. In addition, another major General Foods facility was located in Hoboken, not far from Franklin Baker. General Foods' Maxwell House Coffee-processing plant in Hoboken is the largest in the world, and it was expected that some Franklin Baker employees could be transferred (or reassigned) to the Maxwell House plant. Openings were eventually found for about fifty Franklin Baker workers. In point of fact, there are four other General Foods facilities in the New York City metropolitan area. Corporate headquarters are located in White Plains, New York; the corporation's research and technical center is located in Tarrytown, New York; a machine development plant is located in Port Chester, New York; and a nut equipment assembly plant is located in Garden City on Long Island. However, primarily because of their size or because the facilities required highly skilled or specialized labor, few transfers from Hoboken could be arranged.

Within twenty-five miles of the LeRoy plant were three small Bird's Eye facilities (Medina, Avon, and Wayland, New York). It was impracticable to consider these facilities as a means of absorbing the displaced workers from the LeRoy shutdown. Eleven salaried employees from LeRoy were transferred across the state to a fairly new carton and container plant located in Saratoga Springs.

There was some hope that the Atlantic Gelatin plant, located in Woburn, Massachusetts, would be able to absorb some of the workers from Walter Baker. In fact, not more than four were able to make the transfer. Outside of the Woburn plant and a facility for quick-freezing fish in Gloucester, there were no other important General Foods units in New England to which transfers would have been possible.

In summary, the four production facilities had been located in their communities from a little under forty years to almost two hundred. All four organizations were among the first acquired by Postum in the formation of General Foods. Two of the communities (Orange and LeRoy) were small, rural towns in which General Foods was one of the major employers. The two other plants (Walter Baker and Franklin Baker) were located in major metropolitan areas. With the exception of the Hoboken plant, transfer opportunities to nearby General Foods operations were extremely limited.

The Decision to Shut Down

General foods as a corporation prides itself on its marketing ability[8] and technical proficiency. Technical expertise enables Gen-

---

[8]As an index of the emphasis on marketing at General Foods, one can look at General Food's advertising expenditures. According to *Fortune*,

(Footnote continued)

eral Foods to develop new food products; marketing ability insures that the new products -- or, at least, most of the new products -- will find success with the consuming public.[9] The constant development of new products -- and the improvement of old products -- requires continual investment in new plant and equipment. Over the years, General Foods has been an industry leader in capital expenditure. In fact, in 1959 General Foods assumed the industry lead in annual spending on new plants.[10] Still, many older plants continued to operate.

(Footnote continued)

General Foods spent $113 million on advertising in 1963, making it the fourth largest advertiser in the United States after General Motors, Procter and Gamble, and Ford. See Fortune, op. cit., p. 164. Another indication is the recent development by General Foods of a system of regional warehouses, which, according to Forbes, "have set a new standard for customer service in the industry." Forbes, op. cit., p. 23. See also, Business Week, op. cit., p. 74.

[9]"General Foods' corporate skill consists largely in knowing enough about American tastes to foresee what products will be accepted. Nor surprisingly, General Foods spent $14 million last year (1963) on product research, over 11 per cent of the industry's total, although General Foods has only 2 per cent of this vast industry's total sales." Fortune, op. cit., p. 117.

[10]The record, as given in Standard and Poor's Industry Surveys, 1965, is as follows:

Year	Capital Expenditures (in millions)	Capital Expenditure as Per Cent of Gross Plant
1964	$53.6	11.2
1963	69.9	16.0
1962	56.9	15.2
1961	41.6	12.7
1960	39.9	13.8
1959	34.6	14.0
1958	23.6	11.7

(Footnote continued)

About 1960 the Jell-O Division of General Foods was faced with a key decision concerning four of the oldest plants within the corporation -- those at Dorchester, Massachusetts, Orange, Massachusetts, Hoboken, New Jersey and LeRoy, New York. A decision had to be made whether to continue to make marginal improvements on these old facilities or to close any or all of them down and build new facilities. A task force composed of one man from each of the Division's major operating areas, one from the Division controller's office, and one from the corporate manufacturing and engineering area was assigned to make an exploratory investigation.

According to Whitman and Schmidt, in a study for the American Management Association,

> . . . the task force started its study with no predisposition toward a massive shutdown and consolidation. Improvement of existing facilities was still

---

(Footnote continued)

According to _Fortune_, "General Foods is fast modernizing plant and equipment wherever it can expect a reasonable payback. . ." _Fortune, op. cit._, p. 115. However, this policy apparently has its drawbacks. According to C. W. Cook, chief executive officer of General Foods, "While we have been plowing in on two programs this past year -- an accelerated capital expansion plan and large-scale new product introductions -- . . . their costs necessarily restrict earnings in the year in which they are made. . ." _New York Times, op. cit._ Undoubtedly, Mr. Cook is referring, in part, to the construction of the Dover plant.

> very much in the picture, and the idea of abandoning one or more of the old plants was approached with caution. However, consolidation quickly leaped to the forefront of task force thinking as it became clear that the investment of more and more money in the outmoded plants would be unsound.[11]

The first formal report of the task force was submitted in February, 1961. In part, it concluded:

> It became apparent that the most significant savings were obtainable through overhead reductions by consolidation of existing Jell-O plants into fewer plants. The overhead savings that have been identified represent approximately 80 per cent of the total savings of this study. Direct and transportation savings represent the remainder.[12]

Actually, several consolidation plans were considered. The task force projected transportation, construction, overhead, and direct costs; shutdown, employee-termination, and start-up costs; and profit and loss estimates on everything from a two-plant to a four-plant consolidation, involving any combination of five plants. (Jell-O's Calumet Baking Powder plant in Chicago, founded in 1889, was considered in addition to the four other plants.) Finally, by

---

[11]Whitman and Schmidt, *op. cit.*, p. 15. Mr. Schmidt is senior public relations specialist for General Foods. Mr. Whitman is a free-lance writer.

[12]Quoted in Whitman and Schmidt, *ibid.*, p. 16.

July, 1961, using the criteria of (1) maximum cost reductions, (2) minimum payback time on the invested capital, and (3) optimum profit potential, the task force settled on the shutdown of the four old Eastern plants of the Jell-O Division and their consolidation into one new facility at a new location.

The decision would present the corporation with the problem of closing four long-established plants, thus affecting not only the lives of nearly 1,800 workers but also the economies of the communities in which the plants were located. But potentially the most serious risk of the consolidation plan was the possibility that by concentrating production of so many of General Foods' products at one location, the corporation might one day be faced with a work stoppage (*e.g.*, because of a strike) that would cut off the supply of products that "were found in more homes in the United States than any other brands of grocery items."[13]

The task force recommended that its proposition be given further study. As a result, the management of General Foods set up a "Facilities Improvement Group" to develop firm estimates on the costs of the project, and a possible timetable for its completion.[14]

---

[13] *Ibid.*, p. 18.

[14] *Ibid.*, pp. 19-27.

By February, 1962, this group had not only confirmed the earlier recommendation of the task force, but had prepared a fairly detailed report to be submitted to the Board of Directors of the corporation, which explained the advantages of the consolidation plan, the source of savings to be realized, and presented a timetable to be followed in implementing the transition.[15] The report reached the following conclusion:

> After consideration of the adverse effect the proposed move will have on GF's profits for fiscal 1964 and 1965, as well as the adverse effect on the present employees and the communities of LeRoy and Orange, the Jell-O Division believes that the profit improvement and provision for future growth to be derived from a new Eastern plant justifies the large capital expenditure. If management agrees with the foregoing, we recommend that funds be authorized now for preliminary engineering and site selection; that employee announcements and public relations plans be developed; and that capital funds for the new facility be appropriated by midsummer 1962.[16]

The Board approved the plan in March, 1962, and decided immediately to announce the corporation's plans to the employees and the workers.

On March 7, 1962, each employee at the old plants was handed a letter, accompanied by a press release, informing him of the impending shutdown of his place of employment. Despite the fact that there

---

[15] *Ibid.*, pp. 27-37.

[16] Quoted in Whitman and Schmidt, *op. cit.*, p. 37.

were many questions that still needed to be determined -- where the new plant would be located, what the engineering requirements of the relocation were, what precise personnel policies would be used for the move -- General Foods had a fairly clear conception of what its basic shutdown decision would involve:

1. The four old plants were to be shut down; their operations would be consolidated in a new facility to be built on a new site.

2. The new plant would require at least fifty acres, twenty of these to be under a roof, the remaining acres to be set aside for parking, shipping, and transportation activities, and future expansion needs.

3. The new plant site would be within 250 miles of New York City. Although the precise location had not been determined, General Foods executives were fairly certain that most advantageous locations lay south of New York. This, of course, narrowed the possibilities considerably.

4. The cost of the new plant would be in the neighborhood of $36 to $38 million -- the largest capital outlay in General Food's history. (As it turned out, the cost of the new plant was closer to

$50 million.) It would take two years to complete, with the first relocation of production lines to take place late in 1963. (Again General Foods underestimated the time required for the construction of the plant and transfer of equipment.)

5. Other plants in the General Foods system -- and particularly in the Jell-O Division (at Chicago, Illinois; Evart, Michigan; Woburn, Massachusetts; and Hollywood, California) would not be affected by, or involved in, the move.

6. General Foods did not anticipate any substantial changes in the methods and means of production at the new plant. Essentially the same machines and equipment being used in the old plants would be used in the new installations. Major cost reductions would be realized from the fact of the combination of the four operations -- resulting in significantly lower overhead costs. The new plant would not require the maintenance and housekeeping of the old plants. More than that, an efficient one-floor plant layout would eliminate the costly materials handling required at the old locations. The antiquated character of the old plants had necessitated a more or less improvised design of production flows for many years. Additionally, General Foods expected to save on transportation costs and also, possibly, on wage costs.

7. General Foods executives estimated that the new plant would provide employment for more than 1,200 people. By contrast, the four old plants were employing about 1,800. From the evidence, it appears that General foods officials assumed from the first that transfer opportunities would be offered to at least some of the employees affected by the plant shutdowns. The earliest communiqués on the shutdown decision imply the provision of such opportunities.

Still, it must be emphasized that, at the time of the shutdown announcement in March, 1962, corporate management had not yet decided on the extent to which transfer rights would be offered. Over the succeeding months, as the workers and the communities adjusted themselves to the news of the impending shutdowns, corporate officials had to construct a viable set of personnel policies in this complex area.

In the next chapter, we analyze the logic of personnal policies for plant shutdowns, with specific reference to those policies developed by General Foods.

CHAPTER IV

PERSONNEL POLICIES FOR PLANT SHUTDOWNS

In this chapter the personnel policies which General Foods used in shutting down the four old plants in the Jello-O Division are described and analyzed. An attempt is made to provide a more generalized framework for analysis extending beyond a mere discussion of the specifics of the policies chosen by General Foods. Why is one set of personnel policies used and not another? What is the range of possibilities? What possible criteria can a company use in the selection of appropriate policies? How do the circumstances of the plant shutdown affect the selection of personnel policies? In general, what is the _logic_ behind the selection and implementation of a set of personnel policies for plant shutdowns? These are a few of the questions to which this chapter addresses itself.

It is not sufficient simply to ask: What determines which policies a company will use for plant shutdowns? As it stands, this question is ambiguous. First, it implies that special and unique policies must be developed and used in the event of a plant shutdown. This is not necessarily so. It may be that already existing company policies -- developed with or without a union -- are sufficient. In the area of personnel relations companies have a strong predilection to develop policies, or rules, which are then held to apply to the fullest extent in all possible situations. As Dubin has written:

> In a large company with multiple plant operations, the most obvious consideration affecting labor relations decisions is the need for standardization and uniformity. . . The emphasis is . . . on the fact that administration in the big firm necessitates standardization through rules and uniform procedures as a basis for prediction of future events. Management must be in a position to predict what will be the outcome, granting a given personnel situation . . . The "reign of rules" is the administrative answer to the problems of governing in large-scale organizations. This rule-making habit is all-pervading. . .[1]

It follows, then, that rules and policies designed to govern day-to-day relations and contingencies in the firm are not likely to be altered by the fact of a plant shutdown. These same rules will be used, to the extent possible, to govern the disposition of workers affected by plant shutdowns. This tendency may be reinforced if there is an established collective bargaining relationship.

On the other hand, it is obvious that policies designed for day-to-day relations are not likely to be fully applicable to a plant

---

[1]Robert Dubin, "Imperatives Affecting Industrial Relations Decisions," _Human Relations in Administration_ (Englewood Cliffs, N. J.: Prentice-Hall, 1951), Robert Dubin, ed., pp. 218-219.

shutdown situation, and there will be a need to develop special policies for this special kind of situation. In the past, little attention was paid to the development of plant shutdown policies. The contingency was usually so remote and so final that coping with such an eventuality was not considered necessary. In recent years, however, the possibility of plant shutdowns has apparently become more of a reality, at least in the minds of those concerned with the effects of shutdowns; and in many industries policies have been developed to deal with such an eventuality. Several factors can be pointed to as lending support to the development of policies for plant shutdowns. One of the major factors is, of course, the fear that technological change is accelerating, and consequently is more of a threat today than in the past. Technological change may <u>not</u> be the onerous specter that some people fear. But because they do fear it, this has been one factor leading to the development of policies for plant shutdowns.

A Summary of the Policies Used by General Foods

In this section the complex of personnel policies used by General Foods to effect the termination and transfer of employees at the four eastern plants will be summarized. Remaining sections of this and the following chapter will be devoted to a detailed discussion of many of the policies mentioned here.

Before proceeding, certain essential points should be made clear. First, the policies used by General Foods were uniform in the sense of being applicable to all employees at all four plants. Aside from minor qualifications, no account was taken of possible unique characteristics associated with one or another of the plants. On the other hand, there were some policies applicable to salaried personnel and not to hourly.

Second, the policies were almost wholly developed by the corporation with minimal union participation. The limited role of the unions involved is discussed thoroughly in a later section.[2] Some of the policies had been used for many years by the corporation (*e.g.*, severance pay) and a few had their origin in earlier, comparable experiences of the corporation (*e.g.*, advance notice of the shutdown). The detailed development of all policies used, however, did not come until *after* the shutdown announcement had been made.

Third, and probably most important to the case, all workers had a fundamental choice to make between two options. They could either relocate with all (or nearly all) expenses paid, retaining full seniority and benefit rights, to a job which in the majority of cases was identical to the one they had been performing; or they could elect to terminate with a "fair" severance allowance and the company's promise to help them find new work. (A few workers who had reached age 55 and

---

[2]See Chapter V.

had at least fifteen years of service, had a third choice of early retirement.) Simply put, every worker had a choice of moving or staying. The unique characteristic of the General Foods case is that the moving option was made more attractive and less costly than it typically is.

The General Foods policies, with a brief explanation, are as follows:

1. Advance Notice of Plant Shutdown. Each worker was informed at least two years in advance of his termination or transfer, giving him adequate time to plan ahead and make his choice of terminating or relocating.
2. Extensive Employee Communication Program. From the shutdown announcement to the final move, employees were kept fully informed of every new development. In addition to letters and literature on living and working in Dover, employees received a series of fifteen bulletins between September, 1962, and July, 1964, under the masthead, "On the Move to Dover." These "On the Move" bulletins kept the workers up to date on progress in shutting down the old plants and constructing the new.
3. Employee Counseling and Interviewing. The task of counseling individual employees was assigned to a "relocation

desk," established at each of the closing plants. The relocation desks informed employees of the various opportunities available to them in Dover. Each employee was provided with an "estimate of benefit" form. This form, prepared individually for every employee, informed him of the various benefits open to him under the corporation's retirement, life insurance and severance pay plans. His rights under the corporation's medical insurance plan and an optional employee's investment plan were also outlined.

Salaried employees were more thoroughly canvassed than hourly workers. A detailed survey of each salaried employee's skills, abilities, experience, education, and job interests was carried out.

If there was a weak point in the set of policies used by the corporation, the employee counseling service was probably it. While useful in terms of acquainting the workers with their transfer and termination rights and providing the company with a survey of its employees' skills and aptitudes, the counseling program did little in the way of helping terminating workers to find new jobs. No canvass of job opportunities in the local labor market was made, and, although there was talk of seeking the aid of the local public employment services, such plans never came to fruition. Letters of recommendation were written for the displaced workers; but in the sample of interviews with displaced Walter Baker employees, not one reported that the company had been of any help at all to him in finding new work.

Admittedly, as the Armour experience has shown,[3] there are difficulties in implementing an effective service that will be of significant help to displaced workers. Nevertheless, little effort was applied to the task in the General Foods case.

In summarizing the corporation's employee counseling services, the personnel manager of the Jell-O Division wrote:

> (Counseling and interviewing services were) provided at the four plants for employees who chose not to move to Dover. These undoubtedly varied in quality from one plant to another. For example, at Hoboken about sixty employees were given jobs in the General Foods coffee plant nearby and others were considered for employment at our warehouse in Clifton, New Jersey. This fact alone undoubtedly had a positive impact on the general attitude toward the company.
>
> At LeRoy the Lapp Insulator Company was growing rapidly at the time our plant was closed down. It absorbed a number of our people as did Sylvania Electric in nearby Batavia. Our Personnel Manager (at LeRoy) helped employees make contact with these potential employers.
>
> At Orange there was never more than a handful of people who were out of work because of our move. . .

---

[3]George P. Shultz and Arnold R. Weber, *Strategies for the Displaced Worker* (New York: Harper and Row, 1966), pp. 97-124; Edwin Young, "The Armour Experience: A Case Study in Plant Shutdown," *Adjusting to Technological Change* (New York: Harper and Row, 1963), Gerald Somers *et al.*, eds., pp. 144-158.

> As far as Walter Baker is concerned, the problem was more difficult, since the employee group was larger, older and had longer service. Nevertheless (counseling) services were provided to the best of our ability, including the provision of contacts with other potential employers. . .[4]

4. Severance Pay and Retirement Plans. Both plans had been in effect for many years. Participation in the retirement plan was optional, open to all employees after one year of continuous service. Most employees participated. The plan was supported by company and employee contribution. As pointed out earlier, there was an early retirement plan option. Terminating employees could also elect to have the sum of their contributions, plus interest, refunded.

   Benefits under the severance pay plan were graduated for age and seniority. The maximum benefit was fifty-two weeks of pay. A later section is given over to an extended discussion of issues and problems in severance pay policies.

5. Transfer to the New Plant. Every employee was guaranteed a job at the new plant. The corporation fully realized that many would not accept transfer. Few anticipated that men nearing retirement or married women would be interested in relocating. In fact,

[4]Letter from Mr. Harry Chandler to the author, August 6, 1965.

about 25 per cent eventually transferred to Dover, a figure which is higher than is typical for comparable cases. (One assistant personnel manager remarked that he expected 90 per cent to transfer! Other executives were doubtlessly more realistic.)

A series of transfer policies was elaborated. The policies for hourly employees are summarized below:

a. Visit to Dover. Employees were invited to visit Dover, with the company paying expenses up to $70. The visit had to be made on the employee's own time. When arriving in Dover the employee would report to a company representative who would have a brief orientation talk with him.

b. One week off with pay. At the time of the employee's move to Dover, he received one week with pay to allow him to move and settle his family.

c. Reimbursement for bona fide transfer expenses. The employee was reimbursed for the total cost of packing and carting his household furniture. The company chose the carrier. Also, the company paid for the transportation of the worker and his family from their old home to Dover (8 cents a mile plus toll charges, meals and lodging en route, if an automobile was used).

d. <u>Reimbursement for expenses resulting solely from the transfer.</u> Under this heading the company would pay for a wide variety of expenses connected with the move. Examples of the kinds of expenses covered include: real estate brokerage fees and legal fees (not capital losses on sale of home, however); attorney's fees and other reasonable costs incurred by the buyer in the purchase of a new home; telephone installation costs; alteration of rugs and draperies; service costs of connecting transferred household equipment (stoves, washers, etc.); pro-rated expenses of unused portions of an automobile license plate and operator's license, etc. The company's maximum reimbursement for <u>all</u> transfer expenses (both c and d) was set at $1,000.

e. <u>More liberal transfer policies for salaried personnel.</u> Essentially the relocation policies for salaried personnel differed from those for hourly personnel in three respects. First, there was no upper limit placed on the amount of moving and travelling expenses covered by the company. Second, the salaried worker could take more than one incidental trip to Dover (<u>e.g.</u>, to find new housing) and there was no upper limit on expenses covered by the company for such trips. Third, the company was more generous to salaried employees in terms of housing aid offered. For example, General Foods would buy the relocated salaried worker's old home outright, if the worker so desired.

f. Dover housing assistance. One of the "On the Move" bulletins provided employees with information on the Dover housing market. Terms available on FHA insured mortgages and VA guaranteed mortgages were carefully explained. In addition, the corporation hired an experienced Delaware real estate consultant to advise and guide employees on the rental and sale of homes and apartments in the Dover area. The real estate consultant met and talked with all visiting General Foods employees, and also offered to tour the Dover area with them. As it happened, many of the transferees, particularly those from the Dorchester and Hoboken areas, had rented in the past, found that rentals were slim in the Dover area, and consequently were buying homes for the first time in their lives.

Our interviews with relocated workers reveal that this service saved many first-time buyers both time and money, and was greatly appreciated by all the transferred workers.

6. Seniority, Benefit, and Wage Policies at the New Plant. Briefly, transferred employees were to retain their full seniority and benefit rights. However, the problem of integrating the four previously separate plant seniority systems into one presented management with several difficulties. Wage policy for the new plant was a no less difficult problem. General Foods intended to pay wages comparable to the prevailing level in the Dover area. However, this meant that many transferring workers would suffer a wage cut. This was especially true of the Walter Baker plant, which paid an average base rate considerably higher than the anticipated Dover average, and, on top of that, provided production workers with additional earnings through the plant incentive system, which management intended to eliminate in Dover.

Seniority and wage policies are discussed more thoroughly in Chapter V.

The Personnel Costs of Plant Relocation

Economic theory tells us that General Foods' motivation for the shutdown and consolidation decision was the belief that the rate of return on the expected future net income stream was higher than any alternative rate of return arising from some other use of the amount of the investment. Put in another form, the investment was made because the discounted present value of the future returns from the use of the new plant was expected to be in excess of the cost of the new plant.

Actually, General Foods relied on the simplified version of the above rules: the Task Force assigned to study the corporation's options used the payback period rule, calculating the number of years necessary to pay off the capital investment from the earnings of alternative consolidations. Needless to say, the four-plant Dover consolidation proved to be extraordinarily attractive. Based on the Whitman and Schmidt report, the payback period on the multimillion dollar investment was probably in the neighborhood of ten years.[5]

In making these calculations, corporate officials had to make an adequate allowance for the personnel costs associated with alternate plans. These personnel costs would include:

---

[5]Edmund S. Whitman and W. James Schmidt, Plant Relocation (New York: American Management Association, 1966), pp. 16-17.

1. Costs arising from the termination of employees at the old plants. Included would be termination allowances, added vacation pay expenses, employee counseling and other administrative expenses, life insurance rebates and early retirement benefits above normal levels for which the corporation was liable, etc.
2. Costs arising from the relocation of employees from the old plants to Dover. Included would be pre-relocation Dover visits (also available to those who terminated), transportation allowances and moving expenses, costs associated with the company's employee real estate services, Dover interim living expenses, training transferred employees at Dover, employee counseling and other administrative costs, etc.
3. Costs of recruiting and training new workers at the Dover plant. Included would be all the costs associated with recruiting, selecting, placing, and training new workers, including newspaper advertising, test administration, interviewing, and employee orientation programs.
4. Costs associated with the phase-out of production activity at the old locations. Included would be costs associated with above-normal attrition rates, possibly necessitating the hiring of new workers, payment of overtime in connection with necessary inventory accumulations, costs of lost time, inefficiencies and

lowered productivity of terminating workers, etc.

5. Costs resulting from the transfer of production lines and start-up of production at Dover. Included would be the lost time and inefficiencies associated with the start-up phase, the need to pay overtime at Dover to attain desired production levels, costs from possible higher turnover rates at the new plant, etc.

Account would have to be taken of a wide range of miscellaneous personnel expenses arising from the relocation. For example, the costs associated with the allocation of many man-hours to the planning and implementing of the move itself; some corporate officials had to devote full time to matters related to the move, whereas usually they were active in more ordinary pursuits.

For General Foods, all such personnel costs probably totaled at _least_ \$5 million, including \$2 million for severance allowances and \$1.2 million in direct employee transfer expenses. Table 4.1 shows the total cost arising from direct transfer expenses only. It shows these expenses for employees transferring from the four old plants, plus about fifty workers who were transferred to Dover from other General Foods units. Note that the average cost of relocating exempt (salaried) employees (\$3,880) was about 170 per cent greater

TABLE 4.1

PERSONNEL COSTS ARISING FROM RELOCATION OF GENERAL FOODS EMPLOYEES TO DOVER, DELAWARE

	EXEMPT EMPLOYEES			NONEXEMPT EMPLOYEES		
	Cost	No. of Emplys. by Category	Average Cost	Cost	No. of Emplys. by Category	Average Cost
Residence selling expenses	$144,495	108	$1,338	$ 42,167	76	$ 555
Interest, taxes, insurance	2,780	17	164	388	4	97
Lease cancellation costs	4,946	29	171	1,830	18	102
GF loss on house sales	127,185	39	3,261	-	-	-
Closing costs	70,052	181	387	34,787	113	308
Service, alteration, install.	26,618	202	132	5,814	100	58
Unexpired auto & driver license	1,047	84	12	337	32	11
Pre-Dover interim living costs	16,186	30	540	225	2	113
Dover interim living costs	145,738	204	714	36,018	140	257
Personnel & family travel	56,267	225	250	40,605	183	222
Subtotal*	$595,314	-	-	$162,171	228	$ 711
Moving household furnishings	181,697	221	822	108,466	191	568
Supplemental salary	51,752	217	238	25,779	198	130
Expenses not identifiable**	83,000	-	-	30,000	-	-
Total	$911,763	235	$3,880	$326,416	228	$1,432

*Total of items limited to $1,000 for nonexempt employees. It should be pointed out that some employees may have spent the major portion of their $1,000 on one or two items (*e.g.*, selling and closing costs), thus limiting the amount reimbursable in the remaining categories.

**Expenses paid to transferred employees at other plants.

Source: Company records

than the cost of relocating non-exempt (hourly) employees ($1,432) and reflects the more liberal provision of benefits to salaried personnel. General Foods lost $127,185 on the purchase and resale of homes of salaried workers, whereas this service was not offered to hourly workers. The largest single item of cost to General Foods was the payment of moving household furnishings. About $290,000 were spent to move the furniture of both hourly and salaried workers, representing almost 25 per cent of the total expense of the relocation program.

As pointed out in Chapter III, it was anticipated that the new plant would cost $36 to $38 million, and actually cost $50 million. Hence, actual personnel costs were about 14 per cent of anticipated total costs, and 10 per cent of actual total costs. The importance of making a proper allowance for personnel costs is quite obvious. Underestimation by any significant amount might have easily diminished the profitability of the investment to a point where some alternative use of the money would have been more advantageous.

However, it is clear that General Foods must have had only an unclear notion of what personnel costs would be associated with the shutdown decision, since appropriate personnel policies were not developed until <u>after</u> the shutdown decision had been reached. It is true that corporate planners could anticipate that existing personnel policies would be extended to cover the requirements of the shutdown. General Foods had shut down other facilities in the past, and those experiences could provide some guidelines for expectations about future experience. The corporation had offered limited transfer opportunities in the past in similar situations, and had a firm policy on the payment of termination allowances. Nevertheless, it remains true that essential policies were not developed and details on existing policies were not clarified at the time of the shutdown decision itself. In addition, if the corporation expected that workers at the old locations would be allowed a free choice between possible alternatives, as, in the end, they were allowed, then the uncertainty surrounding the magnitude of the personnel costs of the shutdowns could only be compounded.

A Classification of Policies for Plant Shutdowns

A large number of various kinds of personnel policies has been used for plant shutdowns. It may provide us with some additional insights if an attempt is made to classify these policies. Such a classification is attempted, based in part on certain *a priori* notions about worker behavior. The validity of our classification is limited, therefore, but may be useful in achieving the objective of this chapter of describing the logic behind the selection and implementation of a particular set of personnel policies for plant shutdowns.

The central contention is that each policy used for a plant shutdown may be suitably classified in two dimensions. In the first dimension, policies can be classified on the basis of whether they are procedural in nature[6] or whether they are substantive. A procedural policy is one which merely describes or prescribes some method or manner to achieve a certain objective. Often it will take the form of a service; hence, placement counseling is a procedural policy. A substantive policy is, by definition, simply more "substantial" than a procedural policy and consequently the line between the two cannot be clearly established. Usually a substantive policy will involve some form of compensation, direct or indirect, for the employee. Hence, severance pay is a substantive policy.

The second dimension on which policies can be classified is as follows: every policy can be viewed, to a greater or lesser extent, as being designed either to (1) facilitate the transition of the worker to the external labor market or (2) facilitate his relocation within the company -- or, stated more broadly, facilitate his adjustment to internal opportunities. For convenience we shall refer to them as "external" and "internal" policies. Thus, severance pay is an external

---

[6]Jack Barbash, "The Impact of Technology on Labor-Management Relations," Somers _et al._, _op. cit._, pp. 47-48.

policy, while the whole range of possible policies used in an interplant transfer system is of an internal nature.

In Table 4.2 the various policies which have been or may be used for a plant shutdown are classified on an internal-external basis and on a procedural-substantive basis. It is not claimed that the classification is perfect or that the listing of policies is complete. Also, it is recognized that many shutdowns have occurred (more so in the past than today) for which *none* of the policies listed were used. However, the more commonly used policies are listed and, as pointed out earlier in this chapter, companies are more and more devising a package of such policies when faced with the prospect of a shutdown.

It is important to note that certain policies can be classified on neither an internal nor an external basis. They are "neutral" policies: *i.e.*, they neither facilitate the worker's adjustment to internal opportunities, nor his transition to the external labor market. Thus, advance notice is listed both in the procedural-internal cell and in the procedural-external cell. However, it may be argued that few policies, when taken in the context of a given shutdown, are not ultimately directed to either an internal or external aim. Hence, an advance notice which incorporates the steps a worker is to follow to effect termination is of a different order from one which empha-

TABLE 4.2

A CLASSIFICATION OF PERSONNEL POLICIES FOR PLANT SHUTDOWNS

	Policies Designed to Facilitate Worker Adjustment to Internal Opportunities	Policies Designed to Facilitate the Worker's Transition to the External Labor Market
Procedural Policies	Advance notice Joint consultation with union to develop transfer rights Information and communication on relocation opportunities Employee counseling on relocation opportunities Housing advice for transferring employees	Advance notice Joint consultation with union to develop separation procedures and employee benefits Information and communication on separation benefits Canvas of area employers for information on the availability of job openings Cooperation with local employment services, *e.g.*, in testing and counseling terminating employees
Substantive Policies	Relocation allowance and payment of wages for time used to move Payment of transportation and moving expenses Guaranteed job at new location Guaranteed seniority and/or modified seniority units, *e.g.*, interplant seniority "Flow-back" provisions (see Ch. V) Provision of pre-move trip(s) to new location	Severance pay (dismissal compensation) Job retraining Early retirement benefits Supplemental pension benefits Vesting of fringe benefit rights Supplemental unemployment benefits

sizes the availability of transfer opportunities. Our impression is that nearly all neutral policies are of a procedural nature.

Now it may be objected that many companies do not design a set of plant shutdown policies with either the objective of facilitating the worker's adjustment to internal opportunities or his transition to the external market. Certainly, companies design policies for shutdowns with other aims in mind. However, it may be asserted that, whether consciously designed or not, the net effect, or vector, of any set of plant shutdown policies is in either an internal or external direction.

The judgment of the direction of policies may be difficult for the observer to detect. This is true in the General Foods case. Both internal and external policies were used liberally by General Foods -- and it is conceivable that the net effect of a set of policies is neutral. But after close study of the General Foods case, an observer is forced to the conclusion that the net direction of policies was in an internal direction.

Several points need to be made clear in the analysis before moving on. First, it is clear that workers, when offered the alternatives of termination or relocation, do not make their choice solely on the basis of the policies put into effect by management. There are obviously many forces playing on this kind of decision. The direction of plant shutdown policies is just one force working on the worker's decision. Secondly, often the worker has no options when it comes to plant shutdowns. Relocation is not offered to him; termination is the only alternative. Taken together, the two above points simply mean that the availability of relocation opportunities (*i.e.*, the provision of internal policies) is a necessary but not sufficient condition for relocation.

Whether in fact the worker does have the opportunity of choosing between options and which policies a company selects for a plant shutdown, are largely determined by the *type* of plant shutdown. For example, one is hard put to imagine circumstances under which a company, shutting down its only plant in order to go out of business, would be likely to implement policies to facilitate worker adjustment to internal opportunities. If any policies are used, they will be those designed to ease the worker's transition to the local labor market. On the other hand, whenever a multi-plant company closes one of its plants, there may be very good reasons why it would want to provide relocation opportunities and other forms of "internal" adjustment opportunities for its workers.

For example, the General Foods case demonstrates why a company may elect a set of policies designed primarily to facilitate the worker's adjustment to internal opportunities. General Foods' management was concerned for the goodwill and the image of the corporation. Management felt the guarantee of jobs in Dover to all threatened workers would overcome much of the onus that might be attached to the corporation because of the four shutdowns. Since General Foods was already committed to a fairly generous severance pay plan, the extra costs associated with relocating a large number of workers would be negligible and perhaps even non-existent. It was clear that in some job classifications, particularly the highly skilled categories, the new area would not necessarily be able to fill General Foods' needs. The corporation could go to the expense of recruiting the needed skilled workers (including "white collar" talent) in the new area, with the possibility that the price of grades of labor in short supply might be bid up in the process, or it could attempt to transfer as many of the needed workers as possible. Given the fact that the relocation costs of the personnel transferred would be largely offset by the savings in termination allowances (and other administrative costs of severing workers), the saving which would result from <u>not</u> having to recruit and train new labor in the new area would be a pure plus for the company.

In sum, General Foods found itself in a situation in which it could add to the company's reputation for being a "considerate employer" and "good member of the community," help meet its labor needs at the new plant, and, in the process, not add significantly to the costs the company would be incurring anyway. In the preceding section it was shown that the corporation spent $1.2 million on direct employee transfers. If those who transferred had terminated instead, General Foods would have incurred additional severance pay costs of about $700,000. Not counting the added cost that would have resulted from the corporation's need to recruit and train new workers to replace those who did not transfer, the net cost of the relocation program, *given* the corporation's previous commitment to a severance pay plan, was about $500,000.

The Nature and Extent of Transfer Rights

At this point, it becomes useful to introduce concepts on the nature of transfer rights, first used by Weber.[7] As Weber points out, "In practice the nature of such 'transfer rights' may vary from a limited statement of opportunity whose availability is largely subject to managerial discretion to a *bona fide* 'right' that can be asserted to 'bump' another employee in a specified unit of the same company."[8] Within our framework, the closer the transfer opportunity is to being a *bona fide*

---

[7] Arnold Weber, "The Interplant Transfer of Displaced Employees," Somers, *et al.*, *op. cit.*, pp. 95-143.

[8] *Ibid.*, p. 97.

"right," the more likely it is that the vector of shutdown policies is in an internal direction. Weber divides the range of transfer rights into four possible types.

1. Preferential hiring

> Preferential hiring arrangements usually give employees who have been laid off from one plant the right to preferential consideration when applying for a job at another plant of the same firm. In effect, this means that displaced employees will be given preference over applicants who have no previous record of employment with the company. It should be noted, however, that the extension of preferential hiring rights to displaced employees is usually contingent upon the recall of all employees of the second, or "receiving," plant who are currently on lay-off status.[9]

Weber also points out that preferential hiring rights are hardly ever "absolute" and are usually subject to some management control. In addition, such rights are often limited by geographic considerations and can apply only in a given labor market, *e.g.*, Detroit, as in the automobile industry.

> When there is concentration of production facilities within a limited geographical area, the parties have almost always used the labor market approach as a continuing aspect of the hiring program. However, when employment opportunities for displaced workers are present *in some numbers* outside the affected employees' labor market, then preferential rights are often extended over a wider area on a specific plant-to-plant basis. . . Because preferential hiring programs are devices for the reallocation of labor, they necessarily must encompass the available units of employment opportunities.[10]

---

[9] *Ibid.*

[10] *Ibid.*, p. 101. Italics are Weber's.

Fairly explicit in the above is the proposition that the extension of internal opportunities is closely related to the type of plant shutdown (and hence the company's manpower requirements).

2. Attrition Rights

> The distinctive feature of the concept of attrition rights is that it gives high-seniority employees who have been displaced from one plant preferential hiring rights at other plants of the same company before all employees who are on lay-off status at those plants have been recalled to work.[11]

The only example that Weber can cite of the use of attrition rights is an agreement between Chrysler and the UAW, in effect in 1959 and 1960.

3. The Transfer-of-Operations Principle

This third type of transfer right is of particular interest because it is the type which applies to the General Foods case.

> The transfer-of-operations principle involves a relatively firm commitment on the part of management that employees affected by the shift of a given set of operations from one plant or facility to another will have the right to transfer with the operations and associated job opportunities. . . The application of the transfer-of-operations principle normally does not mean that every employee displaced by the shift is given the right to a job at the plant to which the particular operation is transferred. More precisely, it usually

---

[11] *Ibid.*

> means that the jobs related to the operation will be made available to employees at the old plant who are displaced by the transfer. Such a situation often arises when the transfer of operations is the occasion for the introduction of new or improved technology which has reduced manpower requirements. In this case, transfer rights generally are given only to enough employees to man the operation at the second plant. If more employees indicate a desire to move than there are jobs available, transfer rights will usually be distributed among the displaced employees on the basis of seniority. . . The transfer of operations principle has been applied to two types of situations: those involving the shift of operations to an established plant and those involving a transfer to new plants. . .[12]

Note that the transfer-of-operations principle is only applicable in shutdowns "involving the shift of operations to an established plant" and "those involving a transfer to new plants." Weber points out that the principle has been used on the railroads and in the automobile industry. The General Foods case is probably its first application in the food products industry. However, unlike the railroad and automobile industries, General Foods was able to extend the right of transfer (and the concomitant guarantee of a job at the new facility) to _every_ employee at the shutdown plants. It was never anticipated, nor was it found necessary, to use seniority as an allocating device.

---

[12] _Ibid._, pp. 103-104.

4. Interplant Bumping Rights

> Interplant bumping rights may be considered the strongest form of transfer rights. Under this arrangement, an employee laid off from one plant could displace a junior employee in another plant of the same company. This right could be exercised without the transfer of operations or other enabling conditions. . . In all the cases investigated in detail, no instance was brought to light which involved the use of unconditional interplant bumping rights.[13]

The General Foods case is no exception to this finding. Theoretically, the establishment of such rights would have expanded the employees' opportunities significantly. However, as was pointed out in Chapter III, there were very few General Foods facilities in the vicinity of the four shutdown plants. Hoboken was the exception; but there a relatively large number of transfer opportunities were made available in nearby General Foods units. It can be conjectured that the provision of interplant bumping rights would have had a significant impact on the Walter Baker situation, where the large number of senior workers might have bumped more junior workers at the Atlantic Gelatin plant in nearby Woburn.

There is very little information available on the extent to which companies have instituted interplant transfer systems. As pointed out in Chapter I, such "systems" have been installed

---

[13] *Ibid.*, p. 106.

within recent years in a few collective bargaining relationships, particularly in the steel and automobile industries. In a 1964 survey by the American Management Association, an effort was made to determine to what extent companies reimbursed personnel for relocation expenses.[14] The AMA randomly selected 800 firms, stratified on the basis of company size, from Poor's Register of Corporations, Directors and Executives. However, only 41 per cent responded to the survey. Of the 329 responding, 256 reported having "definite policies covering benefits for employees transferred to other locations." It was found that most of these policies were of fairly recent origin: 77 per cent in the 1953-64 period. Most of the policies applied to individuals or small groups transferring: only 20 per cent of the companies using such policies transferred more than 100 employees in a year. It is not clear that the same transfer policies would be used in the event of one or more plant shutdowns involving large numbers of employees. Furthermore, it is clear that blue-collar personnel do not receive the same consideration as do white-collar personnel. According to the report:

---

[14]K. K. White, Reimbursing Personnel for Transfer and Relocation Costs (New York: American Management Association, 1964), AMA Research Study 67, 61 pp.

> The rank-and-file employees . . . are not covered to the extent accorded the (salaried) personnel. . . In fact, only half of the respondents include them in their policies; but when they are covered they generally receive comparable benefits. Frequently, the rank-and-file worker is excluded from policy statements simply because it is not the practice of the company to move him, or because his benefits are carefully defined in union contracts. . . (When) rank-and-file employees are transferred, the benefits to which they are entitled (in most cases) are incorporated in the labor-union agreement; benefits are not necessarily provided for nonunion employees.[15]

General Foods' Severance Pay Plan in Perspective

Of the 1,800 workers employed by General Foods at the four eastern plants in March, 1962, 986 were to accept termination rather than relocate in Dover. Of this number of terminations, 827 were hourly employees. About 69 per cent of the hourly employees accepted termination, against only 27 per cent of salaried personnel. But whether hourly or salaried personnel, all but a very few of the terminated workers were given severance pay, in accordance with a long-standing General Foods policy.

As pointed out above, General Foods spent approximately $2 million on severance pay. Hourly employees received an average allowance of about $1,800 apiece, whereas salaried employees averaged about $3,100 per employee. These figures can be compared to the average

---

[15] *Ibid.*, pp. 13-15.

costs of relocation: $1,432 for hourly workers and $3,880 for salaried workers.

Severance pay had been offered to hourly employees for at least twenty years. When the corporation's Fairport, New York, plant had shut down in 1946, displaced workers were provided with termination pay. Similarly, when the corporation shut down a Maxwell House Coffee plant in Los Angeles in 1950, all displaced workers were given termination allowances.[16]

General Foods' policy was to give the severing worker a number of weeks of pay. The number of weeks was graduated on the basis of both age and seniority. The latest schedule of termination allowances had been adopted in July, 1961, and is reproduced in Table 4.3. The schedule indicates that workers had to have at least one year of continuous service before they would be eligible for severance pay. Anywhere from one to fifty-two weeks of pay would be granted to the terminated worker. The same schedule was used for both hourly and salaried personnel. The considerable difference in average severance pay between terminated hourly and salaried workers is attributable to differences in pay scales, rather than to significant differences in seniority or age distributions. Workers were paid the lump sum amount, except in those cases where

---

[16] Whitman and Schmidt, op. cit., pp. 101-102.

TABLE 4.3

SCHEDULE OF TERMINATION ALLOWANCES • GENERAL FOODS CORPORATION

Maximum = 52 weeks

Attained Age at Termination	Number of Weeks' Earnings To Be Paid As Termination Allowance or Wage/Salary Continuation																																	
63-65	2	3	5	6	8	9	11	12	14	16	17	18	19	20	21	22	23	24	25	26	27	28	29	30	33	36	39	42	45	48	51	52	52	52	52
60-62	2	3	5	6	8	9	11	12	14	15	16	17	18	19	20	21	22	23	24	25	26	27	28	29	32	35	38	41	44	47	50	52	52	52	52
57-59	1	2	3	4	5	6	8	10	12	14	15	16	17	18	19	20	21	22	23	24	25	26	27	28	31	34	37	40	43	46	49	52	52	52	52
54-56	1	2	3	4	5	6	7	9	11	13	14	15	16	17	18	19	20	21	22	23	24	25	26	27	30	33	36	39	42	45	48	51	52	52	52
51-53	1	2	3	4	5	6	7	8	10	12	13	14	15	16	17	18	19	20	21	22	23	24	25	26	29	32	35	38	41	44	47	50	52	52	52
48-50	1	2	3	4	5	6	7	8	9	11	12	13	14	15	16	17	18	19	20	21	22	23	24	25	28	31	34	37	40	43	46	49	52	52	52
45-47	1	2	3	4	5	6	7	8	9	10	11	12	13	14	15	16	17	18	19	20	21	22	23	24	27	30	33	36	39	42	45	48	51	52	52
42-44	1	2	3	4	4	5	6	7	8	9	10	11	12	13	14	15	16	17	18	19	20	21	22	23	26	29	32	35	38	41	44	47			
39-41	1	2	3	3	4	5	6	6	7	8	9	10	11	12	13	14	15	16	17	18	19	20	21	22	25	28	31	34	37						
36-38	1	2	3	3	3	4	5	6	6	7	8	9	10	11	12	13	14	15	16	17	18	19	20	21	24	27									
33-35	1	2	3	3	3	4	4	5	5	6	7	8	9	10	11	12	13	14	15	16	17	18	19												
30-32	1	1	2	2	2	3	3	4	4	5	6	7	8	9	10	11	12	13	14	15															
27-29	1	1	2	2	2	2	3	3	3	4	5	6	7	8	9	10	11																		
26 & under	1	1	1	2	2	2	2	2	3	3	4	5	6	7																					
	1	2	3	4	5	6	7	8	9	10	11	12	13	14	15	16	17	18	19	20	21	22	23	24	25	26	27	28	29	30	31	32	33	34	35
	Attained Years of Continuous Service																																	

An employee's "Attained Age" and "Attained Years of Continuous Service" will be determined as of the time of layoff, termination, or commencement of wage/salary continuation, whichever occurs first.

The number of weeks' Termination Allowance will not exceed the number of weeks remaining to an employee's normal retirement date.

July 3, 1961

the number of weeks of the allowance exceeded the number of weeks remaining in the year of termination. In those cases, terminating workers would receive a first payment equal to the number of weeks remaining in the year, and a second payment covering the remaining weeks in January of the next year. Workers preferred the tax advantages of this method of payment.

The definitive study in this area is still Everett D. Hawkins' 1940 book, Dismissal Compensation.[17] Hawkins provides a useful definition which bears repeating:

> Dismissal compensation may be defined as the payment of a specific sum, in addition to any back wages or salary, made by an employer to an employee for *permanently* terminating the employment relationship primarily for reasons beyond the control of the employee. . . Normally an employee who voluntarily quits is not entitled to compensation. . . Dismissal compensation is paid for breaking the valuable employment relation rather than for the period of unemployment. Payments, therefore, are not as a rule contingent upon the dismissed worker remaining unemployed. The essential feature of dismissal compensation is a payment made in a whole, or in part, by the employer who permanently severs the employee-employer relationship.[18]

The genesis of union-negotiated severance pay plans can be traced to Sidney Hillman's Amalgamated Clothing Workers. The ACW negotiated

---

[17] Everett D. Hawkins, Dismissal Compensation (Princeton: Princeton University Press, 1940), 390 pp.

[18] Ibid., pp. 5-6. Italics are Hawkins'.

a plan with Hart, Schaffner and Marx in the 1920's whereby displaced cutters received a lump sum dismissal wage out of a fund jointly established by the union and company.[19] However, the practice of paying terminated workers an additional week or two of wages is a practice which management unilaterally instituted years before the rise of trade unionism. Weber and Taylor point out that the payment of dismissal compensation was often made in lieu of an advance notice of displacement.[20] In any event, it is instructive to note that the practice of paying dismissal wages does not necessarily represent a response to trade-union demands. Many unorganized companies have provided severance pay as a matter of policy, even when forced with going out of business.

General Foods apparently instituted a severance pay program complete unilaterally, without any compulsion from a union. In fact, the unions involved in this case had not negotiated an explicit severance pay provision with the company. However, the Butcher Workmen had bargained the following clause into their contract with Walter Baker:

---

[19] Philip Taft, "Organized Labor and Technological Change," Somers, et al., op. cit., p. 39.

[20] Arnold R. Weber and David P. Taylor, "Procedures for Employee Displacement: Advance Notice of Plant Shutdown," The Journal of Business, Vol. XXXVI, No. 3, July, 1963, p. 303.

> So long as they are in effect, employees shall have the benefit of and be subject to all provisions of insurance, retirement, sick benefit and _other benefit plans and policies from time to time promulgated by the company._ Any liberalization of benefit plans or reduction in employee contribution rate which may be granted to any other hourly employees of General Foods Corporation throughout the United States and its territories shall become applicable to employees represented by this bargaining unit effective as of the same date.[21]

This clause, which might be compared with a "most-favored-nation" clause in an international treaty, may be interpreted to include severance pay plans, and, indeed, any "benefit plan" for employees, such as the employee transfer system used by the corporation.

It is difficult to estimate the extent of the use of severance pay in American industry, because so many "plans" are actually either informal arrangements or _ad hoc_ plans developed to meet specific contingencies. A company may merely intend to provide workers with severance pay, should mass layoffs ever become a necessity. Obviously there is a world of difference between a statement of intent by an unorganized company and a formally negotiated plan contained in a collective bargaining agreement.

---

[21] _Meatcutters and Butcher Workmen, Amalgamated, AFL-CIO, and The Walter Baker Chocolate Company, General Foods Corporation, Agreement between,_ August 27, 1961, Paragraphs 101 and 102. Emphasis added.

The National Industrial Conference Board and the Bureau of Labor Statistics have made continuing studies of the use of severance pay plans in American industry. The NICB has attempted to evaluate the use of non-negotiated as well as negotiated plans, by surveying manufacturing and non-manufacturing firms. The NICB's results are limited because of the possibly ephemeral nature of non-negotiated plans, and also because the survey samples are restricted in size and limited primarily to large firms. Nevertheless, a NICB survey revealed that between 40 and 60 per cent of the large manufacturing firms had some type of severance pay arrangement in 1958.[22] A later study of non-manufacturing firms showed that severance pay plans were perhaps more common in financial institutions and utilities than in manufacturing firms, and perhaps less common in wholesale and retail trade firms.[23]

The BLS has published four comprehensive studies of severance pay plans in collective bargaining agreements.[24] The fourth study

---

[22]National Industrial Conference Board, Severance Pay Patterns in Manufacturing, Studies in Personnel Policy, No. 174 (New York: NICB, 1959).

[23]National Industrial Conference Board, Severance Pay Patterns in Non-manufacturing, Studies in Personnel Policy, No. 178 (New York: NICB, 1960).

[24]The four studies published by the Bureau of Labor Statistics are Dismissal Pay Provisions in Union Agreements, December, 1944 (BLS Bulletin 808, 1945); "Dismissal Pay Provisions in Union Agreements, 1949," in Labor-Management Contract Provisions, 1949-50 (BLS Bulletin 1022, 1951); Collective Bargaining Clauses: Dismissal Pay (BLS Bulletin 1216, 1957); and Severance Pay and Lay-Off Benefit Plans (BLS Bulletin 1425-2, 1965).

concluded that the BLS surveys had revealed "a steady upward trend in the per cent of agreements with such plans, and a particularly marked rise since the 1955-56 survey."[25] Major plans were added to agreements in the automobile, aerospace, and rubber industries after 1957. The BLS surveys showed that the percentage of agreements with severance pay plans increased from 5 per cent in 1944 to 8 per cent in 1949 to 16 per cent in 1955-56 to 30 per cent in 1963. The BLS surveyed 1,773 major agreements in 1963 and found that 525 had severance pay plans covering about 40 per cent (3.1 million) of the workers under the agreements studied.[26]

The BLS further found that 46 per cent of all severance pay plans had been negotiated by only five unions: the Steelworkers, Automobile Workers, Communications Workers, Ladies Garment Workers, and Electrical Workers (IBEW).[27] In the communications industry 76 out of 81 agreements had severance pay plans. In fact, four industries account for 43 per cent of all negotiated severance pay plans: communications (76), primary metals (56), transportation equipment (52) and food and kindred products (40).[28]

---

[25] U. S. Department of Labor, Bureau of Labor Statistics, Severance Pay and Lay-off Benefit Plans (Bulletin No. 1425-2, 1965), p. 5.

[26] Ibid., pp. 5-7.

[27] Ibid., p. 1.

[28] Ibid., p. 13.

Using the BLS findings, it is possible to compare General Foods' severance pay plan with other negotiated plans in the food products industry. Although General Foods unilaterally established its plan, as it turns out, it compares favorably with union-negotiated plans. For example, of the thirty-three plans in the food products industry studied in detail by the BLS, all required at least one year of service, and fifteen required two or more years of service, before a worker became eligible for payment. At the outset General Foods required only one year of service, and later that was removed for some workers. Table 4.4 compares the minimum and maximum weeks of payment after various years of service under the General Foods plan (taken from Table 4.3) against the average number of weeks of payment in the food and kindred products industry and in all manufacturing industries. It appears that the negotiated plans in the food products industry are a bit more liberal than the average for all manufacturing, and it is fair to say that the General Foods plan, although not negotiated, is typical of its industry.

A Note on the Rationale of Graduated Severance Benefits

In the 1965 BLS study of severance pay plans, the Bureau found that 354 of the 377 plans studied provided for graduated benefits on the basis of length of service: the longer the service, the higher

TABLE 4.4

A COMPARISON OF GENERAL FOODS' SEVERANCE PAY PLAN WITH THOSE IN MANUFACTURING AND THE FOOD INDUSTRY

(Weeks of Payment)

	(1) Average Weeks, All Manufacturing (194 Agreements)	(2) Average Weeks, Food and Kindred Products (29 Agreements)	General Foods (3) Minimum Number of Weeks	General Foods (4) Maximum Number of Weeks
After 1 year of service	0.3	0.8	1	2
After 5 years of service	5.1	4.6	2	8
After 10 years of service	8.4	9.3	3	16
After 15 years of service	11.1	16.5	9	21
After 20 years of service	13.9	23.6	15	26
After 25 years of service	16.5	30.5	24	33

Source: Columns (1) and (2), BLS, Severance Pay and Layoff Benefit Plans (Bulletin No. 1425-2), p. 51, Table 11.

the benefit.[29] As we have seen, the General Foods plan graduated severance payments on the basis of both length of service and age. What is the explanation for the practice of graduating severance benefits on the basis of age and/or seniority?

Such rationalizations as have been made for this feature of severance pay plans rest, at least implicitly, on the concept of property rights in jobs. The layman's explanation that the worker is being "rewarded" for long service is extended and interpreted to mean that the accumulation of seniority rights represents a form of property for which the worker should be compensated. The long-service employee is the beneficiary of certain added rights and privileges; therefore, he should be justly compensated for relinquishing those rights and privileges. Presumably the employer responds by offering higher severance benefits because he is fair-minded and recognizes the equity in the worker's claim. Alternatively the employer may respond because of union pressure.

Both are possible explanations. However, a third explanation is also possible. This argument is based on the possible incompatibility between the use of a seniority system for internal labor allocation and the management of a plant solely on the efficiency

---

[29]Ibid., p. 39.

principle. As Chamberlain[30] and others have pointed out, most managers are convinced that the use of seniority reduces worker incentives and plant efficiency; unions naturally argue the contrary. We are not about to argue either side of the question. If employers simply <u>believe</u> that there is a conflict between seniority and efficiency, it is enough to justify the employer's provision of higher severance benefits to longer-service employees.

The employer, recognizing the element of choice present in the majority of severance pay plans, would seek to design a plan that would provide stronger incentives for less efficient employees to terminate. An employee's efficiency is a relative matter, based on the wage-productivity nexus. The employer, other things being equal, would prefer to have those employees terminate whose productivity was not commensurate with their wage levels. If it were true -- or if the employer merely thought it true -- that the more senior employee received additional wages and benefits not justified by his level of productivity, then the employer would prefer to have the more senior employee terminate, and would be willing to offer a higher severance benefit in order to induce him to do so.

If the employer also incurs added pension costs with senior employees, he has another inducement to design his severance plan

---

[30]Neil W. Chamberlain, <u>Labor</u> (New York: McGraw-Hill, 1958), pp. 265-268.

to appear relatively more attractive to long-service workers. Thus, seniority-related severance benefit plans may be at least partly the result of the employer's search for lower costs.

Advance Notice of Plant Shutdown

This chapter concludes with a brief discussion of General Foods' advance announcement of plant shutdown. Weber and Taylor have already provided a comprehensive analysis of the procedures, objectives, and problems of advance notices.[31] As these authors point out:

> In recent years, a growing concern over employee displacement arising from plant closings has led to further innovations in the procedural aspects of labor relations. In a dynamic economy, changes in technology and market structure have always taken their toll of production facilities that have lost their economic usefulness. Whereas in the past the unit usually suffered a swift, unheralded demise, an impending plant shutdown may now involve a variety of measures to inform, and perhaps comfort, the affected parties. By themselves, these procedures for advance notice of plant shutdown do not alter the economic facts. Considerable evidence reveals, however, that they can contribute to sound labor-management relations by facilitating an orderly adjustment to employee displacement and by providing a framework for developing other remedial measures.[32]

---

[31] Weber and Taylor, op. cit.

[32] Ibid., p. 302.

The decision when to announce to employees and the public the impending shutdown of the four obsolescent plants was, chronologically speaking, the first personnel policy decision that the management of General Foods needed to make. When the decision was made to carry through with the shutdown and consolidation, management decided almost simultaneously that immediate notification was the most efficacious policy. Management feared the possible consequences if notification were withheld and word of the shutdown would leak out. It was decided from the first that the corporation should, within reason, withhold nothing from the various publics affected by the initial decision, and that all future decisions and developments should be announced as soon as it was feasible to do so.

The two-year advance notice provided by General Foods is not typical of the duration of notice provided by companies in similar situations. Weber and Taylor studied thirty-two cases of plant shutdowns or "major dislocations" and found that the median period of advance notice for all cases was ten months. The shortest period was three weeks, while a telephone company provided an exceptional three-year notification.[33]

On March 7, 1962, letters were sent to all employees of the four old plants over the signature of E. Burke Giblin, Vice-President

---

[33] Ibid., p. 307.

of the Jell-O Division. One such letter follows:

> TO EMPLOYEES OF FRANKLIN BAKER, HOBOKEN:
>
> After thorough study and consideration of all the factors involved, General Foods has decided to consolidate four of the Eastern plants of the Jell-O Division into one modern production facility which probably will be located within 250 miles of New York City. This will mean the eventual closing of our plant at Hoboken, as well as the Jell-O plant in LeRoy, the Walter Baker plant in Dorchester, and the Minute plant in Orange.
>
> The attached press release, which is to go to the newspapers for publication tomorrow, will explain the scope of the move and give you an idea of the general background. Here, however, I would like to talk more at length about family matters.
>
> At the outset, let me assure you that you will be kept fully informed of developments as they occur, particularly of any move that may affect your future, and to begin with we'll want to tell you where the plant will be built just as soon as we know ourselves.
>
> Since the first relocation is more than a year away, we have plenty of time to establish the policies which will guide the move and to discuss the effect of the move with you personally. As soon as the site of the new plant is selected, and the engineering is far enough along to plan operating procedures, we can begin to talk about what jobs will be open, what qualifications will be needed, and how personal costs of transfers will be met. We hope that everyone who can transfer to the new plant will then express a wish to do so.

For those who do not transfer to the new plant when the time comes, we will, of course, arrange suitable termination allowances based on age and length of service. Assistance to find other employment also will be available if needed.

I realize that you will have many questions. Let me assure you that you will have a good opportunity to discuss your individual problems and that every consideration will be given each individual case.

Jell-O and General Foods reached the important decision to consolidate our Eastern plants into one new facility with high hopes on one hand but with a great deal of regret on the other. We have long enjoyed friendly relations in Hoboken, and our roots in this community go very deep. We are aware that the move will cause everyone a certain amount of inconvenience and will greatly inconvenience some.

We will do all we can to minimize personal inconvenience, and we believe that advance planning, shared with you, will help the most. Careful, forehanded, and shared plans certainly held personal inconvenience to a minimum when the General Offices moved from New York to White Plains, in 1954, and that was a major move, too, involving about as many people as will be involved in our move. We will follow the same pattern, and I would like to emphasize again these three points:

First, no job should be affected for more than a year, or longer.

Second, in good time you will have your opportunity to discuss your personal future with us and learn precisely how the move will affect you.

Third, you will be fully informed of developments as they occur.

Several points about this communication should be noted:

1. Employees at the four old plants were the first to hear of the decision. General Foods was careful to do this in order to minimize hard feelings at the four old plants.
2. However, by so doing, the corporation was informing the employees before personnel policies had been formulated, before the site for the new plant had been selected, and before the technical and manpower requirements of the new plant were fully known.
3. On the other hand, even though firm personnel policies had not yet been devised, the corporation was already advising its employees that transfer opportunities would be available: "We hope that everyone who can transfer to the new plant will . . . express a wish to do so."

Interviews with displaced and relocated workers reveal general satisfaction with and gratitude for the long advance notice. Workers indicated that it allowed them an adequate period within which to plan for the impending dislocation. A few employees postponed major purchases they had been planning to make, or otherwise attempted to provide for themselves a financial cushion to help them through the transitional period. Some employees began to canvass the labor market for alternative job opportunities. However, most workers did not *immediately* begin to make adjustments for the coming shutdown, or search out available jobs in the local area. In fact, the overwhelming majority of workers electing termination did not begin an active job search until *after* their displacement. To management's satisfaction, turnover or attrition was not higher after the shutdown notification than before. Workers were induced to remain in employment by the opportunity to earn higher wages and increase their incomes through abundant overtime opportunities available in the shutdown phase, and also by the fact that quitting before the date prescribed by management disqualified the worker for any severance benefits. Loyalty to the company, miscalculation about the ease of finding alternative employment, and simple inertia were other factors that possibly helped to control excessive attrition.

A few displaced workers indicated in interviews that the long advance notice was unsettling. They reported feeling "nervous" or "upset" living with the knowledge that their source of livelihood was to be abruptly cut off in the near future. But, while a very few might have reacted with anxiety and apprehension, the great majority appreciated the company's directness and openness. Additional evidence on worker attitudes to advance notice is presented in Chapter VII.

Chapter Summary

In this chapter the personnel policies used by General Foods to provide relocation opportunities and severance benefits to workers affected by the shutdown of four plants have been examined. Highlights of the discussion are listed below.

1. Details on the precise nature of the policies implemented by General Foods were first presented. In essence, every worker affected by the plant shutdowns was guaranteed a job at the new plant to be built in Dover, Delaware. Workers had the choice of either relocating with all (or nearly all) expenses paid, retaining full seniority and benefit rights, to a job which in the majority of cases was identical to the one they had been performing, or terminating with a reasonable severance allowance and the company's promise to help them find new work. All employees had the opportunity to visit Dover at company expense. Hourly employees electing transfer received one week off with pay at the time of their relocation and reimbursement up to $1,000 for expenses growing out of their move.

2. The personnel costs incurred by the corporation arising from the plant relocation were found to be substantial and were estimated at about $5 million, including $2 million for severance allowances and $1.2 million for direct employee transfer expenses. The average

cost of relocating salaried employees was $3,880; the average for hourly employees was $1,432. The difference reflects the more liberal provision of benefits to salaried personnel.

3. In order to provide a more general framework for the understanding of personnel policies for plant shutdowns, a classification of such policies was developed. Two types of distinctions were made: between policies of a procedural or substantive nature, and between policies designed to facilitate the transition of the worker to the external labor market, or policies designed to facilitate his relocation with the company. General Foods used a variety of all types of policies, but the net effect of the design of the policies used by the corporation was judged to be of an "internal" nature.

4. The nature of transfer rights, as first analyzed by Weber, was next discussed. The General Foods case was shown to be an application of the "transfer-of-operations" principle.

5. The average amount of severance pay received by terminating hourly employees was $1,800. The average received by salaried employees was $3,100. It was pointed out that General Foods severance pay plan was employer-instituted. Nevertheless, it was shown to compare very favorably with union-negotiated plans in the food industry,

which, in turn, appear to be a bit more liberal than the average negotiated plan in force in manufacturing in general.

6. The long advance notice of the plant shutdowns given by the corporation to its employees was found to be exceptional. Interviews with workers revealed that, with a few exceptions, they appreciated the company's directness and openness.

CHAPTER V

PERSONNEL POLICIES AND PROBLEMS IN STARTING THE DOVER PLANT

In the start-up phase of the Dover plant, the General Foods Corporation had at least four general problems to deal with in the area of personnel relations.

First, the company had to recruit, select, train, and place a large number of workers needed to supplement those transferring in from outside the Dover area.

Second, the company had to decide on an appropriate wage policy, seniority system, and complex of working rules to govern the workforce of the new plant.

Third, the company had to face the possibility of union organization of the new plant, and be prepared to negotiate in case a union did succeed in achieving representation.

Finally, the company had to be prepared to handle the problems that the relocated workers would face in orienting themselves to a new work and community environment; for a successful plant operation, the "outsiders" and "natives" would have to be successfully integrated, at least in the plant community.

The sample of relocated workers surveyed in Dover was asked a series of questions designed to determine the degree of their accommodation to and integration in the new plant and the Dover community. The results of the survey are analyzed in Chapter VII; therefore the discussion of this aspect of the personnel problems of starting a new plant is deferred to that chapter. Here we will be concerned with a discussion and analysis of the first three personnel problems of starting a new plant mentioned above.

Recruitment, Selection, and Placement at Dover

After the initial shutdown announcement of March 7, 1962, the corporation set about finding a suitable site for the new plant.[1] While the Dover area quickly came to the foreground as fulfilling the company's site selection criteria, it was not until September, 1962, that the final decision on Dover was made. In October, ground breaking ceremonies were held, and temporary offices were opened in the Dover business section. The first transfer took place in May, 1963, when the Franklin Baker machine accounting department moved into temporary Dover quarters.

---

[1]A complete account of the site selection process is given in Whitman and Schmidt, *op. cit.*, pp. 41-51.

By September, 1963, about 100 employees were working in Dover (including 30 new hires), and a few had been able to move into the new offices at the plant site. In February, 1964, limited production at the new plant was begun, sixteen months after the ground-breaking ceremonies. By June, 1964, 830 employees were at work at the Dover plant (365 salaried and 465 hourly). In the meantime all Hoboken transferees had arrived, and the Hoboken plant was closed in April, 1964. LeRoy transfers came in during the summer and the original Jell-O plant was closed in August.

By September, the plant had nearly reached full strength. There were 1,509 at work, 553 salaried and 1,056 hourly employees. The final Walter Baker workers moved in over the winter, and the Baker plant was closed in the spring (to be re-opened briefly in April -- see above). On May 5, 1965, the Chairman of General Foods, Charles G. Mortimer, dedicated the new Dover plant. Employment soon reached the combined strength of the four old plants -- 1,800.

The company faced the necessity of hiring more than 1,300 (1,000 production and 300 office) workers for the new facility. There is no doubt that a liberal inter-plant transfer system was established in large part because of company fears of a shortage of skilled labor in the Dover area. The company foresaw no difficulty in recruiting the large number of semi-skilled workers needed to run the mechanized and semi-mechanized production lines, but did anticipate that certain grades of blue-collar labor, particularly skilled maintenance men, might be in short supply. By offering to <u>all</u> hourly workers an attractive opportunity to move with the company, management hoped to induce enough <u>skilled</u> workers to transfer so that no problems would result from possible shortages in the Dover area.

Probably fewer skilled workers transferred than the company might have hoped for. The highly skilled millwrights, toolmakers, electricians, and others were benefited by the availability of good -- and even higher paying -- jobs in their expanding local economies (particularly Boston and Hoboken). On the other hand, there turned out to be less of a shortage of general labor in the Dover area than the company had forecast. In fact, company officials were literally astonished at the deluge of employment applications that they received -- from as far away as Philadelphia and Baltimore. The temporary Jell-O office in Dover began issuing employment applications in May, 1963. Completed applications began being returned at the rate of 150 a week. By September, 3,100 had been received (2,200 for hourly employment). By November and December, 1963, employment applications were rolling in at the rate of 500 a week. It was obvious that the company was going to be faced with a massive selection problem.

The company, therefore, was able to implement rigid hiring standards. In addition to setting up a rigorous interview and screening process, the company enlisted the aid of the Delaware State Employment Service which administered the General Aptitude Test Battery (GATB) to applicants. Through December, 1964, the company had issued more than 17,000 applications to potential employees. Of these, 11,256 were returned; 10,190 were applications for hourly work; 9,220 were asked to take the GATB; 4,886 appeared for testing; 3,550 were interviewed; 1,456 were tentatively accepted; 1,284 passed the physical examination; 1,236 passed the reference check; and 1,113 were hired.

Despite all this, the company still had problems finding needed, skilled, maintenance men. Want ads were placed in Philadelphia, Baltimore, and Wilmington papers. Additional maintenance men were brought in on temporary assignment from other General Foods units. Production men with apparent mechanical abilities were trained and promoted. The major problem, according to Whitman and Schmidt, was that skilled tradesmen in the Dover area had their past work primarily in residential construction and were not interested in working at rates more than $1.50 below construction industry levels.[2]

Another hiring problem which concerned the company but never really materialized centered on General Food's long-standing policy

---

[2]Whitman and Schmidt, pp. 119-120.

of equal opportunity in hiring and employment. The company had every intention of carrying through with this policy in Dover, despite a survey by a consulting firm which indicated that some resentment and resistance to integration existed in Dover. The company decided to state its policy clearly at the outset. It was later determined that Negroes had applied and were accepted for positions in about the same proportion as the number of Negroes in the population of the area. All in all, there was little, if any, friction on the matter.[3]

Wage Policy at Dover

Turning now to the problems of establishing wage policies for the new plant, let it be noted that these policies were originally devised in late 1962 and early 1963, so that workers were fully able to include such considerations in making their decision to move or not.

General Foods informed the workers that it was the company's policy to "pay salaries as good as prevail for similar work under similar conditions in the communities where our plants and offices are located."[4] While the company expected some savings in the area of

---

[3] *Ibid.*, pp. 48-49 and p. 119.

[4] Company memo dated November 15, 1962.

wage costs, by far the largest saving resulting from the consolidation was to come from lowered overhead costs. Nevertheless, in selecting a site for the plant, one possibility was eliminated because of high wage levels. Dover, on the other hand, held the promise of lower wage levels than nearby metropolitan areas.

It might have been the company's policy to pay prevailing community standards in wages. But by settling in Dover, and thereby becoming one of the major employers of southern Delaware, the company itself could rightfully expect to become one of the area's wage leaders. The company's "prevailing standards" policy was instrumental in making a site selection, but was bound to become less important by virtue of the company's selection of Dover.

What does a "prevailing standards" policy really mean? It is a simplified surrogate for a behavioral approach which follows the conventional economic model. The company will pay wages just high enough to attract the labor it needs. It will be sufficient to pay the "prevailing" wage, for this wage will approximate the equilibrium wage for the area. A wage which is a bit lower will fail to attract sufficient labor; a wage which is a bit higher will be unnecessarily costly.

What are the implications of the fact that the company was deluged with job applicants,[5] and was able to impose high hiring

---

[5]With the exception of skilled maintenance men, as discussed above.

standards? There are several possible explanations.

1. The company was actually offering wages above the community level; company officials had miscalculated the prevailing community standards and had set wages too high. This is unlikely, as the company had undertaken a careful survey of wages in the Delaware area.

2. The area was actually a depressed one: there was unemployment and surplus labor available. Not true: Delaware, like most areas of the country, was enjoying a sustained economic expansion. If anything, labor markets tended to be tight over the 1963-64 period.

3. The prevailing area wage itself was "too high," *i.e.*, the area labor market was in disequilibrium. One symptom of a market in disequilibrium would be the existence of unemployment, which was not true of Dover unless one wants to make some allowance for the presence of hidden unemployment, a possibility in an area which is largely rural. We might expect a wage to be sustained at a level above equilibrium if strong unions (and employers) are present, but this was patently not the case for the southern half of Delaware.

4. There were other significant market imperfections; workers miscalculated where their net advantage lay, or were simply irrational in desiring employment at Jell-O Dover. Of course, allowance must always be made for labor-market imperfections, but there is no indication

that they were any greater in the Dover area than elsewhere. Some workers might have miscalculated, but there is no compelling evidence to suggest that many acted irrationally.

5. General Foods was indeed offering the correct prevailing money wage, but workers were responding not only to the wage offered but to the total net advantages of employment at the Jell-O plant. There is good reason to believe that workers estimated the net advantages of Jell-O employment, given the prevailing wage, to be greater than the net advantages in other employment in the southern Delaware area. There was a good deal of excitement created by the coming of General Foods to Delaware. The local Dover newspaper called it "the best news Dover has had in many a year . . ."[6] The corporation was given much publicity, and the beneficial effects of the Jell-O plant on the local area economy were stressed. By such occurrences as the participation of Delaware Governor Elbert Carvel in the ground-breaking ceremonies, the new plant was granted a kind of official esteem. There is little doubt that an effective public relations program can have a beneficial feedback effect on a company's employment situation. There seems to have been a transferral from the importance of the plant to the local area to the importance of the individual who is employed by the plant. There was an aura of excitement surrounding the possibility of employment at a new, modern, important manufacturing facility that other employers

[6]Quoted in Whitman and Schmidt, p. 132.

could not match. Such an appeal might seem exaggerated to the outsider, and may in fact be transitory, but there is little doubt that it aided the corporation in acquiring needed labor (excepting skilled tradesmen).

Moreover, there were definite advantages to employment at the Jell-O plant not indicated by the wage offered. There was a promise of security and stability of employment at General Foods, not offered by alternate area employers (in retail trade, the services, and farming). The first to be hired would be able to acquire rights through seniority accumulation, below the transferred workers, to be sure, but above those who would subsequently be hired. General Foods did offer attractive fringe benefits plans, usually only available in large concerns, and the perceptive or intuitive worker probably realized that, as one of the area's largest employers, General Foods would probably become one of the area's wage leaders. Such was the sum of net advantages offered by the new plant.

But while the prevailing Dover wage was sufficient to attract more semi-skilled and clerical labor from the local area than General Foods could use, such a wage level happened to be below the existing wage levels at the two old Baker plants, and slightly above the levels existing at LeRoy and Orange. Table 5.1 compares wage levels on six representative jobs at the four old locations with the rates estab-

TABLE 5.1

COMPARISON OF HOURLY RATES PAID AT THE FOUR SHUTDOWN PLANTS AND DOVER

Job	LeRoy	Orange	Franklin Baker	Walter Baker*	Dover
Fork Truck Operator	$2.18	$2.10	$2.85	$2.42**	$2.30
Janitor	2.00	1.94	2.53	2.12	2.00
Maintenance "A"	2.58	2.36	3.33	2.82	3.00
Mixer	2.18	2.10	2.85	2.36**	2.30
Operator-Female	1.89	1.94	2.38	1.94	1.80
Package Machine Operator	2.18	2.20	2.41	2.42**	2.45

* Walter Baker had an incentive system. Those on incentive earned, on the average, 18 per cent more than the base rate.

** An incentive job at Walter Baker.

SOURCE: Company records.

lished on the jobs at the Dover plant. If these six jobs are truly representative of the hourly wage levels existing among and between the old plants and the new plant, then the Dover hourly rate was on the average about 6 per cent above the LeRoy average and 9 per cent above the Orange average, but 18 per cent below the Franklin Baker average and 8 per cent below the Walter Baker average (if the Walter Baker average is computed with due consideration for the incentive jobs). The over-all difference is about 3 per cent in favor of the four old plants, as compared to the Dover plant. However, this figure may be misleading since we are dealing with unweighted averages. If each of the hourly averages at the old plants is weighted by the number of hourly workers employed, we find that the Dover hourly wage level is about 6.5 per cent below the average wage paid at the four old plants. Short of having the actual figures (which are not available), this is about the best estimate which can be made of the savings in wage costs enjoyed by General Foods as a result of the transfer of operations.

Seniority Integration at the New Plant

According to the personnel manager of the Jell-O Division, management "anticipated great problems in the area of seniority as we integrated four systems under the one plan at Dover. As a matter of fact, we had a lot of difficulty reaching our own conclusions about what the best seniority system would be. . ."[7]

Problems of seniority integration have been particularly acute in cases in which the transferring employees move to an already established plant. In such situations the incumbent employees may feel their job security threatened by the incursion into their plant of "outsiders" with greater seniority.[8] The problem may be less serious in cases in which a new plant has been built and there are no incumbent employees. On the other hand, in the General Foods case, the welding together of four previously separate seniority systems implied that, if there was to be plant-wide seniority at Dover, some transferring employees would lose relative to others. A man at the top of the seniority list at the Dorchester plant might find himself behind others transferring from any of the other three plants.

One possible solution might have been to offer transfer, but without the retention of accumulated seniority. Relocated workers could have been treated as new employees, with seniority commencing on the date of their entry into the new plant. Of course, relocation would then have been much less attractive to the affected employees, and it is conceivable, if not likely, that many who did accept trans-

[7]Letter from Harry Chandler to the author, August 6, 1965.

[8]Arnold Weber, "The Interplant Transfer of Displaced Employees," Adjusting to Technological Change (New York: Harper and Row, 1963), Gerald Somers, et al., eds., pp. 123-132.

fer would not have done so had their seniority been eliminated. Indeed, we have the testimony of many of the relocated workers to substantiate that possibility. It was precisely to retain their seniority rights that induced many to transfer to the Dover plant.

Another variant would be to allow transferring employees to retain their full seniority with respect to pensions, vacations, and other fringe benefits, but to treat them as new employees for purposes of determining lay-off, recall, promotion, and work assignments. Another possibility would have been the pegged date-of-entry approach, whereby all transferring employees would have been given a single date-of-entry.[9] Since the relocation of workers took place over a period of several months, the pegged date-of-entry would put all transferred employees on an equal footing, and would eliminate advantages accruing to relocated workers who happened to arrive at an earlier date. The pegged date-of-entry might have been designated as a date in advance of the date of hiring of any new workers from the Dover area, so that, while transferred employees would all be on an equal footing, they would have an advantage over the new hires.

The seniority policy which General Foods intended to use for hourly employees at Dover was finally released on January 11, 1963,

---

[9] *Ibid.*, p. 126.

more than a year after the initial announcement of the relocation. According to the "On the Move to Dover" Bulletin which employees received on that date, "This Seniority Policy has been developed with due consideration for policies currently in effect at our four plants and anticipated operating requirements at our Dover plant. Protection of present employees has been a principal consideration in deciding upon these rules."

General Foods offered to all transferring employees their full seniority, computed from the date of their employment by the corporation. New employees at Dover were to have their seniority computed from the date of their employment after completing a probationary period of sixty days. "When fitness and ability are equal," seniority was to govern such matters as job and shift assignments, layoffs, recalls, and promotions. However, the company avoided the provision of a plant-wide seniority unit, and thus some of the problems of seniority integration, by creating four separate seniority units within the Dover plant. The four seniority units or departments were to be organized as follows:

(1) East - including most of the operations carried on by the Jell-O, Minute, and Franklin Baker plants.

(2) West - to include primarily the chocolate operations of the Walter Baker plant.

(3) Maintenance and utilities

(4) Receiving and shipping

In addition, the policy statement stipulated that seniority rules were to apply separately to men and women.

As already noted, the majority of transferring employees were able to stay on the same jobs that they had held at the old plants. For those workers for whom this was not possible, the company provided that the choice of department and job classification was to be determined on the basis of seniority. At the same time, those employees performing the same jobs that they had held at the old plants could not be bumped out of those jobs by other transfers with greater seniority who had never performed the job.

When a job vacancy occurred, a "posting-and-bidding" system was to be used to fill the job. But only those employees within the seniority unit (department) in which the vacancy occurred were eligible to bid for the job. There was to be no plant-wide bidding on jobs. Departmental seniority units had, in fact, been used at three of the old plants, the exception being the Hoboken plant. The collective bargaining agreement at Walter Baker provided that

> Promotions, demotions and transfers of Employees shall be made on the basis of departmental seniority, provided such Employees are capable of performing efficiently and fulfilling adequately the job requirements.[10]

Nevertheless, the existence of four separate seniority units caused some discontent among the employees. Mr. D. E. Normoyle from the Personnel Department of the Jell-O Division described the problem in a letter to the author:

> One provision of the seniority system which caused a sizeable problem during startup was the restriction on plant-wide job bidding. Initially, the plant was divided into four departments. . . When job openings occurred in one of these departments, only those employees assigned to the department in which the opening existed were eligible to bid.
>
> This had a very disturbing effect on many of our transferees (particularly those from Hoboken who were accustomed to plant-wide bidding) as well as many of our new hires. We modified the policy to the extent of permitting inter-department bidding, but only at the labor grade 5 classification (at that time \$2.10/hr.). This modification was more advantageous to the new employee than to the transferees, since most of the latter were at higher rated jobs and would not bid down to get into another department.[11]

---

[10] Meat Cutters and Butcher Workmen of North America, Amalgamated, AFL-CIO, Local 451, and the Walter Baker Chocolate Company, Agreement between, August 27, 1961, p. 28.

[11] Letter from D. E. Normoyle to the author, August 16, 1965.

In the next section of this chapter some attention will be paid to union relations at the old plants and at Dover. Suffice it to say here that organization of the Dover plant by the Butcher Workmen and by the Teamsters occurred in May, 1964, a few months after the startup of the first manufacturing lines. Mr. Normoyle explains the effect of unionization on the seniority question:

> Management expected that if we became organized unrestricted plant bidding would be a major proposal of the union. Our expectations were fulfilled. Plant-wide bidding was a critical issue and it was not resolved until the final sessions of that "long hot summer" of negotiations. . . (Plant-wide) bidding is now a fact of life in the Production and Maintenance areas in Dover, with some minor restrictions. However, this is not a provision of the agreement with the Teamsters. Shipping and Receiving employees are still limited to bidding on job openings in the S & R Department.[12]

According to the agreement signed with the Butcher Workmen, October 1, 1964, plant-wide bidding was to be used within the bargaining unit represented by the Butcher Workmen to govern manning of job openings above the base rate (provided that "fitness and ability are equal") and to make shift assignments, provided that the employees fell within the same job classification.[13]

---

[12] Ibid.

[13] Meat Cutters and Butcher Workmen of North America, Amalgamated, AFL-CIO, Amalgamated Food and Allied Workers Local 56, and the Jell-O/Dover Operations, General Foods Corporation, Agreement between, October 1, 1964, p. 20.

Strictly speaking, the lay-off procedure was not to be governed by the plant-wide principle, since it was entirely impractical to allow semi-skilled production workers to bump into skilled maintenance jobs. However, the contract did allow for the least senior employee whose job is being cut back to bump a more junior employee performing in the same job classification in his plant "division" (Chocolate, Jell-O, and Maintenance) provided the employee demonstrates that he is capable of "normal performance" within two days.[14]

According to Mr. Normoyle, "There have been some grievances regarding the interpretation of the 'normal performance after two days' aspect of the curtailment procedure. . . Possibly this could become an issue when we negotiate next year."[15] Aside from this point, however, Mr. Normoyle expressed the belief that no major changes would be made in the seniority provisions at the next negotiations. Harry Chandler, the personnel manager of the Jell-O Division, writing on the matter of seniority policy, concluded, "I suspect that in the future there may be other minor changes. I would not expect any of the basic ingredients of the seniority policy to change, however."[16]

---

[14] Ibid., pp. 24-25.

[15] Normoyle to author, op. cit.

[16] Chandler to author, op. cit.

The Role of the Unions in the Plant Shutdowns

Another problem that the company faced in starting the Dover plant was the possibility of union organization of the new facility. Before dealing with that problem, however, we need to retrace our steps a bit to outline the role of the unions in the shutdown phase of the plant relocation process. This discussion has been delayed until now because in part the role of the unions in the shutdown of the old plants was a limited one, and, by discussing the role of the unions here, rather than earlier, we are able to present a more comprehensive view of their role in both the shut-down and start-up phase of the relocation. Unions have been concerned traditionally with the threat to workers of displacement, and have sought to devise rules and policies to mitigate the effects of plant shutdowns.

It is not clear whether the union factor was important in the General Foods case. In the first place, only two of the plants shut down were unionized. Secondly, the policies were developed by General Foods after little or no consultation with the union. It is paradoxical that one of the most liberal interplant transfer systems put in effect in recent years was evolved with minimal union participation.

It is almost axiomatic in industrial relations that "generous" employee benefit policies are the result of either a strong collective bargaining relationship or a paternalistic employer. Neither seems to be true in the General Foods case. This is neither to blame nor praise the corporation, but is intended merely as a conclusion reached after close study of the case. There were strong reasons why General Foods implemented a relatively liberal set of policies; some of the reasons were susceptible to economic justification, and all were the product of what one corporate official called "enlightened self-interest."

It may be argued that the fact of union growth in general may have had an *indirect* effect on the process of policy formation at General Foods. In addition, General Foods admittedly had to reckon with the *presence* of unions at Hoboken and Dorchester, and at other facilities throughout the nation.

The Hoboken and Dorchester unions would be capable of exercising a veto on corporate intentions. The corporation hoped to maintain production at desired levels at the four old plants until the day they were finally shut down. In fact, there was a need to increase production in certain product areas in order to build up inventories so that individual production lines could be shut down and transferred to Dover with no effect on the supply of the product to the grocery shelf. Dissatisfied unions might very well be able to stymie that objective. But the provision of fair and generous shutdown policies might well "steal the union's thunder."

Unions at other General Foods facilities would be watching developments within the Jell-O Division. On the one hand, General Foods might well want to demonstrate to these unions and their members the fairness and generosity of the corporation. On the other hand, the corporation would want to be careful not to set any dangerous precedents which would be difficult to follow in other situations.

In fact, union relations had, for the most part, been stable and trouble-free. There had been one strike at Walter Baker, none at Franklin Baker. And as the shutdown of the old plants proceeded, the unions cooperated -- seeming to feel that the shutdowns were inevitable and that there was little they could do.

Contract Negotiations at Walter Baker, 1962, and at Franklin Baker, 1963

When the announcement of the shutdown was made in March, 1962, it happened that new contract negotiations were being carried on at the Franklin Baker plant with the Butcher Workmen and the Teamsters. Company officials were concerned about what effect the announcement would have on negotiations. The company, anxious to win union cooperation for the phase-out period, apparently acceded to many of the demands of the union. The personnel manager of the Jell-O Division put it this way:

> Negotiations were in progress at Franklin Baker when the initial announcement was made that the plant was to be closed. It was our intention to convey to the union the true circumstances and not be trapped by a feeling of mistrust which might have developed had our announcement been delayed until negotiations were completed. This is about the way it worked out.[17]

A contract settlement was reached at Franklin Baker shortly after the shutdown announcement. The Jell-O personnel manager summarized its terms:

> The contract settlement negotiated at Franklin Baker in March, 1962, did provide for a substantial increase of 15¢ an hour with some selected jobs going as high as 21¢ an hour. This amounted to about a 7 per cent raise in rates. In addition, the new contract called for a termination of the contract when the plant was closed by the company or at the end of three years, whichever happened first. There was no provision for a wage reopening during the term of the contract which accounts in part for the sizeable increases.[18]

Another possible reason for granting the generous wage increases was the company's desire to retain as many of the workers as

---

[17]Letter from Harry Chandler to the author, August 6, 1965.

[18]Letter from Harry Chandler to Fred Foulkes, December 17, 1965. Mr. Foulkes served as research assistant to Professor Robert Livernash of the Harvard Business School and helped prepare a case on the General Foods experience. Mr. Foulkes and the author exchanged research materials pertaining to the General Foods case.

possible until their scheduled termination or transfer. Premature attrition of a large portion of the work force might cause production to fall below desired levels. That, in turn, would have unwanted effects on the need to insure the steady supply of goods to food retailers and on the timetable for the shutdown. The wage increases served as an extra inducement to the workers to remain on their jobs.

The contract between the Butcher Workmen and the Walter Baker Company was due to expire in August, 1963. By that time all the personnel policies to be used for the shutdown had been developed in detail. Many of the workers had already visited Dover and had decided to transfer. Firm offers of jobs had been made to those transferring in June. The union virtually was faced with a *fait accompli*.

There was one area of great concern to the union, however. General Foods had provided workers with the opportunity to transfer to Dover at the expense of the company. Should the transferred worker become disenchanted with his new job or community and desire to return to his former location, he could of course do so, but at the loss of his severance pay. The union was anxious to establish "flow-back" rights for transferred employees.

Flow-back rights often, but not always, accompany the establishment of an interplant transfer system. According to Weber,

> The general principle in evidence is that flow-back rights are extended to employees who have transferred some distance from one city to another, but not to those employees who have moved to a different plant in the same labor market. . . The leading consideration in the establishment of flow-back rights appears to be that employees who transfer to a new community should be given a period of grace to determine their ability to adapt to the new environment.[19]

The Jell-O personnel manager described the establishment of "flow-back" rights for Walter Baker workers:

> The single (case in which the union played a role in establishing policy) . . . concerns the 90-day privilege which was extended to Walter Baker hourly employees -- providing an opportunity for Walter Baker bargaining unit employees to return to Dorchester without loss of termination pay. In order to qualify for this, however, they had to make application before December 31, 1964. Only a handful availed themselves of the privilege which was not extended to other units.[20]

---

[19] Weber, op. cit., p. 122.

[20] Chandler to author, August 6, 1965.

The General Foods experience with flow-back rights confirms the earlier conclusion reached by Weber: "Although the establishment of flow-back rights has sometimes been a subject of controversy, the excessive use of this prerogative does not seem to be a major problem."[21]

In the 1963 negotiations, the Butcher Workmen also sought a provision which was more or less the counterpart of the flow-back privilege. The union proposed that General Foods permit employees to terminate with severance pay and the option of returning to work at the Dover plant with full seniority rights. The option would hold good for one year. This would allow the terminated worker to test the local market for a period of time. If the worker discovered he was unable to obtain the kind of job he desired, he could then elect to relocate to Dover.

There is little record in the literature of a similar privilege being granted to terminated workers. It is a general principle that by the acceptance of severance pay, the worker relinquishes any rights he may have had with his employer, and the employer is relieved of any obligation he may have had to the worker. Few principles are ever absolute, however. When the Walter Baker plant resumed partial operations in the spring of 1965 (to last only through July), General Foods rehired a small group of workers who had

---

[21] Weber, op. cit., p. 123.

terminated with severance pay. They returned without seniority, however, and were fully aware of the temporary nature of the work.

There is one recorded case in which terminated workers were subsequently permitted transfer rights. Armour and Company shut down its Sioux City, Iowa, plant in June, 1963. Subsequently, the company decided to build a new plant in West Point, Nebraska; the plant was scheduled to open in early 1964. The company agreed to offer preferential hiring to terminated Sioux City workers at its West Point plant and, on a more limited basis, at its Sterling, Illinois, plant. The former Armour workers who accepted new jobs at West Point and Sterling would start with full seniority _only if_ they repaid their separation pay; otherwise, they would have new employee status.[22]

General Foods would not consent to extending transfer rights beyond the payment of a termination allowance. The corporation did consent to a union request for an increase in severance pay. Severance pay was calculated on the basis of average weekly wage. The union requested that only the highest average obtained within the previous twelve months be used to compute an individual's

---

[22]Norman M. Bradburn, _Inter-plant Transfer: the Sioux City Experience_ (Chicago: National Opinion Research Center, 1964), pp. 1-2.

severance pay. The company was also requested to disregard all but full work weeks in establishing the average to be used. In essence, the company agreed to the union's demands. In fact, termination allowances were computed on the basis of average weekly wages (excluding bonus and overtime payments) for the last quarter of 1963 -- after the new contract went into effect and the workers were enjoying the wage increase negotiated by the union. In addition, the company agreed to pay at least one week of severance pay to every terminated worker, regardless of length of service.

General Foods granted a 17 cents an hour across-the board wage increase to all Walter Baker hourly employees in the new 1963 agreement. Once again the company might have been relying on a substantial wage boost to hold the workers to their jobs. It might be pointed out that most of the Walter Baker workers had an opportunity to work many additional overtime hours over the final months that the plant was in operation. Consequently, most of them were bringing home more money than they ever had before in the period just prior to their termination.

The union agreed that the 1963 contract would terminate when operations were suspended at the Walter Baker plant, or at the end of two years, whichever came earlier. In fact, because both parties recognized that their relationship was temporary, they agreed not to go to the expense of printing up new contracts. A few copies of the contract changes were mimeographed to serve as a supplement to the expired contract.

It is clear that the General Foods experience was not an exercise in "creative collective bargaining." In this respect it is exceptional, since the comparable experiences of the Armour Company, Kaiser Steel, International Harvester, and other cases described in the literature were all promulgated to a large extent because of the presence of a highly active union. Union participation in policy-making at General Foods was minimal. The president of the local at Walter Baker agreed that his union had little to do with the shutdown and relocation.[23] On the other hand, it is hard to imagine the development of such a set of policies prior to the rise of the union movement. Whether recognized by management and union participants in the General Foods case or not, it is likely that the environment created by thirty years of evolving union-management relations had at least an indirect influence on the seemingly unilateral development of plant shutdown policies. Moreover, the presence of unions at two of the shutdown plants, and the hope for constructive labor relations at the new plant, no doubt were factors prompting General Foods to act as it did.

---

[23] I should like to thank Mr. Fred Foulkes for passing on the results of his interview with the president of the Butcher Workmen local at Walter Baker.

Still, the personnel manager of the Jell-O Division was entirely accurate when he summarized the unions' role in the following fashion:

> Actually, with one exception (the 90-day flow back provision at Walter Baker), the unions played no part in establishing policies. The policies which were unilaterally developed were discussed and reviewed with the unions, however. Most of our policies were based on long-standing General Foods practices, although . . . some of them were adapted specifically for the Dover move. . .
>
> We expected the unions to be reasonably cooperative, but actually they exceeded our highest expectations in this respect. I believe they were responding to our openness with them.[24]

Union Organization at Dover

General Foods management had good reason to believe that the new Dover plant would not be unionized. The union movement has not made strong inroads in the Delaware area. In a pre-move survey, the corporation discovered strong anti-union sentiment on the part of some of the Dover residents. The leading newspaper in Dover is staunchly anti-union. Furthermore, a significant number of transfers would be coming from plants with no history of unionization.

---

[24]Chandler to author, August 6, 1965.

Nevertheless, shortly after production had begun at the new plant, both the Butcher Workmen and the Teamsters began an organizing drive among the Jell-O/Dover workers. The Butcher Workmen submitted a petition to the National Labor Relations Board to represent the production and maintenance workers; the Teamsters submitted a petition to the NLRB to represent warehouse employees. The NLRB ordered certification elections to be held simultaneously in the two bargaining units on May 28, 1964. In fact, employment in these areas was not more than 25 per cent of what the corporation expected total employment to be when all production lines were fully operational.

In the certification elections, both unions won. There were 34 eligible voters in the warehouse unit; 31 voted for the Teamsters Local 876, and three voted against the union. Of 334 eligible production and maintenance employees, 330 cast ballots. The Amalgamated Food and Allied Workers, Local 56, of the Amalgamated Meatcutters and Butcher Workmen received 282 votes. One vote was cast for the IBEW and 47 voted against the union. Accordingly, the two unions were duly certified by the NLRB.

Throughout the summer of 1964 the company carried on negotiations jointly with the two unions. The corporation had announced that, as a matter of policy, it could not accept the union shop.

In fact, the unions had had maintenance of membership union security clauses in their contracts at the Dorchester and Hoboken plants. In the end, the Dover unions accepted maintenance of membership as the appropriate form of union security for the new plant. As discussed in an earlier section, the problem of seniority also received much attention in the contract negotiations. On other issues the company agreed to eight paid holidays, whereas the Dorchester contract included eleven paid holidays. A five-step grievance procedure was also agreed upon. The last step was arbitration; in return, the union agreed to a no-strike clause for the term of the contract. Finally, the company agreed to grant wage increases of between eight and fourteen cents per hour in each year of the contract. The agreement covered a period of two years and was signed October 1, 1964.

A Summary of the General Foods Experience

A comprehensive picture of the General Foods experience is given in Tables 5.2 through 5.6. Essentially, the five tables show the disposition of employees at the four old plants by various employment categories. Table 5.2 gives the disposition of the total of employees at the four old plants. Tables 5.3 and 5.4 contrast the experience of hourly (non-exempt) with salaried (exempt) employees.

TABLE 5.2

TOTAL EMPLOYMENT AT FOUR GENERAL FOODS PLANTS, MARCH, 1962, AND DISTRIBUTION OF EMPLOYEES AFTER THAT DATE

	(1) Employment 3/62		(2) Terminations after 3/62		(3) Transfers to Dover		(4) Others*		(5) Transferred to Other GF Units		(6) Total Transfers Col. (3)+(5)	
	Number	Per Cent	Number	Per Cent	Number	Per Cent	Number	Per Cent	Number	Per Cent	Number	Per Cent
Walter Baker, Dorchester, Mass.	825	100.0 (45.9)	460	55.8 (46.7)	187	22.7 (44.2)	167	20.2 (59.6)	11	1.3 (13.3)	198	24.0 (39.1)
Franklin Baker, Hoboken, N. J.	513	100.0 (28.5)	286	55.8 (29.0)	114	22.2 (27.0)	55	10.7 (19.6)	58	11.3 (69.9)	172	33.5 (34.0)
Jell-O LeRoy, N. Y.	365	100.0 (20.3)	229	62.7 (23.2)	88	24.1 (20.8)	37	10.1 (13.2)	11	3.1 (13.3)	99	27.2 (19.6)
Minute, Orange, Mass.**	96	100.0 (5.3)	11	11.5 (1.1)	34	35.4 (8.0)	21	21.9 (7.6)	3	3.1 (3.5)	37	38.5 (7.3)
Total, 4 Plants	1799	100.0	986	54.8	423	23.5	280	15.6	83	4.6	506	28.1

* Include: 1. Retired and deceased, but not including those who elected early retirement at their termination date.
2. Temporary and casual employees, not eligible for severance pay or transfer to Dover.
3. Quits, resignations, discharges and layoffs.

** As of Summer 1965, 27 of the 96 employed at Orange in March, 1962, were still on the job.

TABLE 5.3

TOTAL HOURLY EMPLOYMENT AT FOUR GENERAL FOODS PLANTS, MARCH, 1962
AND DISTRIBUTION OF HOURLY EMPLOYEES AFTER THAT DATE

	(1) Hourly Employment 3/62		(2) Terminations after 3/62		(3) Transfers to Dover		(4) Others*		(5) Transferred to Other GF Units		(6) Total Transfers Col. (3)+(5)	
	Number	Per Cent	Number	Per Cent	Number	Per Cent	Number	Per Cent	Number	Per Cent	Number	Per Cent
Walter Baker, Dorchester, Mass.	518	100.0 (43.1)	376	72.6 (45.5)	69	13.3 (40.6)	68	13.1 (40.6)	5	1.0 (9.8)	74	14.3 (33.5)
Franklin Baker, Hoboken, N. J.	330	100.0 (27.5)	215	65.1 (26.0)	51	15.5 (30.0)	21	6.4 (16.3)	43	13.0 (84.3)	94	28.5 (42.5)
Jell-O LeRoy, N. Y.	285	100.0 (23.7)	225	78.9 (27.2)	41	14.4 (24.1)	19	6.7 (14.7)	0	0.0 (0.0)	41	14.4 (18.6)
Minute, Orange, Mass.**	68	100.0 (5.7)	11	16.2 (1.3)	9	13.2 (5.3)	21	30.9 (16.3)	3	4.4 (5.9)	12	17.6 (5.4)
Total, 4 Plants	1201	100.0	827	68.9	170	14.2	129	10.7	51	4.2	221	18.4

* Include: 1. Retired and deceased, but not including those who elected early retirement at their termination date.
2. Temporary and casual employees, not eligible for severance pay or transfer to Dover.
3. Quits, resignations, discharges and layoffs.

** As of Summer 1965, 24 of the 68 hourly employees at Orange in March, 1962, were still on the job.

TABLE 5.4

TOTAL SALARIED EMPLOYMENT AT FOUR GENERAL FOODS PLANTS, MARCH, 1962 AND DISTRIBUTION OF SALARIED EMPLOYEES AFTER THAT DATE

	(1) Salaried Employment 3/62		(2) Terminations after 3/62		(3) Transfers to Dover		(4) Others*		(5) Transferred to Other GF Units		(6) Total Transfers Col. (3)+(5)	
	Number	Per Cent	Number	Per Cent	Number	Per Cent	Number	Per Cent	Number	Per Cent	Number	Per Cent
Walter Baker, Dorchester, Mass.	307	100.0 (51.3)	84	27.4 (52.8)	118	38.4 (46.6)	99	32.2 (65.6)	6	2.0 (18.8)	124	40.4 (43.5)
Franklin Baker, Hoboken, N. J.	183	100.0 (30.6)	71	38.8 (44.7)	63	34.4 (24.9)	34	18.6 (22.5)	15	8.2 (46.9)	78	42.6 (27.4)
Jell-O LeRoy, N. Y.	80	100.0 (13.4)	4	5.0 (2.5)	47	58.8 (8.6)	18	22.5 (11.9)	11	13.7 (34.3)	58	72.5 (20.4)
Minute, Orange, Mass.**	28	100.0 (4.7)	0	0.0 (0.0)	25	89.3 (9.9)	0	0.0 (0.0)	0	0.0 (0.0)	25	89.3 (8.7)
Total, 4 Plants	598	100.0	159	26.6	253	42.3	151	25.3	32	5.4	285	47.7

* Include: 1. Retired and deceased, but not including those who elected early retirement at their termination date.
2. Temporary and casual employees, not eligible for severance pay or transfer to Dover.
3. Quits, resignations, discharges and layoffs.

** As of Summer 1965, 3 of the 28 salaried employees at Orange in March, 1962, were still on the job.

TABLE 5.5

TOTAL MALE HOURLY EMPLOYMENT AT FOUR GENERAL FOODS PLANTS, MARCH, 1962, AND DISTRIBUTION OF THOSE EMPLOYEES AFTER THAT DATE

	(1) Male Hourly Employment 3/62		(2) Terminations after 3/62		(3) Transfers to Dover		(4) Others*		(5) Transferred to Other GF Units		(6) Total Transfers Col. (3)+(5)	
	Number	Per Cent	Number	Per Cent	Number	Per Cent	Number	Per Cent	Number	Per Cent	Number	Per Cent
Walter Baker, Dorchester, Mass.	458	100.0 (52.6)	318	69.4 (56.1)	67	14.7 (44.4)	68	14.8 (68.0)	5	1.1 (15.2)	72	15.8 (39.1)
Franklin Baker, Hoboken, N. J.	220	100.0 (25.3)	141	64.0 (24.9)	45	20.5 (29.8)	9	4.1 (9.0)	25	11.4 (75.8)	70	31.9 (38.0)
Jell-O LeRoy, N. Y.	139	100.0 (15.9)	99	71.2 (17.5)	31	22.3 (20.5)	9	6.5 (9.0)	0	0.0 (0.0)	31	22.3 (16.9)
Minute, Orange, Mass.**	54	100.0 (6.2)	9	16.7 (1.5)	8	14.8 (5.3)	14	25.9 (14.0)	3	5.6 (9.0)	11	20.4 (6.0)
Total, 4 Plants	871	100.0	567	65.1	151	17.3	100	11.5	33	3.6	184	20.9

*Include: 1. Retired and deceased, but not including those who elected early retirement at their termination date.
2. Temporary and casual employees, not eligible for severance pay or transfer to Dover.
3. Quits, resignations, discharges and layoffs.

** As of Summer 1965, 20 of the 54 male hourly employees at Orange in March, 1962, were still on the job.

TABLE 5.6

TOTAL FEMALE HOURLY EMPLOYMENT AT FOUR GENERAL FOODS PLANTS, MARCH, 1962, AND DISTRIBUTION OF THOSE EMPLOYEES AFTER THAT DATE

	(1) Female Hourly Employment 3/62		(2) Terminations after 3/62		(3) Transfers to Dover		(4) Others*		(5) Transferred to Other GF Units		(6) Total Transfers Col. (3)+(5)	
	Number	Per Cent	Number	Per Cent	Number	Per Cent	Number	Per Cent	Number	Per Cent	Number	Per Cent
Walter Baker, Dorchester, Mass.	60	100.0 (18.2)	58	96.7 (22.3)	2	3.3 (10.5)	0	0.0 (0.0)	0	0.0 (0.0)	2	3.3 (3.4)
Franklin Baker, Hoboken, N. J.	110	100.0 (33.3)	74	67.3 (28.5)	6	5.5 (31.6)	12	10.9 (41.4)	18	16.4 (100.0)	24	21.9 (64.9)
Jell-O LeRoy, N. Y.	146	100.0 (44.2)	126	86.3 (48.5)	10	6.8 (52.6)	10	6.8 (34.5)	0	0.0 (0.0)	10	6.8 (27.0)
Minute, Orange, Mass.**	14	100.0 (4.3)	2	14.3 (0.7)	1	7.1 (5.3)	7	50.0 (24.1)	0	0.0 (0.0)	1	7.1 (2.7)
Total, 4 Plants	330	100.0	260	78.8	19	5.8	29	8.8	18	5.5	37	11.3

* Include:
1. Retired and deceased, but not including those who elected early retirement at their termination date.
2. Temporary and casual employees, not eligible for severance pay or transfer to Dover.
3. Quits, resignations, discharges, and layoffs.

** As of Summer 1965, 3 of the 14 female hourly employees at Orange in March, 1962, were still on the job.

A further breakdown of the hourly workers by sex is given in Tables 5.5 and 5.6. Unfortunately, the records do not allow a breakdown of the salaried employees by sex.

The figures should be interpreted as the best estimates possible. They are constructed from several company sources, some of which are contradictory. The contradictions in the records never amount to more than a few workers in any given category. The unbracketed percentages are row figures, calculated for a given row on the number in column (1); the bracketed percentages are calculated on the totals in each column.

The over-all picture for the four-plant shutdown is given in Table 5.2. There were 1,799 employed at the four old plants at the time of the shutdown announcement in March, 1962. The Walter Baker plant alone employed 46 per cent of the 1,799 workers. The Minute plant, on the other hand, with just 96 workers, comprised just over 5 per cent of total employment at the four plants. About 55 per cent (986) of all the employees elected termination with severance pay after March, 1962. About 24 per cent (423) of the workers transferred to Dover. Adding the 83 workers who transferred to other General Foods units, one finds that 506 employees, or 28 per cent, were able to continue in employment with the corporation by transferring to either Dover or another GF unit. Column (4) includes all those who cannot be classified as either transfers or terminations. A good number of those included in Column (4) would not have been eligible for transfer to Dover -- e.g., the temporary help at the four old plants. Making allowances for those who were not eligible for transfer, it can be estimated that better than 30 per cent of those who were eligible elected to transfer to another General Foods facility.

For a more accurate picture of what actually happened in the General Foods case, it is necessary to examine the contrasting distributions of hourly and salaried personnel. Looking at Tables 5.3 and 5.4 one finds, first, that two-thirds (1,201) of the total employment at the four old plants were engaged in non-exempt work. Roughly, this represents the blue-collar work-force. Of this number, nearly 70 per cent (827) elected termination with severance pay. On the other hand, only 27 per cent (159) of the salaried personnel elected to terminate. One hundred and seventy of the hourly workers transferred to Dover. This represents 14.2 per cent of total hourly employment at the four old plants. Another 51 transferred to other General Foods units. This number consists primarily of Franklin Baker hourly workers who were able to secure employment at General Foods' Maxwell House plant in Hoboken. In all, 221 of 1,201 hourly employees, or 18.4 per cent, were able to transfer to Dover or another GF unit.

Of the 598 salaried employees, only 26.6 per cent (159) terminated with severance pay, whereas 253 elected to transfer to Dover, and 32 transferred to other General Foods units. That is, 285 salaried personnel, or 47.7 per cent, transferred in the face of the plant shutdowns.

Thus, of the 506 transferring as a result of the shutdown of the four old plants, 43.7 per cent (221) were hourly personnel and 56.3 per cent (285) were salaried. Of the 423 transferring to Dover, 40.2 per cent (170) were hourly workers and 59.8 per cent (253) were salaried.

One clear conclusion is that employment status was a primary determinant of transfer. On a relative basis, the transfer rate among salaried workers was two and one-half to three times greater than that among hourly workers. This result squares with correlative evidence from other geographic labor mobility studies. For example, a survey by the Survey Research Center of the University of Michigan found that of 750 "white-collar" workers (professional, technical, managerial, clerical, sales; not including the self-employed), 25 per cent had moved to their current area of residence within the preceding five years. Among 940 "blue-collar" workers (craftsmen, foremen, operatives, laborers, and service workers), 14.6 per cent had moved to the area within the preceding five years.[25] The lowest rate among the white-collar group (clerical and sales) was still higher than the highest rate among the blue-collar group (laborers and service workers): 19 per cent to 16 per cent. However, it should be pointed out that, for many reasons, the Michigan survey results are not strictly comparable to this study. Among other differences, the geographically mobile group in the Survey Research Center study may have _also_ changed industries, occupations, employers, not to mention labor force status (for example, from an unemployed status to an employed status). This study involves a "pure" geographic shift -- with no change in the labor force status, industry, occupation, employer, and, indeed, specific job assignment of the transferring employee.

Tables 5.5 and 5.6 give a breakdown of hourly employees by sex. More than 72 per cent (871) of the hourly employees at the shutdown plants were male. On the other hand, there were more female hourly workers at the LeRoy plant than males: 146 to 139. As expected, the transfer rate among males was significantly higher than the transfer rate among females. Of the 170 hourly employees transferring to

---

[25]Computed from Table III-7, p. 64, of John B. Lansing, _et al._, _The Geographic Mobility of Labor, A First Report_ (Ann Arbor, Michigan: Survey Research Center, 1963).

Dover, only 19 were women. Many of the 19 who did transfer accompanied husbands who also worked for General Foods. The transferring women represented 5.8 per cent of total female hourly employment at the four old plants. Almost 80 per cent of the female hourly workers elected to terminate. Another 18 women in Hoboken transferred to the Maxwell House plant in that city, so that a total of 37 out of 330 hourly women (11.3 per cent) transferred to either Jell-O/Dover or Maxwell House.

Among the hourly men, 17.3 per cent (151) transferred to Dover. Another 33 transferred to other GF units, most going to the Hoboken Maxwell House plant. Thus, nearly 21 per cent of the hourly men were able to continue in employment with General Foods by transferring to another GF unit. In terms of the larger implications of the General Foods experience, the transfer rate among hourly men is a key figure. The provision of a liberal interplant transfer system induced about one in five male production and maintenance workers to make a geographic shift.

Passing now to a consideration of the disposition of General Foods employees on a plant-by-plant basis, note must first be made of the fact that the corporation did not find it necessary to shut down the Orange plant. About 30 per cent of those employed at Orange in March, 1962, were never laid off, but continued in employment through

1965. General Foods began to use the Orange plant for experimental production work. A high proportion of the remaining Orange workers transferred to Dover. Indeed, none of the salaried personnel terminated at Orange: three continued in employment and the rest -- 25 -- relocated to Dover.

The other three plants were, in fact, shut down. All things considered, the experience of these three plants, in terms of terminations and relocations, was remarkably similar. For example, the over-all Dover transfer rate (Column 3, Table 5.2) varied from 22.2 per cent at Walter Baker to 24.1 per cent at Jell-O/LeRoy. The transfer rate among hourly employees varied from 13.3 per cent at Walter Baker to 15.5 per cent at Franklin Baker.

The total transfer rate, including transfers to other GF units (Column 6, Table 5.2), was highest for the Orange plant, reflecting the fact that most salaried employees at Orange transferred to Dover. About one-third of the Franklin Baker employees continued in General Foods' employ by transferring, reflecting the presence of job opportunities at the Hoboken Maxwell House plant. About one-fourth of the employees at the two Baker plants transferred to Dover or another GF unit.

It may also be noted that only four salaried workers terminated at the Jell-O plant, compared to significant numbers at the two Baker plants. The almost non-existent termination rate among salaried employees at Orange and LeRoy, as compared to Dorchester and Hoboken, may be attributable to the relative scarcity of alternative job opportunities in office, clerical, professional, and managerial occupations in these two semi-rural locations, as compared to available "white-collar" opportunities in the Boston and New York City metropolitan areas.

The rates of terminations among hourly employees (with the exception of the Orange plant) varied from 65 per cent at Franklin Baker to 79 per cent at LeRoy. Among only the male hourly employees the termination rate ranged from 64 to 71 per cent.

Some Comparisons with Other Plant Relocation Cases

It is instructive to compare the results of the General Foods experience with comparable cases of interplant transfer. However, as noted in Chapter I, there are very few published reports recounting the incidence of relocation. Smith and Fowler report on the shutdown of a Ford assembly plant in Buffalo, New York, in the middle of the 1957-58 recession.[26] Operations were being transferred to Lorain, Ohio, some 200 miles southwest of Buffalo. All

---

[26]Luke M. Smith and Irving A. Fowler, *Do Workers Move When Their Plant Is Relocated? The Case of the Ford Motor Company Plant Relocation* (Buffalo: Department of Sociology, University of Buffalo, 1960), 19 pp. See also, Luke M. Smith and Irving A. Fowler, "Plant Relocation and Worker Migration," *Blue Collar World* (Englewood Cliffs, N. J.: Prentice-Hall, 1964), Arthur B. Shostak and William Gomberg, eds., pp. 491-497.

production workers at the Buffalo plant were offered jobs in Lorain with seniority and job classification rights. Within two months of the shutdown, Smith and Fowler interviewed a sample of 145 affected families and found that 20 per cent were planning on moving to Lorain. Seven months later Smith and Fowler found 140 of the original 145 families still living in Buffalo. Obviously, less than 20 per cent had moved, although 11 per cent reported that they still anticipated relocating.

Beaumont and Helfgott summarize several cases of interplant transfer.[27] In another case of a shutdown of an automobile assembly plant, about 24 per cent of the hourly employees accepted transfer, with retention of seniority, to other company plants -- mainly to one located 115 miles away.[28] Perhaps a more typical case involved a chemical company in the North Central region of the United States. As a result of technological improvements, more than 150 workers were displaced by the chemical company in the mid-1950's. The company offered to transfer the affected workers expense-free to another facility some 500 miles away. Eight accepted transfer; that is, 5.3 per cent.[29] In other instances Beaumont and Helfgott report

---

[27]Richard A. Beaumont and Roy B. Helfgott, Management, Automation, and People (New York: Industrial Relations Counselors, 1964), 60 pp.

[28]Ibid., p. 78.

[29]Ibid., p. 79.

transfer rates of as high as 40 per cent. However, not enough information is provided by the authors to insure a meaningful interpretation. Many cases of plant relocation permit the employee to transfer without a geographic shift of his residence.

Bradburn reports on the shutdown of an Armour meatpacking plant in Sioux City, Iowa, in June, 1963.[30] Of all the reported cases of the establishemt of an interplant transfer system, Armour's Sioux City experience most closely parallels the General Foods experience. Also, Bradburn's provision of a complete description of the Armour interplant transfer plan, the circumstances surrounding its imposition, and the results obtained, permit some meaningful comparisons to be drawn with the General Foods experience. Some 1,178 workers were affected by the shutdown of the Sioux City plant. A three-month advance notice was given of the impending shutdown (compared to two years in the General Foods case). Under an agreement between the United Packinghouse Workers and the Armour Company, all workers at the plant with more than eighteen months of seniority were offered the choice of termination with severance pay or relocation to another Armour plant. The company would pay up to

---

[30]Norman M. Bradburn, _Inter-plant Transfer: The Sioux City Experience_ (Chicago: National Opinion Research Center, 1964), 60 pp.

$500 in moving expenses, and the worker would have some choice of plants, depending on his seniority. In addition, as described in an earlier section, workers were provided with flowback rights of six months. A new development occurred some five months after the shutdown of the Sioux City plant: Armour opened two new plants (one in West Point, Nebraska, some 60 miles from Sioux City, and one in Sterling, Illinois, 380 miles distant), and offered preferential hiring at the new plants to displaced Sioux City employees. A worker could accept transfer and retain his previously accumulated seniority, <u>provided</u> he repaid the full amount of his separation pay, <u>or</u> he could keep his separation pay and transfer to West Point or Sterling as a new employee. For workers who had already relocated to other Armour plants, transfer to West Point or Sterling was possible with full seniority, <u>provided</u> the amount of reimbursement for moving expenses was repaid, <u>or</u> if they agreed to take termination with severance pay and accept employment at the new plants as new employees.

Citing the Sioux City experience, Shultz and Weber note that 234 of 1,150 employees transferred after that plant shutdown.[31] That would be a transfer rate of 20 per cent, exactly matching the trans-

---

[31]George Shultz and Arnold Weber, <u>Strategies for the Displaced Worker</u> (New York: Harper and Row, 1966), pp. 59-60.

fer rate among General Foods hourly employees. However, Shultz and Weber do not present enough data on the composition of the Armour Sioux City work force (particularly its sex composition) to make the comparison very meaningful.

On the other hand, Bradburn obtained interviews with a sample of 390 male employees from the Sioux City plant. The sample was selected from the male master seniority list. (Presumably the sample consists of only hourly or non-exempt employees.) By using company records, Bradburn was able to check on the distribution of his sample in March, 1964, some nine months after the closing of the Sioux City plant. Of the 390 men in his sample, Bradburn found that 267 (68 per cent) had elected separation, 58 (15 per cent) were still working at the plant to which they had originally transferred, and 53 (14 per cent) were working at the new Sterling and West Point plants.[32] Thus, 29 per cent of the sample of male hourly employees had completed transfer to other Armour facilities, compared to 21 per cent of the male hourly employees in the General Foods case.

The higher proportion of Bradburn's sample of Armour employees electing transfer can be attributed to many factors which distinguish the Sioux City case from the General Foods experience. For example,

[32] Bradburn, op. cit., pp. 32-34.

as already noted, the Sioux City workers had the guarantee of flow-back rights, whereas such rights were only granted to the workers at one of the General Foods plants, and then very late in the game. Secondly, Sioux City workers had the option of transferring to one of several Armour plants, all in the same region of the country. General Foods employees had a more restricted choice: for most only the Dover option was available -- a choice which meant moving from the Northeastern section of the country to a border state with strong southern ties. Thirdly, the lack of employment opportunities in Sioux City exerted a strong "push" on the Armour workers to transfer. Alternative employment opportunities were quite good for many of the General Foods employees, especially for those living in the Boston and New York City metropolitan areas. Finally, the union in the Sioux City case had a major role in implementing the transfer plan and made a strong effort to inform the workers of the features of the plan. The union had a much smaller role in the General Foods case.

It is difficult to assess the significance of the difference in the length of the advance notice in the two cases (three months *versus* two years). A longer advance notice allows the worker more time to either (1) seek out alternative job opportunities in the local labor market or (2) make the necessary preparations and adjustments needed to relocate. The evidence of these two cases suggests that perhaps the former effect was predominant in the General Foods experience. On the other hand, it is clear that more financial compensation was available for transferring General Foods employees than for Armour's Sioux City workers. However, to attempt to estimate the impact of this factor, one should also know the relative amounts of severance pay available to Sioux City workers. Bradburn does not supply such data. We know that the amounts of severance pay available to General Foods workers were enough to induce a good number of them to terminate. Hypothetically, the absence of such amounts would have convinced an additional number to transfer to Dover.

Shultz and Weber also cite the experience of several other Armour plants which shut down, totally or partially, and instituted an interplant transfer system. Again, the absence of sufficient data makes comparisons tenuous. Nevertheless, all the reported cases are remarkable for the limited number of workers accepting transfer. In the shutdown of an Armour Birmingham plant in 1961, 150 workers terminated, three accepted transfer, and two of the three later returned to Birmingham. The 1962 shutdown of a Fort Worth plant resulted in 800 "potential" transferees; six actually moved, and three returned.[33] The partial shutdown of Armour's Kansas City plant

---

[33]Shultz and Weber, _op. cit._, p. 57.

in 1964 threatened 1,000 workers with displacement. Armour had 400 jobs to offer the threatened workers in three new plants, all within 300 miles of Kansas City. A total of 227 moved; 50 later returned to Kansas City.[34]

Chapter Summary

In this chapter the personnel policies and problems of starting the Dover plant were examined. In addition, an overview of the General Foods experience and some comparisons with other cases of plant relocation were presented. The chapter's major areas of discussion are summarized below.

1. General Foods received more than 11,000 applications for about 1,100 openings at the new Dover plant. Unfortunately the company still had problems finding skilled maintenance men. Not enough skilled workers transferred to meet the company's needs in Dover, and recruiting them in the local area proved to be difficult.

2. The company's wage policy in Dover was examined. The wage structure established for the new plant was found to be higher than the wage structure at the old LeRoy and Orange plants,

---

[34] *Ibid.*, pp. 61-64.

and lower than the wage structure at Hoboken and Dorchester. It was estimated that the company saved in the neighborhood of six per cent in wage costs by the move to Dover.

3. Seniority policy at the new plant had to be shaped so as to integrate successfully four previously separated seniority units. General Foods transfers retained whatever seniority they had accumulated at the old plants. Some of the problems of integrating seniority units were avoided by the establishment of four separate seniority units, or departments, in the new plant. However, after the plant was organized, the Butcher Workmen asked for, and received, a modified version of plant-wide seniority. The problems of seniority integration were minimal, and the company felt that "the basic ingredients of the seniority policy" would remain unchanged.

4. The General Foods inter-plant transfer system was employer-instituted, the unions at two of the shut-down plants playing almost no role at all. The single exception was the successful effort by the Butcher Workmen during contract negotiations in 1963 to establish "flow-back" rights for Walter Baker workers. The added provision had little impact, however, and only a "handful" of Walter Baker workers exercised

flow-back rights. Although the unions played a minimal role in policy-making, they remained cooperative in the closing phase of the plant relocation.

5. At Dover in May, 1964, the NLRB held certification elections in which the Butcher Workmen and Teamsters were chosen as collective bargaining representatives of the production and maintenance workers, and the warehouse workers, respectively. The first union contract at the new Dover plant was signed on October 1, 1964.

6. Of the 1,800 workers employed at the four General Foods plants in March, 1962, nearly 30 per cent were able to remain with the corporation despite the plant shutdowns. Nearly one-quarter -- 423 workers -- transferred to the new Dover plant. Of the 600 salaried workers, more than 40 per cent went to Dover. However, of the 1,200 hourly employees, only about 15 per cent, _i.e._, 170 workers, relocated to Dover. Among 871 male hourly workers, more than 17 per cent went to Dover, and four per cent or so went to other GF facilities. Thus, 21 per cent of the male hourly General Foods employees remained with the company despite the plant shutdowns.

7. The General Foods case was contrasted with other cases of inter-plant transfer reported in the literature. Typically, only a small proportion of workers affected by plant shutdowns elect to transfer to another plant when such relocation opportunities are offered to them. The exact number of workers electing relocation in any given case depends upon a wide array of factors: the precise nature of the transfer opportunity, the inducements and guarantees offered, the distance to be travelled, the composition of the work force, the availability of jobs in the local labor market, the severance benefits offered, and many other factors. The proportion of General Foods workers transferring was found to be roughly comparable to, if not a bit higher than, the proportion transferring in other similar cases.

CHAPTER VI

CHARACTERISTICS OF THE RELOCATED WORKER

What were the characteristics of the relocated General Foods workers? How did the relocated (or transferred) worker compare with the displaced (or terminated) worker? Was the relocated worker a "typical migrant?" Did the relocated worker fit the profile we have come to expect of those who are geographically mobile? It is to these questions that this chapter addresses itself.

In this chapter a large number of economic and social characteristics of the relocated worker will be discussed, such as age, occupation, family income, home ownership, education, and seniority. The analysis will proceed primarily by comparing the relocated worker with other groups of workers. For example, the relocated General Foods worker will be contrasted with the displaced General Foods worker. In addition, it will be possible in this chapter to compare the relocated worker with all migrants who move for any reason.

This latter comparison will be possible because of a comprehensive study of the geographic mobility of American family heads, undertaken and published by the Survey Research Center (SRC), Institute for Social Research, Ann Arbor, Michigan, in 1963.[1] As noted

[1]John B. Lansing, et al., The Geographic Mobility of Labor: A First Report (Ann Arbor, Mich.: Survey Research Center, 1963), 315 pp.

in Chapter II, the questionnaires for this study duplicate many of the questions used in the SRC survey. Therefore, direct comparisons will be possible at several points.

While many significant studies of geographic mobility have been published over the years (including several based on Census data),[2] the most exhaustive survey made to date has been that of the Survey Research Center, sponsored by agencies of the United States Departments of Commerce, Health, Education, and Welfare, and Labor. Over the year 1962, interviews were conducted with 2,669 individuals, the sample selected in order to constitute a probability sample of all families in the United States living in private dwelling units (houses, apartments, trailers).[3] Of this number of interviews, 16 per cent of the family heads had moved to their present area within the previous five years -- that is, within the 1958 to 1962 period.[4] The characteristics of this group of recent migrants give us a profile of the geographically mobile.[5] It is to this group that we shall be comparing the characteristics of relocated General Foods workers.

---

[2]See, for example, United States Bureau of the Census, 1960 Census of the Population, Supplementary Reports, May 18, 1962, PC(S1)-19, _Geographic Mobility of the Population of the United States, April, 1960._

[3]Lansing, _et al._, _op. cit._, p. 3.

[4]_Ibid._, pp. 56-57.

[5]A migrant is defined as an individual who makes an inter-country move. See, for example, Seymour Wolfbein, _Employment and Unemployment in the United States_ (Chicago: Science Research Associates, 1964), p. 219.

The scheme of the chapter is to attempt to differentiate the salient characteristics of the GF relocated worker, not only from the "immobile" (the displaced worker) but also from others who were also mobile (those in the SRC sample who were migrants in the 1958 to 1962 period). The relocated or transferred worker is a mobile worker _only_ in the sense that he changes his area of residence. Transferred workers typically do not change their employer, industry, occupation, labor force status, or even their job assignment. In a sense, the terminated worker can be considered more "mobile" than the transferred. The terminated worker re-enters the labor market or leaves the labor force completely. He must, necessarily, change employers and this move will probably mean a change of industry and often a change of occupation. Are these changes of a higher or lower order of mobility than geographic movement? Who faces greater uncertainty and risk, the displaced worker or the relocated worker? We usually associate risk-taking with the migrant -- but is this really true of the General Foods worker?

The typical migrant changes not only his place of residence but also his employer, his industry, and very often his occupation. "Labor mobility responds to opportunity,"[6] and this has been found

---

[6]Gladys L. Palmer, "Interpreting Patterns of Labor Mobility," _Labor Mobility and Economic Opportunity_, E. Wight Bakke, _et al._, eds. (New York: The Technology Press of M.I.T. and John Wiley and Sons, 1954), p. 62.

true for migrants. For example, migration rates are higher for the unemployed than for the employed.[7] But is it true of the transferred worker? Does the transferred worker seek economic opportunity -- or economic security?

It is because of these obvious differences between the transferred worker and the migrant in general that we shall proceed to compare the characteristics of GF relocated workers with migrant family heads in the SRC sample, as well as the displaced GF workers.

In the United States in 1964, approximately 38 million people changed their place of residence. Of this number, approximately 6.1 million moved between states, representing 3.3 per cent of the total population.[8] The SRC survey revealed that, of the total number of moves made within the 1958-62 period, 16 per cent were "triggered" by a transfer or reassignment.[9] Assuming that this percentage is stable and applicable to the country as a whole, it appears that just under one million people changed their state of residence in 1964, as a result of a job transfer.

---

[7]Wolfbein, op. cit., p. 222.

[8]United States Bureau of the Census, Statistical Abstract of the United States, 87th ed. (Washington: Government Printing Office, 1966), p. 32. The "year" is actually the twelve-month period between March, 1964, and March, 1965.

[9]Lansing, et al., op. cit., p. 125.

The question arises: are the characteristics of the transferred or relocated worker comparable to the characteristics of the worker who makes a geographic shift for other reasons than job transfer?

It cannot be claimed that the characteristics of the relocated General Foods workers are representative of the thousands of workers who move between states every year in response to a transfer by their employer. In fact, because of the somewhat atypical employer transfer policies implemented by General Foods, and the other unique circumstances surrounding this case, it is probable that there are substantial differences between the group of relocated workers surveyed for this study, and relocated workers in general. Given the nature of employer policies and the known proclivities of the blue-collar worker, it is entirely likely that the overwhelming majority of all transferred workers are white-collar, managerial, technical, and other skilled personnel. As has been demonstrated in this study, even in the face of highly attractive relocation opportunities, blue-collar workers are extremely reluctant to move.

Another likely difference between the workers surveyed in this case and all relocated workers concerns the number of workers transferred to one location by a single employer. It is unlikely that a shift of more than 400 workers to one location is representative of relocations in general. It is more likely that most transfers are made singly or in small groups -- especially when the distance of the relocation is considerable.

Despite these differences, however, there are good reasons for contrasting the workers of this study with the more generally mobile. First, such a comparison has simply not been made before. Second, some of the differences suggested by this study between the transferred worker and the geographically mobile in general are so substantial that it seems unlikely that the unique facets of this case can be entirely responsible. Third, and probably most important, the growth of interplant transfer systems in American industry may portend more similar shifts of large numbers of workers -- including the unskilled and semi-skilled -- in the future.

In the absence of earlier studies, there is no way of knowing whether the SRC figure of 16 per cent has been a stable figure, or whether the percentage of moves due to transfers has been growing through the years. Yet, all evidence points to a growing tendency for industry to promote relocation whenever feasible. To understand fully the implications of this presumed trend, we ought to know how the transferred worker -- particularly the blue-collar transferred worker -- differs from all interstate migrants.

Access to Information

The first and most obvious difference is that the relocated or transferred worker has his job arranged before he moves. The fact that the job is there and guaranteed is indeed the real reason for the move. On the other hand, of all heads of families who move to a new area, not all move because of job opportunities. Many move in order to retire, or for reasons of health. Of those who do move to a new job, only 59 per cent succeed in arranging the job before moving.[10] And while it is obvious that 100 per cent of the General Foods workers "arranged" their jobs through their employer, those heads of families in the SRC survey who moved to a new area to work in the 1958-62 period arranged jobs with their employers, either before or after their move, in only 22 per cent of the cases.[11] All this points to one of the most significant differences between the transferred General Foods workers and the geographically mobile in general: the transferred workers had maximum access to information concerning the employer and the new job situation; on the other hand, when jobs were not pre-arranged, the generally mobile had no information at all about jobs and employers in the new area in 47 per cent of the moves.[12]

---

[10] Ibid., pp. 131, 135.

[11] Ibid., p. 138.

[12] Ibid., p. 136.

<u>Occupation</u>

It has previously been pointed out that a far larger percentage of General Foods salaried personnel transferred to Dover than hourly personnel.[13] The question arises as to whether the occupational composition of transferred General Foods workers is similar to the occupational composition of migrants in general. This question can be analyzed through Table 6.1. For example, it has long been known that the geographic mobility of professional and technical workers is greater than that of other occupational groups.[14] That finding is confirmed for the 1958-62 period by the SRC data. Of all migrants in that period, by far the largest group were professional and technical workers (23.1 per cent of all migrants in that period).

In order to derive a relative measure of the geographic mobility of each occupational group, a ratio was computed by dividing Column (2) by Column (1). This ratio is equal to the ratio of all SRC migrants, 1958-62, in a particular occupation to all SRC family heads in a particular occupation, weighted (<u>i.e.</u>, multiplied) by the ratio of all family heads to all migrants. The resulting ratio appears in Column (6). A ratio equal to 1.0 indicates that

---

[13]See Chapter V.

[14]Herbert S. Parnes, <u>Research on Labor Mobility</u> (New York: Social Science Research Council, 1954), pp. 83-85.

TABLE 6.1

GEOGRAPHIC MOBILITY BY OCCUPATIONAL CLASSIFICATION:
COMPARISON OF FAMILY HEADS WHO WERE MIGRANTS IN SRC.
SAMPLE OF ALL FAMILY HEADS WITH TRANSFERRED GENERAL FOODS WORKERS

	(1) All SRC Family Heads[1] Per Cent	(2) All SRC Migrants 1958-62[1] Per Cent	(3) G F Workers, Four Old Plants (Est.) Per Cent	(4) Sample, G.F Transferred Workers No.	(5) Sample, G F Transferred Workers Per Cent	(5) (2) ÷ (1)	(7) (5) ÷ (3)
Professional, Technical	11.1	23.1	16	51	23.7	2.1	1.5
Managerial	5.8	8.1	10	24	11.2	1.4	1.1
Clerical, Sales	11.2	13.6	13	22	10.2	1.2	.8
Craftsmen, Foremen	12.6	11.9	16	62	28.8	.9	1.8
Operatives	13.1	10.9	35	50	23.3	.8	.7
Laborers, Service Workers	9.6	9.8	10	6	2.8	1.0	.3
Self-employed	8.0	4.5	--	--	--	.6	--
Farmers, Farm Mgrs.	3.9	2.4	--	--	--	.6	--
Housewives, Retired Students	24.7	15.7	--	--	--	.6	--
Total	100.0	100.0	100.0	215	100.0		

[1]Computed from data supplied in Table III-7 of John B. Lansing, *et al.*, *The Geographic Mobility of Labor: A First Report* (Ann Arbor, Mich.: Survey Research Center, 1963), p. 64.

a particular occupational group has a mobility rate equal to the population as a whole. The higher the ratio, the more geographically mobile the members of a particular occupation are <u>relative</u> to the population as a whole. Hence, professional and technical workers, with a mobility ratio equal to 2.1, are more than twice as mobile as the entire population. The two other "white-collar" groups, managerial personnel and clerical and sales workers, are also above the population average in terms of geographic mobility.

The mobility ratio for the blue-collar occupations taken as a group is just under 1.0; *i.e.*, blue-collar workers are almost as mobile as the average of all family heads. Perhaps a surprising result is the mobility ratio of laborers and service workers, which is somewhat higher than that of the more skilled blue-collar workers and about equal to the average of all family heads.

Less surprising is the finding that the relative mobility rate for the self-employed, housewives, retired persons and students is about 60 per cent of that of the population as a whole. On the other hand, the finding for farm workers and managers severely contradicts the generally accepted belief that farm workers are more mobile than the average.[15] The SRC data reveal that farm workers

---

[15] *Ibid.*, p. 84.

are among the least mobile of all the occupational groups. While this interesting result deserves further examination, our major purpose here is to contrast mobility by occupation of the relocated workers with all migrants.

To analyze the geographic mobility by occupation of the General Foods workers, a comparable mobility ratio has been computed by dividing Column (2), showing the percentage distribution by occupation of the sample of General Foods workers interviewed for the study, by Column (3), which is the estimated percentage distribution by occupation of all General Foods workers employed at the four shutdown plants. The resulting ratio appears in Column (7) and, analogous to the ratio computed for all migrants, is equal to the ratio of GF transfers in a given occupation to all GF workers in a given occupation at the old plants, weighted (*i.e.*, multiplied) by the ratio of all GF workers employed at the shutdown plants to all relocated GF workers. A mobility ratio of 1.0 indicates that a group of GF workers in a given occupation had a rate of transfer equal to the rate for all GF workers affected by the plant relocation.

Exact comparisons between Columns (6) and (7) cannot be made because of the natural absence of the last three occupational groups listed in the table from the GF sample. What is significant is the difference in the rankings of the occupations. Column (7) shows a very altered pattern of geographic mobility by occupation from what one might expect, given the pattern for the population as a whole. The most mobile workers by our relative measure are the craftsmen (or highly skilled blue-collar workers) and the foremen. The 1.8 ratio for this group indicates that craftsmen and foremen were 80 per cent more mobile than the average for all GF workers. In contrast, the mobility rate for all migrants who are craftsmen and foremen is a bit less than the average for the entire population.

GF professional, technical, and managerial personnel are also revealed to have above average mobility rates. By contrast, the rate for unskilled GF workers (laborers and service workers) is just 30 per cent of the average for all GF workers, and probably lower than one might expect, given the national data.

It has been pointed out that General Foods implemented an elaborate inter-plant transfer system largely in order to induce more skilled personnel to accept transfer. In an absolute sense, the corporation was frustrated in that objective. Not nearly enough skilled blue-collar workers transferred to fill the company's needs. But the findings in Table 6.1 demonstrate clearly that, in a relative sense, the corporation did indeed succeed in inducing a relatively greater proportion of skilled, blue-collar help to transfer than other types of workers employed by the corporation -- and more than one might expect on the basis of the geographic mobility patterns of the entire population. At the same time, the semi-skilled operatives and unskilled workers -- the need for which the company had the least difficulty in meeting -- were relatively the least likely to move.

Sex

Brief note should be made of the sex composition of the relocated workers. Of all hourly workers employed at the four old plants, 27.5 per cent were women. Of all transferred workers, only 10.1 per cent were women. The figures are comparable for the salaried group. Those females who did transfer fall roughly into one of two categories: (1) single or unattached women and (2) wives of other relocated GF workers. Interviews with displaced GF employees revealed that most of the terminated women were secondary earners in their households. It is quite clear that the geographic mobility of the female employees was substantially less than that of the males. For all inter-state migrants the evidence is less compelling. Parnes points out that

> . . . the persistence of slightly higher migration rates for men in numerous Census surveys . . . provides a basis for belief that there are real though perhaps slight differences in the geographic mobility of men and women . . . [However] the Census Bureau has been somewhat guarded in drawing definite conclusions from its data because the differences . . . have not been statistically significant.[16]

Age

It has long been recognized that there is a very strong relationship between age and geographic mobility. Studies have shown that age and geographic mobility are negatively related.[17] How does the age distribution of the relocated General Foods workers compare with the pattern for all migrants? Again, through the use of SRC data, an analysis of this question is possible. The procedure used in the analysis of occupational differentials in geographic mobility is again followed in Table 6.2. Columns (1) and (2) give the percentage age distributions of all SRC family heads. Column (3) shows the estimated percentage age distribution of all General Foods workers at the four shut-down plants. Columns (4) and (5) give the number and percentage of the sample of relocated General Foods workers in each age category. In Columns (6) and (7) ratios are computed analogous to those computed by occupa-

---

[16] *Ibid.*, p. 115.

[17] *Ibid.*, pp. 104-105. See also, Lansing *et al.*, *op. cit.*, pp. 55-60; Wolfbein, *op. cit.*, pp. 220-221; U. S. Department of Labor, Office of Manpower, Automation and Training, *Mobility and Worker Adaptation to Economic Change in the United States* (Manpower Research, Bulletin No. 1, July, 1963), p. 22.

TABLE 6.2

AGE AND GEOGRAPHIC MOBILITY: A COMPARISON OF FAMILY HEADS WHO WERE MIGRANTS, 1958-62, IN SRC SAMPLE OF ALL FAMILY HEADS WITH TRANSFERRED GENERAL FOODS WORKERS

	(1)	(2)	(3)	(4)	(5)	(6)	(7)
Age	All SRC Family Heads [1] Per Cent	All SRC Migrants 1958-62 [1] Per Cent	G F Workers Four Old Plants (Est.) Per Cent	Sample, G F Transferred Workers No.	Sample, G F Transferred Workers Per Cent	(2) ÷ (1)	(5) ÷ (3)
18-24	5.7	14.7	2.2	9	4.2	2.6	1.9
25-34	19.7	37.7	17.9	42	19.5	1.9	1.1
35-44	20.9	20.0	22.2	52	24.2	1.0	1.1
45-54	19.8	15.1	30.8	74	34.4	.8	1.2
55-64	15.2	7.7	26.9	38	17.7	.5	.7
65 or over	18.7	4.8	0.0	0	0.0	.3	--
	100.0	100.0	100.0	215	100.0		
Mean Age	55.4	37.5	45.7		43.7		

[1] Computed from Table III-2 in John B. Lansing *et al.*, *The Geographic Mobility of Labor: A First Report*, (Ann Arbor, Mich.: Survey Research Center, 1963), p. 58.

tional groups. The ratio in Column (6) indicates the rate of geographic movement of family heads in a particular age category relative to that of all families. The ratio in Column (7) indicates the rate of geographic movement of GF relocated workers in a particular age category relative to that of all GF relocated workers.

The inverse correlation between age and geographic mobility is once again confirmed by the SRC data. The movement of those aged 18 to 24 is more than two and one-half times the rate for all family heads. For those aged 25 to 34, geographic movement is almost twice as great as for the entire population. Those 65 and over have a rate of geographic mobility which is just 30 per cent of the over-all rate. There is a substantial difference between the mean age of the migrant (37.5 years) and the mean age of all family heads (55.4 years).

The age-mobility relationship for General Foods workers is not quite as clear as that of all family heads. Although the age composition of the work force at the four shut-down plants shows that nearly 80 per cent were aged 35 to 64, compared to about 56 per cent of all family heads, the exclusion of those past the 65-year retirement age from the General Foods work force lowers the average age of the GF worker at the old plants (45.7 years) below that of the average of all family heads (55.4). Yet the mean age of the SRC migrant was only 37.5 years, compared to 43.7 years for the transferred GF employee. The difference between the mean age of the GF relocated worker and the mean age of all GF workers at the closed plants is not statistically significant. And the age distributions between the two GF groups are not very dissimilar. In other words, in terms of age the transferred worker is much more like the group from which he came than the typical migrant is.

The ratios in Column (7) bear out this conclusion. While a negative relationship exists, it is not nearly so clear in Column (7) as in Column (6). There is a particularly marked difference for the 45-54 age category. General Foods transfers in this category are about 20 per cent more mobile than all GF transfers. Migrants in this age category are only 80 per cent as mobile as all migrants.

These findings are consistent with the belief that an interplant transfer system induces larger numbers of older workers to pick up and move to a new location than might be expected, given the mobility propensities of all older workers. The increased relative mobility of those in the 45-54 age category is particularly significant, since it has been found in almost every study of displaced workers (including this one) that those over age 45 have a particularly difficult time achieving re-employment.[18] For this age group the opportunity to remain with a company with which one is likely to have built up fifteen or more years of seniority, can be a most attractive alternative to re-entering the labor market as a job-seeker, especially since assuming the risks of job-seeking are well known to the older worker.

On the other hand, the relative mobility rate for those in the 55 to 64 age category is the lowest of any age group, and about 60 per cent of that of the 45 to 54 age group. The propensity for movement for relocated workers is very close to the relative rate for all migrants in this age group.

How does one explain the disparity between the mobility ratios for those in the 45-54 age group and those in the 55-64 age group? A partial explanation is that those over age 55 were eligible for early retirement (provided that they had fifteen years of service), whereas this alternative was not open for those under age 55.[19] In general, there were too many workers in the older age category just one or two years away from retirement, for whom relocation, no matter how attractive in other respects, was not a

---

[18]See Chapter VIII for the findings of this study and for other sources on the relation of age and unemployment.

[19]Of the 116 displaced Walter Baker employees interviewed for this study, 18 were eligible for, and had accepted, early retirement.

practical alternative. But those workers aged 45 to 54 were too young for retirement -- even early retirement; they had from ten to twenty years of working life ahead of them, and faced hunting for new work under the handicap of their age. While other workers of this age group are reluctant to invest in a move which may very well prove to be futile, the guarantee of a job and the elimination of almost all costs of moving made transfer a practically costless investment for the 45 to 54-year-old General Foods worker. As a consequence, as shown in Table 6.2, the age-mobility relationship was considerably altered for the relocated workers, and especially for those in the 45 to 54 age group.

Table 6.3 shows the age distribution for relocated General Foods workers by hourly-salaried status. The average age for the relocated hourly worker was 46.9 years, compared to 41.3 years for the salaried worker. Thus the average age for the relocated hourly worker was <u>greater</u> than the average age of all the workers employed at the shut-down plants, and nearly equal to the average of all terminations (47.2 years; see Chapter IV). However, before we jump to any conclusions here, we ought to have a breakdown on the age distribution of all GF employees at the four old plants on an hourly-salaried basis -- and that information is not available. Also, the sample of 116 interviewed displaced workers, in addition to being

TABLE 6.3

AGE DISTRIBUTION FOR HOURLY AND SALARIED GENERAL FOODS RELOCATED WORKERS

Age	Salaried Workers		Hourly Workers	
	Number	Per Cent	Number	Per Cent
19 and under	0	0.0	1	1.1
20-24	5	4.0	3	3.3
25-29	12	9.6	3	3.3
30-34	19	15.2	8	8.9
35-39	20	16.0	8	8.9
40-44	17	13.6	7	7.8
45-49	23	18.4	13	14.4
50-54	15	12.0	23	25.6
55-59	12	9.6	18	20.0
60-64	2	1.6	6	6.7
65 and over	0	0.0	0	0.0
Total	125	100.0	90	100.0
Mean Age		41.3		46.9

limited to only former Walter Baker workers, is otherwise not large enough for the purpose of knowing whether there was a significant age difference between displaced hourly workers and displaced salaried workers. The evidence available from the interviews with displaced workers does suggest that there _was_ a difference in the average age of hourly as compared with salaried workers. But whether that difference was on the order of 5.6 years, as it is for the relocated workers, one cannot say for certain.

At any rate, one can see from Table 6.3 that 52.3 per cent of the relocated hourly workers were more than fifty years old, compared to 23.2 per cent of the salaried. Tentatively we conclude that the age-mobility relationship was even weaker for the relocated hourly worker than for the relocated salaried worker.

Marital Status, Dependency Status, and Labor Force Status of Wife

According to Parnes, ". . . there is some evidence that married men living with their wives are somewhat less likely to make intercounty changes of residence than men in other marital status categories."[20] Although Lansing and his associates, in their study based on SRC data, support this proposition, Table 6.4 shows that their evidence is not conclusive. Actually, of all migrant family

[20] Parnes, _op. cit._, p. 120.

TABLE 6.4

MARITAL STATUS OF HEADS OF FAMILIES, HEADS WHO WERE MIGRANTS, 1958-62 AND GENERAL FOODS RELOCATED AND DISPLACED WORKERS

	(1) SRC Sample of all Family Heads[1]	(2) Migrants, 1958-62 in SRC Sample[1]	(3) Salaried G F Transferred Workers		(4) Hourly G F Transferred Workers		(5) Sample G F Displaced Workers	
	Per Cent	Per Cent	No.	Per Cent	No.	Per Cent	No.	Per cent
Married	76.5	79.2	109	87.2	79	87.8	86	74.1
Single	3.9	5.1	14	11.2	10	11.1	25	21.6
Widowed Divorced	19.6	15.7	2	1.6	1	1.1	5	4.3
Total	100.0	100.0	125	100.0	90	100.0	116	100.0

[1]Computed from Tables III-8 and III-9 in John B. Lansing, *et al.*, *The Geographic Mobility of Labor: A First Report* (Ann Arbor, Mich.: Survey Research Center, 1963), pp. 66-67.

heads in the 1958-62 period, a slightly greater percentage were married than of all family heads in the SRC survey. Lansing, *et al.*, rest their conclusion primarily on the finding that of those who are single *and* under 35 years of age, 64 per cent had moved to the area within the preceding five years (*i.e.*, 1958-62). However, of the more than 2,600 family heads surveyed by the Survey Research Center, only thirty were both single and under 35 (and therefore presumably nineteen had moved in the 1958-62 period).[21] The SRC data more clearly support the hypothesis that those who are widowed or divorced are less likely to be geographically mobile than *either* married or single people.

For General Foods workers, Table 6.4 shows that nearly nine out of ten of the relocated workers were married. On the other hand, 74.1 per cent of the displaced Walter Baker workers who were interviewed were married. This comparison indicates that married General Foods workers were more likely to transfer than unmarried. What one probably must conclude on the basis of both the SRC survey and this study is that there are other factors (age and occupation among them) more important than marital status as determinants of geographic mobility. Unless there is some way of holding these other factors constant, the exact effect of marital status cannot be assessed.

---

[21]Lansing, *et al.*, *op. cit.*, pp. 65-67.

Another factor, related to marital status, which probably affects the likelihood of a family's moving, is dependency status. There is little evidence in the literature on the relationship between the size of the living unit and geographic mobility. If "number of dependents" is defined to include the respondent plus all those living in his household who were not active in the labor force (admittedly not a perfect definition, but one which allowed for ease of calculation), then the average number of dependents per relocated General Foods worker was 3.4. For the sample of displaced workers, the average number of dependents per terminated worker was 2.7. About 65 per cent of the relocated workers had children living at home. About one-third of the relocated workers had more than two children at home. For the General Foods employee with children, presumably the need to guarantee an uninterrupted stream of income was greater than for the single worker, couple, or individual who lived in a household with alternative sources of income. Possibly the best way to guarantee an uninterrupted stream of income was to transfer to Dover.

It is generally considered more difficult for married couples to move when both are employed. That is, the labor force participation of a wife is thought to have a dampening effect on the geographic mobility of her household. It is well known that the labor force participation of all wives has been steadily increasing over the years -- from 4.5 per cent in 1890 to 30.7 per cent in 1960.[22] If there is indeed a negative relationship between labor force participation of wives and geographic mobility, then, all other things being equal, there should be a declining trend in the rate of migration. Yet inter-county migration has remained remarkably stable over the post-war period.[23] It is beyond the scope of this study to attempt to assess all the factors that may influence this relationship. Of course, over the post-war period "all other things" were _not_ equal. It is also possible that the postulate has never been true or, alternatively, that it once was true but is less true today. That is, it may be that a working wife once tended to hold down the mobility of a household, but that today, with working wives a more generally accepted part of our pattern of living, with employment opportunities generally good in most parts of the country, and with employment opportunities very possibly increasing for women at a greater rate than for men (given the changing occupational composition of the labor force), a working wife is less a barrier to geographic mobility than she once was.

---

[22] Wolfbein, _op. cit._, p. 152.

[23] _Ibid._, pp. 219-220.

The Survey Research Center survey revealed that 83 per cent of the wives in families in the sample had worked at some time, compared to 92 per cent of the wives in those families which had moved in the 1958-62 period.[24] As Lansing, *et al.*, conclude, "This result does not support the hypothesis that it is more difficult for married couples to move when both are gainfully employed."[25]

Table 6.5 shows that, *at the time of the interview*, 25.8 per cent of the married, relocated workers' wives were participating in the labor force (*i.e.*, working full or part-time, or looking for work), whereas 30.9 per cent of the displaced workers' wives were active in the labor force. (Note again that about 31 per cent of all wives in the early 1960's were participating in the labor force.) What is more relevant in order to estimate the effect of a wife's labor force status on mobility is her labor force status at the time of the relocation opportunity. In a later section we will deal in greater detail with the impact of the relocation on the worker's household, including to what extent wives were forced to give up a job in order to accompany their husbands on the move. Apparently about the same percentage of the wives of relocated workers were in the labor force before the move as after. On the other hand, among the displaced workers there was

---

[24]Computed from Table III-10, Lansing, *et al.*, *op. cit.*, p. 68.

[25]*Ibid.*, p. 65.

TABLE 6.5

LABOR FORCE STATUS OF WIFE OF RELOCATED AND DISPLACED GENERAL FOODS WORKERS (at time of interview)

	Relocated Workers		Displaced Workers	
	No.	Per Cent	No.	Per Cent
Working full-time	23	13.5	11	16.2
Working part-time	12	7.0	8	11.8
Looking for work	9	5.3	2	2.9
Withdrawn from the labor force	127	74.2	47	69.1
Total	171	100.0	68	100.0

some movement of wives into the labor force most probably as a result of the plant shutdowns. Specifically, five of the eight wives working part-time (under fifteen hours a week) had no previous work history whatsoever and entered the labor force after the shutdown announcement of March, 1962. If those five are subtracted from the labor-force participants, the proportion of displaced workers' wives in the labor force in the spring of 1962 becomes 23.5 per cent. Here again, as for the factor of marital status, the effect of the labor force status of the wife on the mobility of the GF worker is unclear; the evidence is inconclusive. Quite possibly a working wife was not a barrier to transfer in the majority of cases.

Education

The relationship of education and geographic mobility, as shown in Table 6.6, is fairly explicit, both for all migrants, 1958-62, included in the SRC survey, and for General Foods relocated workers. It is clear that higher rates of geographic mobility are associated with higher levels of education for both groups.

SRC migrants are shown to be relatively less mobile than all mobile family heads when educational attainment is twelve years (high school completed) or less. A break occurs after twelve years, with those with thirteen or more years of schooling clearly more mobile

TABLE 6.6

EDUCATION AND GEOGRAPHIC MOBILITY: A COMPARISON OF SRC FAMILY HEADS, SRC FAMILY HEADS WHO WERE MIGRANTS, 1958-62, GENERAL FOODS TRANSFERRED WORKERS, AND GENERAL FOODS DISPLACED WORKERS

	(1) All SRC Family Heads [1] Per Cent	(2) All SRC Migrants, 1958-62[1] Per Cent	(3) G F Trans-ferred Workers No.	(4) G F Trans-ferred Workers Per Cent	(5) G F Displaced Workers No.	(6) G F Displaced Workers Per Cent
0-8 (Grade school)	30.8	15.1	11	5.1	28	24.1
9-11 (Some high school; some high school plus non-academic)	18.9	13.4	32	14.9	33	28.4
12 (Completed high school)	15.7	13.5	83	38.6	39	33.6
13-15 (Completed high school plus non-academic; some college)	21.6	27.4	43	20.0	12	10.4
16 and up (College degree)	13.0	30.6	46	21.4	4	3.5
Total	100.0	100.0	215	100.0	116	100.0

than those with less. Family heads who have completed college are about two and one-half times as mobile as the entire population.

A similar relationship is shown for the General Foods workers. For the factors age and occupation, we were able to compare the transferred GF workers against all GF workers employed at the four closed plants, thus allowing a more direct comparison to be made between the GF workers and the SRC migrants. For education, we are restricted to comparing GF transferred workers with our sample of displaced workers. This tends to accentuate the difference in educational attainment between the two groups being compared. Consequently, the point at which the relocated workers become relatively more mobile than the displaced workers is after eleven years of school, compared with twelve when all SRC migrants are measured against all family heads. If the GF relocated workers could be compared with all workers at four old plants, the effect would be to increase the "break," probably to twelve years, if not more. Table 6.6 shows that 38.6 per cent of the relocated workers had completed twelve years of school; the comparable figure for all migrants in the 1958-62 period is only 13.5 per cent. This is largely the result of the fact that the "pool" of GF workers with twelve years of schooling from which the relocated workers came is proportionately larger than the pool of all family heads with twelve years of schooling.

If an adjustment could be made to account for the difference in the size of these pools, it is estimated that the mobility rates for relocated workers and all migrants with twelve years of school would be about equal.

Despite these difficulties in making accurate comparisons, it is clear that the pattern of mobility by education for GF relocated workers is very similar to the pattern for all migrants. Earlier it was discovered that the geographic mobility patterns by age and occupation were different for the relocated worker in comparison with the migrant in general. Education, age, and occupation are all intercorrelated: the older worker tends to be less educated, the less educated worker tends to have a lower-skilled job. It is difficult in any mobility study to isolate the separate effects of these variables. However, when Lansing, et al., attempted to hold age constant, it was found that "the relation between education and mobility remains powerful."[26] For the General Foods workers, the relation between age and occupation, on the one hand, and mobility, on the other, was found to be weaker than one might expect, given the characteristics of all migrants. Yet, for the General Foods workers, education was closely related to mobility. Consequently, we conclude that educational attainment was a prime determinant of relocation.

---

[26] Ibid., p. 60.

This conclusion is supported by Table 6.7. Here data on transferred and displaced workers are broken down on the basis of hourly rated or salaried status, a two-pronged occupational classification roughly corresponding to blue-collar or white-collar work. Table 6.7 shows that within each broad occupational category, education is fairly strongly related to geographic movement. Hourly transferred workers averaged 11.3 years of school, compared to 9.2 for hourly displaced workers; salaried transferred averaged 13.9 years of school compared to 11.6 for the salaried displaced workers.

Birthplace and Years of Residence in Old Area

The great majority of General Foods workers who moved to Dover had been born and raised in the area from which they moved. About 69 per cent of those interviewed were born in the old area. Of all family heads interviewed by the Survey Research Center, 64 per cent were living in an area which was not their birthplace.[27] Only one of the 215 surveyed for this study indicated that the move was a return to the place of his birth, compared to one in ten of all moves made between 1950 and 1962.[28] The distance of the move to Dover was con-

---

[27] *Ibid.*, pp. 8-11.

[28] *Ibid.*, p. 25.

TABLE 6.7

EDUCATION OF GENERAL FOODS TRANSFERRED AND DISPLACED WORKERS; COMPARISON OF HOURLY AND SALARIED WORKERS
(Percentage distribution)

Years of School	Hourly Workers Transferred	Hourly Workers Displaced	Salaried Workers Transferred	Salaried Workers Displaced
0-8	11.1	26.7	0.8	16.7
9-11	28.9	37.2	4.8	3.3
12	42.2	30.2	36.0	43.4
13-15	16.7	5.9	22.4	23.3
16 and up	1.1	0.0	36.0	13.3
Total	100.0	100.0	100.0	100.0
Number of Workers	90	86	125	30
Mean Years of School	11.3	9.2	13.9	11.6

siderable: for those from Hoboken, more than 200 miles; for those from the other three plants, more than 400 miles. For those in the SRC survey, 28 per cent were living 500 miles or more from their birthplace -- however, there is evidence that movement away from one's place of birth is a gradual process, the distance increasing with age.[29] Most of the people who are living more than 400 miles from their birthplace did not move that distance all at once. The majority of family heads in this country have moved away from their birthplace, but, in contrast with the typical, relocated GF worker, they have not moved as far, and have taken a longer period of time to do so.

Table 6.8 shows the percentage distribution of years of residence in the old area for relocated and displaced workers. Both hourly-rated and salaried relocated workers had, on the average, lived fewer years in their old area. Relocated hourly workers had lived an average of 35.1 years in their old area, compared to 42.3 years for those hourly workers who terminated. Relocated salaried workers had lived an average of 27.7 years in their old area, compared to 40.7 years for those salaried workers who terminated. The relocated worker lived fewer years in the area from which he moved, in part because he was younger than the displaced worker. But age differences can account

---

[29]*Ibid.*, pp. 8-11.

TABLE 6.8

YEARS OF RESIDENCE IN OLD AREA FOR DISPLACED AND RELOCATED GENERAL FOODS WORKERS
(Percentage distribution)

Years of Residence in Old Area	Hourly Workers		Salaried Workers	
	Relocated	Displaced	Relocated	Displaced
0-9	2.2	1.2	20.8	0.0
10-19	17.8	5.7	12.8	3.3
20-29	17.8	12.8	16.0	23.3
30-39	21.1	19.8	24.0	20.0
40-49	16.7	25.6	16.8	20.0
50-59	23.3	22.1	8.8	26.7
60 and up	1.1	12.8	0.8	6.7
Total	100.0	100.0	100.0	100.0
Mean	35.1	42.3	27.7	40.7

for only about three years of the difference in average length of residence in the old area for the two groups. The rest must be a reflection of a greater amount of past movement for the relocated worker in contrast to the displaced worker.

But even though the relocated workers had averaged fewer years of residence in the old locations, it is apparent that they had, nevertheless, been long-time residents. About half of the relocated workers had lived more than thirty years in their old area; and this represents a considerable degree of immobility. The Survey Research Center found that of <u>all</u> moves made from 1950 to 1962 "about one out of three were made by people who had lived <u>one year</u> or less in the location from which they had moved."[30] Many of these moves, however, were made by the same people -- chronic migrants, so to speak.

Lansing, <u>et al.</u>, continue,

> This finding is interesting because it suggests that once people have made a move they may make another move quickly. The same forces that led them to move in the first place may operate again, and it may be that they find the second move easier to make once they have "learned how to move" and they have cut themselves loose from any ties to the community from which they originally started.[31]

---

[30]<u>Ibid.</u>, p. 117 (emphasis added).

[31]<u>Ibid.</u>, pp. 117, 119.

If years of residence in an area can be used as a measure of ties to a community, then relocated General Foods workers were closely tied to their former communities. In terms of how long they had lived in one place before moving to another, the General Foods workers present a stark contrast to migrants in general. On the other hand, if the SRC conclusion quoted above is accurate, it may be that many of these relocated workers will move again. Indeed, for some of the workers who had never before moved away from their birthplace, the General Foods relocation may be the first of several moves that they will make in their lifetimes. Certainly General Foods "taught" many of the relocated workers "how to move," and the workers may apply that lesson again in the future.

Indices of Past Mobility: Changes in Residence, Changes in City, and Travel Behavior

As a measure of past mobility, relocated General Foods workers were asked (1) how many times they had changed their place of *residence* since 1950, and (2) how many of these changes of residence involved a change of *city* (not including the Dover move). The results are contained in Table 6.9, for salaried workers, and in Table 6.10, for hourly workers. Rows in the tables indicate the number of changes of city; columns, the number of changes of residence. In Table 6.9,

TABLE 6.9

NUMBER OF CHANGES IN RESIDENCE AND NUMBER OF CHANGES IN CITY SINCE 1950
OF RELOCATED GENERAL FOODS SALARIED WORKERS

Number of Changes of City	Number of Changes of Residence							Total	Per Cent
	0	1	2	3	4	5	6 or more		
0	47	13	5	1	0	1	0	67	53.6
1		18	5	2	2	0	0	27	21.6
2			8	2	0	1	0	11	8.8
3				7	3	0	0	10	8.0
4					2	0	0	2	1.6
5						3	2	5	4.0
6 or more							3	3	2.4
Total	47	31	18	12	7	5	5	125	100.0
Per Cent	37.6	24.8	14.4	9.6	5.6	4.0	4.0		100.0

for example, we see that forty-seven salaried workers had changed neither their residence nor their city since 1950, and before the Dover move. Thirty-one had changed their place of residence once; for thirteen this change did not involve a change of city, and for eighteen it did. For salaried workers, 53.6 per cent had not changed cities from 1950 to the Dover move and 37.6 per cent had not changed residences. But hourly workers, as shown by Table 6.10, had made even fewer moves: 75.6 per cent had not changed cities, and 56.7 per cent had not changed residences. It is clear that, of those who moved to Dover, salaried workers were much more accustomed to making changes in residences and cities than hourly workers.

Exact comparisons with the SRC results are difficult, since that study speaks in terms of moves between "labor market areas." If a change in "labor market area" cam be considered the equivalent of a change between "cities," then the amount of movement by GF relocated hourly workers is very similar to the amount of movement by all family heads: 71 per cent of the surveyed family heads had lived in only one "labor market area" since 1950, 15 per cent had lived in two.[32] It follows, then, that transferred GF salaried workers had made more moves since 1950 than the population as a whole.

---

[32] *Ibid.*, p. 15.

TABLE 6.10

NUMBER OF CHANGES IN RESIDENCE AND NUMBER OF CHANGES IN CITY SINCE 1950 OF RELOCATED GENERAL FOODS HOURLY WORKERS

Number of Changes of City	Number of Changes of Residence							Total	Per Cent
	0	1	2	3	4	5	6 or more		
0	51	10	4	2	0	1	0	68	75.6
1		6	4	4	0	0	0	14	15.6
2			1	1	1	0	0	3	3.3
3				0	0	0	0	0	0.0
4					3	0	0	3	3.3
5						0	1	1	1.1
6 or more							1	1	1.1
Total	51	16	9	7	4	1	2	90	100.0
Per Cent	56.7	17.8	10.0	7.8	4.4	1.1	2.2		100.0

A "trip" is a kind of move, often difficult to distinguish from more permanent kinds of movement. The Survey Research Center found a definite relation between frequency of travel, measured by the number of trips taken 100 miles from an individual's home, and geographic mobility. Cause and effect may be difficult to specify in the relation, however. "It may be that people travel because they have moved, but it may also be that people have moved because they have traveled."[33] Because General Foods workers were interviewed within a few months of their move to Dover, it is clear that most if not all trips taken 100 miles or more from home were necessarily taken <u>before</u> their move to Dover. If time sequence indicates cause and effect, then it may be that a high frequency of travel for General Foods workers (thereby presumably "conditioning" the individual to travel) has led to a greater propensity to relocate in Dover.

Table 6.11 explores the relation between travel behavior and geographic mobility. When migrant family heads are compared with all family heads, it is clear that the migrants were much more likely to have made ten or more trips in the preceding five-year period (51 per cent of all migrant family heads had made ten or more trips, compared to 32 per cent of all family heads). The travel behavior

---

[33] <u>Ibid.</u>, p. 104.

TABLE 6.11

NUMBER OF TRIPS TAKEN TO PLACES 100 MILES FROM HOME FOR ALL FAMILY HEADS, FAMILY HEADS WHO WERE MIGRANTS, 1958-62, AND RELOCATED GENERAL FOODS WORKERS

Number of Trips	(1) All SRC Heads of Families[1] Per Cent	(2) Migrants 1958-62 [2] Per Cent	(3) G F Transferred Hourly Workers Per Cent	(4) G F Transferred Salaried Workers Per Cent
None	16	5	5.5	1.6
1 or 2	21	16	6.7	5.8
3-5	22	20	22.2	15.2
6-9	9	8	18.9	17.6
10 or more	32	51	46.7	60.0
Total	100	100	100.0	100.0

[1] John B. Lansing, *et al.*, *The Geographic Mobility of Labor: A First Report* (Ann Arbor, Mich.: Survey Research Center, 1963), p. 101.

[2] *Ibid.*, p. 108. Computed from Table III-42 on that page.

of relocated General Foods workers is similar to that of all migrants. Of the hourly transfers, 46.7 per cent had made ten or more trips of 100 miles in the preceding five years; of the salaried transfers, 60 per cent had made ten or more trips. In fact, a greater proportion of General Foods workers had made six or more trips than of all migrants: about 66 per cent of the GF hourly workers and 78 per cent of the salaried, compared to 59 per cent of the migrants. Thus the relation between travel behavior and geographic mobility is probably stronger for General Foods workers than for all migrants. This finding suggests that the GF workers might have been willing to move a considerable distance to Dover in part because they had become accustomed to traveling long distances.

Temporary Work Assignments

It was previously shown that the relocated General Foods workers had on the average been long-time residents of their former communities. The interviewed workers were also asked whether they had ever gone away *temporarily* to work. This same question was put to family heads in the Survey Research Center survey. A comparison of the results obtained in that study and the present one are obtained in Table 6.12. Unfortunately, the Lansing report does not indicate whether migrants in the 1958-62 period had in the past been more prone

TABLE 6.12

WHETHER FAMILY HEAD HAS EVER GONE AWAY TEMPORARILY TO WORK: COMPARISON OF GENERAL FOODS WORKERS WITH ALL FAMILY HEADS

	All Family Heads[1] Per Cent	G F Transferred Hourly Workers Per Cent	G F Transferred Salaried Workers Per Cent
Have gone away temporarily	7	31.1	47.2
Followed construction work	2	3.3	0.8
Followed other work	1	2.2	1.6
Took a job at a distance but on a temporary basis	2	2.2	5.6
Brief assignment in another area for G F	--	3.3	15.2
Brief assignment in another area for another company	1	7.8	4.5
For other reasons	1	12.3	19.2
Have never gone away temporarily	92	68.9	52.8
Not ascertained	1	0.0	0.0
Total	100	100.0	100.0

[1]John B. Lansing, *et al.*, *The Geographic Mobility of Labor: A First Report* (Ann Arbor, Mich.: Survey Research Center, 1963), p. 34.

to this form of temporary movement than family heads in general. Nevertheless, we can see from Table 6.12 that, despite long-time residence in the former area, GF workers had done quite a bit of movement in response to temporary job assignments. While only seven per cent of all family heads had ever gone away temporarily to work, nearly one-third (31.1 per cent) of the hourly GF workers and nearly one-half (47.2 per cent) of the salaried GF workers reported going away temporarily to work.

Of particular note is the kind of temporary work assignment prompting movement by the General Foods workers. For example, 15 per cent of the salaried workers had been to another area on temporary assignment for General Foods. Even 3.5 per cent of the hourly workers had had a temporary assignment in another area for General Foods. All told, about 11 per cent of the hourly workers and 20 per cent of the salaried workers had gone away temporarily to work either for General Foods or for another company. This compared to only one per cent of all family heads who had worked for a company in another area on a temporary assignment. In part, this reflects General Foods' policy of freely shifting workers from one plant site to another when a man with a special kind of expertise is needed to help start or maintain a production line.

A relatively large percentage of General Foods workers reported working in another area on a temporary basis for reasons other than those listed. There is no way of telling exactly what the "other reasons" might be, but included in this category are those workers who took summer jobs away from home, or those skilled GF employees (for example, engineers) who might have done consulting work on a free-lance basis.

The large amount of past movement because of temporary work assignments represents another "conditioning" factor which might have increased the General Foods workers' propensity to relocate to Dover.

Family Income

Evidence on the relationship between income and geographic mobility appears to be contradictory. A recent publication of the Department of Labor finds that "there is a noticeable association between increasing mobility of American males and diminishing income."[34] This conclusion is based on census data for 1960 showing the relationship of residential mobility and income. There is also evidence that migration (as opposed to residential mobility) rates

---

[34] *Mobility and Worker Adaptation to Economic Change in the United States*, *op. cit.*, p. 21.

are also inversely correlated with income. Wolfbein reports that the migration rate for men with yearly incomes of $1,000 to $1,999 is 11.7 per cent, and that as income increases the migration rate falls -- to 4.0 per cent for men with $15,000 or more.[35]

Again we are faced with a variable which is intercorrelated with a number of other variables, making it difficult to isolate the effect. Nevertheless, it may seem curious that geographic mobility is more common among professional, managerial, and other highly skilled workers, and among the highly educated -- groups whose incomes are above average -- and yet for income to be inversely related to geographic mobility. One might hypothesize that a reconciliation can be made by considering the relation of age to income, occupation, education, and mobility. Age and income are directly related, the young having lower average incomes, regardless of occupation or educational attainment. Hence, the inverse relation of income and mobility may simply reflect the preponderance of the young among the geographically mobile.

The findings of the Survey Research Center do not clarify the relation of income and migration. As Lansing, <u>et al.</u>, put it, "The interpretation of the relation between income and past mobility is

---

[35]Wolfbein, <u>op. cit.</u>, p. 223.

particularly difficult."[36] Table 6.13 shows, in part, the SRC findings. Comparing migrants in the 1958-62 period with all family heads, there appears to be, if anything, a slightly _positive_ relationship between income and migration. However, the only unequivocal conclusion one can reach from examining Table 6.13 is that "those with family incomes under $2,000 a year are less likely to have moved . . . than the rest of the population."[37] But even this conclusion squarely contradicts Wolfbein's finding, cited above.

Of course, one can scarcely look to the General Foods workers for a definitive answer to this apparent contradiction. In terms of yearly income, the General Foods families differ significantly from migrants and the population in general. First, the level of income for General Foods workers is above the level for migrants and the population. Second, the distribution of families' incomes is more compressed for the General Foods workers. Neither of these differences is very surprising.

Family heads and migrant family heads include in their ranks a number who are or have recently been unemployed. This is not true for the GF workers, and this factor alone accounts for much of the difference between the GF workers and "everyone else."

---

[36]Lansing, _et al._, _op. cit._, p. 74.

[37]_Ibid._

TABLE 6.13

TOTAL FAMILY INCOME, PREVIOUS YEAR: A COMPARISON OF ALL FAMILY HEADS FAMILY HEADS WHO WERE MIGRANTS, 1958-62, GENERAL FOODS HOURLY DISPLACED AND TRANSFERRED WORKERS, AND SALARIED DISPLACED AND TRANSFERRED WORKERS
(Percentage Distribution)

Total Family Income	(1) All SRC Family Heads [1]	(2) SRC Migrants 1958-62[1]	(3) G F Hourly Displaced Workers	(4) G F Hourly Transferred Workers	(5) G F Salaried Displaced Workers	(6) G F Salaried Transferred Workers
Under $2,000	14.5	7.4	0.0	0.0	0.0	0.0
$2,000-2,999	9.2	8.1	0.0	0.0	0.0	0.0
$3,000-3,999	8.4	7.8	1.2	0.0	0.0	0.0
$4,000-4,999	10.4	13.8	5.8	3.3	6.7	1.6
$5,000-5,999	14.0	13.3	7.0	4.5	10.0	4.0
$6,000-7,499	15.8	17.9	36.0	27.8	16.7	10.4
$7,500-9,999	12.4	16.5	26.7	33.3	30.0	32.0
$10,000 or over	15.3	15.2	23.3	27.8	36.6	51.2
Not ascertained	--	--	--	3.3	--	0.8
Total	100.0	100.0	100.0	100.0	100.0	100.0

1. Computed from Table III-16, John B. Lansing, *et al.*, *The Geographic Mobility of Labor: A First Report* (Ann Arbor, Mich.: Survey Research Center, 1963), p. 76.

From Table 6.13 we can determine the median income categories for the six sample groups:

Family heads	$5,000 - 5,999
Migrant family heads	$5,000 - 5,999
GF hourly displaced	$7,500
GF hourly transferred	$7,500 - 9,999
GF salaried displaced	$7,500 - 9,999
GF salaried transferred	$10,000 and over

By dividing the GF workers by hourly or salaried status, we are to some extent, but obviously not completely, holding occupation constant. In terms of median income category, the finding for the hourly and salaried groups is consistent. Transferred workers in both groups were in a higher median income category than displaced workers. On the other hand, both the SRC sample of all family heads and the migrant family heads fell into the same median income category.

While the relation between income and migration in general may be unclear, the evidence from this study suggests that General Foods families with higher incomes had a slightly greater tendency to relocate than did those with lower incomes.

Financial Position

All workers interviewed for this study were asked to indicate everything their family owned (such as real estate, stocks and bonds, savings, cash, checking account, automobiles, and so on), and everything their family owed (except home mortgages; including car loans, charge accounts, installment payment loans, and other debts). Loosely, the results, summarized in Table 6.14, give an indication of the workers' assets and debts. In general, the General Foods workers, whether displaced or transferred, were not in a particularly precarious financial position. The majority reported owning more than $5,000 and owing less than $1,000. It is likely that the probability of prevarication, perhaps by inadvertence, runs higher for these questions than for others.

If a worker's decision to terminate or relocate depends on the relative costs of displacement or relocation, his decision should also be related to his financial capacity to meet the costs incumbent upon his decision. If the costs of displacement are high relative to relocation, one would expect, all other things being equal, workers in a less secure financial position to accept relocation. In most situations the costs of moving are probably greater than the costs of staying. One would then expect those with limited financial

TABLE 6.14

COMPARISON OF EVERYTHING FAMILY "OWNS" AND "OWES"
FOR TRANSFERRED AND DISPLACED GENERAL FOODS WORKERS
(Percentage Distribution)

	Transferred Workers	Displaced Workers
Everything family owns totals less than $1,000	2.3	9.5
Everything family owes totals		
Less than $1,000	1.4	6.0
Between $1,000 and $5,000	0.9	3.5
More than $5,000	0.0	0.0
Everything family owns totals between $1,000 and $5,000	22.3	23.3
Everything family owes totals		
Less than $1,000	11.6	16.4
Between $1,000 and $5,000	8.8	6.9
More than $5,000	1.9	0.0
Everything family owns totals more than $5,000	72.1	67.2
Everything family owes totals		
Less than $1,000	39.5	47.4
Between $1,000 and $5,000	28.4	18.1
More than $5,000	4.2	1.7
Not ascertained	3.3	0.0
Total	100.0	100.0

reserves to stay. One would think that workers, consciously or unconsciously, make calculations of the expected monetary costs of the options before them, and their capacity to meet them, and then decide accordingly.

In the General Foods case, the costs of relocation were lowered significantly for all workers and theoretically eliminated completely for the salaried workers. On the other hand, the typical worker, considering the option of termination, had to contemplate some period of unemployment and the costs associated with unemployment. However, such costs would be mitigated by the company's provision of severance pay and the receipt of unemployment compensation from the state. Therefore, it is difficult to say whether, on balance, for the GF worker, there was any cost advantage to terminating or relocating. The answer, if one is possible, depended largely on the characteristics of the individual worker -- his age, occupation, education, and so on.

An examination of Table 6.14 reveals a weak relationship between relocation and financial position. There is perhaps a tendency for the transferred worker to be slightly better off in terms of the value of his family's possessions. But there is also some tendency for the transferred worker to owe a bit more money than the displaced worker. For example, 72 per cent of the transferred workers owned more than $5,000, compared to 67 per cent of the displaced workers. But within this category, about 33 per cent of the transferred workers owned more than $1,000, compared to about 20 per cent of the displaced workers.

In view of the above, and our reluctance to invest in the figures more precision than is warranted, no conclusion can be reached on the relationship of migration and financial position for the General Foods workers.

Home Ownership

"Home ownership makes people reluctant to move to other areas," Reynolds discovered.[38] Almost without exception, every study on geographic mobility has found home ownership to be a barrier to movement.[39] The Survey Research Center found that, of the migrant family heads in the 1958-62 period, "only 29 per cent owned or were buying their homes. This percentage is substantially below the percentage

---

[38] Lloyd G. Reynolds, The Structure of Labor Markets (New York: Harper and Brothers, 1951), p. 9.

[39] See, in addition to Reynolds, op. cit., Parnes, op. cit., pp. 123-124; Leonard P. Adams and Robert L. Aronson, Workers and Industrial Change (Ithaca, New York: Cornell University, 1957), pp. 97-99; Dale Yoder, "Manpower Mobility: Two Studies," in E. Wight Bakke et al., op. cit., p. 88.

of home owners in the general population, which was in the neighborhood of 60 per cent in 1960, at the time when these moves were taking place."[40]

In the face of this consensus view on home ownership and mobility, one almost feels the need to apologize for reporting the following finding: a greater proportion of those General Foods workers who moved had owned or were in the process of buying a home in the old location (62.3 per cent) than of those who were displaced (52.6 per cent). This relationship holds true when the samples are broken down. For example, 58.8 per cent of the transferred Walter Baker hourly employees owned a home before moving, compared to 50 per cent of the displaced Walter Baker hourly employees.

No finding in this study so contradicts the conventional wisdom on geographic mobility as this one. Wherein lies the explanation? The impact of the transfer policies put into effect by General Foods is most evident in this area. Home ownership is normally a barrier to geographic mobility in part because the process of divesting oneself of a home can be a difficult and onerous task. But General Foods reduced most of the burdens for the home owner, and, as we have seen in Chapter IV, would _buy_ the home from a salaried worker if no other buyer could be found. Furthermore, it happens

---

[40]Lansing, _et al._, _op. cit._, p. 79.

that rental opportunities were limited in the Dover area. There were certainly fewer rental opportunities in Dover than in Hoboken or Boston, and very likely fewer than in the Orange and LeRoy areas. Most workers who moved to Dover had to contemplate the purchase of a home. Although there was very little difference in the financial position of the movers and stayers, it was probably easier for the past home-owner to find the necessary down-payment for a home (for example, by selling his old home) than for the renter. Parnes suggests that there may be "a possible personality difference between home-owners and renters. . . ."[41] Owners may have a stable preference for owning; renters for renting. If this is true, then there was a strong disincentive for renters to move to Dover because of the limited rental opportunities there.

All this suggests that we have perhaps taken a one-sided view of the relation between home ownership and migration. In addition to owner-or-renter status in the old area, the character of the housing market in the area of potential movement must also be examined. Can the worker obtain living quarters in the new area comparable to those in the old? Or will he be forced into a different sort of accommodation than he has been accustomed to? Certainly these are the kinds of matters which workers themselves consider.

In sum, it has been found that proportionately more home-makers moved to Dover than terminated. The explanation seems to reside in

---

[41]Parnes, <u>op. cit.</u>, p. 124.

(1) the nature of General Foods' transfer policies and (2) the character of the Dover housing market.

Seniority

The final characteristic of the relocated worker considered in this chapter is length of service (or "seniority"). Seniority is to some extent a measure of the employee's loyalty, or strength of attachment, to the company. The plant relocation was definitely a test of that attachment. As we have seen, workers electing relocation were guaranteed their full seniority, and all the privileges associated with long tenure of employment. It is to be expected that the longer service employee would be more prone to relocate than the shorter.

Table 6.15 shows that this expectation is fulfilled for the General Foods workers. The average length of service for the transferred worker was 16.1 years, compared to 13.3 years for the displaced worker. More than 50 per cent of the displaced workers had ten or fewer years of service, compared to less than 20 per cent of the transferred workers. When the samples are broken down, the same relation prevails. For example, hourly transfers averaged 15.8 years of service, compared to 12.9 years for hourly terminations. Salaried transfers averaged 16.6 years, compared to 14.7 years for salaried

TABLE 6.15

YEARS OF SERVICE (SENIORITY) OF GENERAL FOODS TRANSFERRED AND DISPLACED WORKERS

Years of Service	Transferred Workers No.	Transferred Workers Per Cent	Displaced Workers No.	Displaced Workers Per Cent
0- 5	28	13.0	18	15.5
6-10	34	15.8	41	35.3
11-15	46	21.4	22	19.0
16-20	44	20.5	15	12.9
21-25	20	9.4	8	6.9
26-30	25	11.6	7	6.0
31-35	16	7.4	2	1.7
36-40	2	0.9	1	1.0
40 or more	0	0.0	2	1.7
Total	215	100.0	116	100.0
Mean		16.1		13.3

terminations. The modal category for hourly transfers was eleven to fifteen years of service, and for salaried transfers, sixteen to twenty years of service. For both hourly and salaried displaced workers, the modal category of service was six to ten years.

Some of the difference between transferred and displaced workers can probably be accounted for by the difference in age for the two groups. As noted, transferred workers were slightly younger, on the average, than displaced workers (forty-seven years to forty-four years). However, the <u>relative</u> difference in years of service between the two groups was greater than the relative difference in age. The relocated workers were asked, "Can you tell me your major reasons for moving to Dover?" The great majority of answers indicated retaining seniority as a major reason for relocating. It can be concluded that length of service was one of the prime determinants of relocation.

Chapter Summary

The General Foods relocated workers have been examined on a number of economic and social factors in an attempt to find out how they differed, if at all, from displaced General Foods workers and migrants in general. Comparisons were based on simple two-way or three-way relationships. It is difficult in such relationships to isolate cause and effect. Moreover, it would have been preferable, perhaps, to apply multi-variate analysis to arrive at a more precise weighting of the importance of the determinants of mobility examined. (Given the size and nature of the samples, however, multi-variate analysis would not add much to the analysis.) Our major findings indicate the following:

1. Managerial and technical personnel, foremen, and highly skilled blue-collar workers were the most likely General Foods employees to relocate. Less skilled blue-collar workers as well as clerical and sales workers were more likely to terminate. On the other hand, the direct relation between occupational skill level and geographic mobility was not as strong for General Foods workers as for migrants in general. In particular, inter-plant transfer policies caused or allowed a greater proportion of higher skilled blue-collar workers to relocate than one might have expected, given the migration pattern by occupation for the population as a whole.

2. Sex was a primary determinant of relocation. Very few women elected transfer to Dover. The relation of sex and geographic mobility was much more pronounced for General Foods workers than for the population as a whole.

3. There was a definite inverse relation between age and geographic mobility for the General Foods workers. Those under age twenty-five were about twice as likely to transfer as those over age twenty-five. On the other hand, the relation was apparently not as strong for the relocated worker as for the population in general. In particular, there was a much greater tendency for the General Foods worker in the forty-five to fifty-four age bracket to transfer than would be indicated by the figures for migrants in general. Furthermore, blue-collar relocated workers tended to be significantly older than white-collar workers.

4. The proportion of workers married was higher among the relocated workers than among the displaced. Moreover, the relocated workers had, on the average, more dependents than the displaced workers. In addition, it is reasonably clear that a working wife was not a barrier to the transfer of a General Foods worker. These results are surprising and contradict popularly-held notions about the geographically mobile. However, the Survey Research Center study revealed a very similar picture for migrants in general. It is likely that other variables are more important in determining the

geographic mobility of workers than marital status, dependency status, and the labor force status of the wife.

5. There was a clear tendency for more educated General Foord workers to be more mobile than less educated. In relative terms, about twice as many relocated workers as displaced workers had gone beyond high school, and seven times as many had completed college. The relation was strong even when some allowance was made for occupation. In terms of educational attainment, and in contrast to occupation and age, General Foods relocated workers were very similar to migrants in general. It must be concluded that educational attainment -- and all that it represents -- was a primary determinant of movement among the General Foods workers.

6. Relocated General Foods workers had lived fewer years in their old area than displaced workers. Yet in absolute terms, the relocated workers had been strongly attached to their former communities (broadly defined), averaging about thirty years of residence. Most of the movement in this country is done by a small proportion of the people, and they, consequently, tend to be short-term residents

of the communities from which they move. Therefore, in terms of years of residence in the old area, the relocated General Foods worker was an extremely atypical migrant.

7. Although they had been long-time residents in their old areas, the General Foods relocated workers had made many intra-area moves over the preceding fourteen-year period. Slightly more than one-half had made at least one change of residence after 1950 and before the Dover move. A salaried worker was more likely to have made a change in residence and/or city than an hourly-rated worker. The number of such moves among both groups was of the same magnitude as the number of such moves for the population.

8. On the other hand, relocated General Foods workers had had more travel experience than migrants in general. About 70 per cent of the relocated workers had made six or more trips of one hundred miles or more in the preceding five-year period, compared to about 60 per cent of all migrants and 40 per cent of all family heads. Past travel behavior might have served as a "conditioning factor" which increased the propensity of the General Foods worker to move.

9. In addition, the General Foods relocated worker was shown to have extensive travel experience in connection with fulfilling a temporary work assignment. Proportionately five times as many relocated workers had at some time gone away on a temporaty work assignment as family heads in general. Many of these assignments were at the behest of the corporation. Many of the relocated workers had become accustomed to traveling in order to work for General Foods, and this undoubtedly served to increase their propensity to accept permanent transfer to Dover.

10. While the relationship between family income and geographic mobility is in general unclear, there appears to have been a tendency for General Foods workers with higher family incomes to transfer to Dover. Family income is another factor which is apparently not as strong a determinant of geographic mobility as, say, age, occupation or education. The same must be said of the factor "financial position." While relocated workers "owned" a bit more than displaced workers, they also "owed" a bit more.

11. Home ownership has long been thought to be a deterrent to geographic mobility. It is surprising, then, that the proportion of home-owners among the relocated workers was higher than the proportion among the displaced workers. This finding is found to have been true even when the samples were broken down by occupation and previous area. It was explained by reference to the company's policies of aid to the transferring home-owner and by the relative lack of rental opportunities in the Dover area.

12. Relocated General Foods workers averaged longer years of service with the company than displaced workers. It is clear that seniority was an important determinant of relocation. Only by transferring to Dover could the General Foods worker retain the privileges attendant on long service. Seniority can also be viewed as a measure of the worker's loyalty to the company. The plant relocation was a test of his attachment to the company vis-à-vis his attachment to his community. There was a tendency for long years of service with the company to dominate long years of residence in the

old area, and thus for seniority to be a crucial variable among those found to be associated with relocation.

In conclusion, the results clearly indicate that the relocated worker differed significantly not only from the displaced worker, but, in several important respects, from other migrants as well.

CHAPTER VII

THE EXPERIENCE OF THE RELOCATED WORKERS: THE PROCESS AND CONSEQUENCES OF MOVING

This chapter will consider the process and consequences of the General Foods workers' relocation to the new Dover plant. Among the questions which will be examined are the following: Did the workers view the company's transfer policies as adequate? To what extent were all of the costs of relocation covered by the company? What impact did the relocation have on the workers' households? What impact did the relocation have on the labor force participation of the workers' wives? Did relocated workers tend to look for work in their local labor market before accepting transfer to Dover; and, if so, what methods of job search did they employ? Who in the workers' households participated in the decision to transfer, and when was that decision made?

Particular attention will be paid to certain consequences of the move. How did household income change as a result of the move? What kinds of financial adjustments were necessary as a result of the move? Finally, were the workers satisfied with the new plant and community? If they had the opportunity to make the transfer decision again, would they still elect to relocate to Dover?

The Impact of Some Company Policies

In a later section of this chapter, we consider whether the costs of the relocation were adequately covered by General Foods' policies. The question of the adequacy of certain other transfer policies is also discussed.

For example, we have seen that the corporation, by making the shutdown announcement in March, 1962, gave its employees a minimum of two years' advance notice of its intentions. For some transfers, the notice was nearer to three years in advance of eventual relocation. As was pointed out in Chapter IV, an advance notice of two years is certainly exceptional; the median duration of such notices in industry generally is closer to one month.

What impact did the two-year advance notice have on the relocated worker? Was it necessary for the company to have notified its employees so much in advance of the relocation? The relocated workers were asked two questions related to the advanced notice of the plant shutdowns:

(1) How far in advance *should* a company notify its employees when *it is* going to shut down a plant?

(2) Would your decision to move have been affected if the company had given notice of the plant's closing only *six* months in advance?

Table 7.1 summarizes in percentage terms the responses to these questions. Nine out of ten of the relocated workers felt that a company should notify its workers at least one year in advance of a plant shutdown. About half the sample thought that a two-year notice was necessary. There were some differences of opinion between the hourly and salaried workers. Close to 70 per cent of the blue-collar group thought that a two-year notice was necessary, whereas less than half of the white-collar workers were of that opinion. The salaried workers were perhaps more realistic than the hourly workers on this question. Most felt that a one-year notice was sufficient, and several chose a shorter period as the appropriate length of time for an advance notice. The salaried group perhaps recognized more than the hourly group that a two-year notice was exceptional, and that often a company cannot possibly notify workers as far as two years in advance of a significant change.

About 45 per cent of the sample indicated that their decision to move would not have been affected by a six-months' advance notice. The rest of the respondents were evenly divided between those who did not know what effect a six-months' notice would have had on their decision and those who indicated that the shorter notice would have affected their decision. While a shorter notice probably would not have caused as many as 25 or 30 per cent of the sample not to transfer, the

TABLE 7.1

OPINION ON HOW FAR IN ADVANCE A COMPANY SHOULD NOTIFY ITS EMPLOYEES OF A PLANT SHUTDOWN BY EFFECT OF A SIX MONTHS' ADVANCE NOTICE ON THE WORKER'S DECISION TO MOVE: A COMPARISON OF HOURLY AND SALARIED RELOCATED WORKERS
(Percentage Distribution)

Opinion on how far in advance a company should notify its employees	Would your decision to move have been affected if the company had given notice of the plant closing only six months in advance?							
	Hourly Workers				Salaried Workers			
	Total	Yes	Don't Know	No	Total	Yes	Don't Know	No
At least two years	68	81	68	55	45	77	35	37
At least one year	29	19	32	36	46	23	56	50
At least six months	3	0	0	9	7	0	6	9
At least three months	0	0	0	0	1	0	0	4
No answer	0	0	0	0	1	0	3	0
Total	100	100	100	100	100	100	100	100
Cases	90	32	25	33	125	26	34	65

size of the group indicating that the shorter notice would or might have had some effect on their decision does demonstrate the importance of the two-year notice and the significant role this policy had in the decision-making process of the respondents.

However, the breakdown of the sample demonstrates that a shorter notice probably would have affected the hourly group more than the salaried. About one-third of the hourly group noted that a six-month notice would have affected their decision, while only about one in five of the salaried group noted that the shorter notice would have had some effect. More than half the salaried group indicated that they would have transferred regardless of the length of the advance notice, compared to about one-third of the hourly group.

Table 7.1 demonstrates the degree of consistency in the answers of the respondents to the two questions. Those who believed that a company should give its employees a two-year notice were much more likely to have indicated that a six-month notice would have affected their decision. About eight out of ten of the respondents who indicated that their decision would have been affected by a shorter notice also thought a company should give its employees a two-year notice. On the other hand, only about half of those workers who either did not know or said that a six-month notice would have had no effect also indicated a preference for a two-year notice.

In sum, the great majority of the relocated workers thought that at least a one-year notice was needed before a plant shutdown, with most of the hourly group believing a two-year notice was needed. At the same time, the hourly group was much more likely to have indicated that a shorter notice would have affected their decision to move than the salaried group, for whom the advance notice was a less important consideration.

We have previously seen how extensive was the employee communication program used by the corporation to inform the workers about the new plant, Dover and its environs, and the mechanics of moving. To what extent did the relocated employees rely on the company's information, and to what extent did they seek additional information about the new community? In view of the extensive portfolio of literature distributed to the employees -- a portfolio which included maps and brochures published by the Chamber of Commerce and various Dover and Delaware agencies listing the various recreational and cultural amenities in Delaware, in addition to company literature -- it may be surprising that eight out of ten of the relocated workers said they sought additional information beyond what the corporation supplied them. It is not so surprising, however, when one considers that only twelve people in the sample indicated that they had any familiarity with the Dover area at all (ten of the twelve had visited

Dover on a vacation, one had been born there, and one had been there as a serviceman). There was a slight tendency for the white-collar (salaried) workers to be more prone to look for additional information than the blue-collar workers. Nine out of ten of the former group and seven out of ten of the latter group sought additional information. Unfortunately no attempt was made to find out what sort of information was sought and to whom the workers turned for this information.

The relocated workers were also asked whether they had taken advantage of the offer of a trip to Dover at company expense. It will be recalled that General Foods offered to pay up to $70 to hourly employees to cover the costs of such a trip. No upper limit on the costs covered was put on the trips of salaried workers, and they could take more than one, with company approval. The only requirement was that employees check in at the corporation's temporary headquarters in Dover after they arrived.

All but six of the sample of 215 relocated workers had made a pre-move trip to Dover at company expense. Of the six who did not go, four were hourly employees and two were salaried. The relocated workers were further asked, "Do you feel (the trip) was absolutely necessary in order for you to make up your mind about moving?" The results are tabulated in Table 7.2.

TABLE 7.2

WAS THE PRE-MOVE DOVER TRIP ABSOLUTELY NECESSARY IN ORDER FOR YOU TO MAKE UP YOUR MIND ABOUT MOVING?

	Hourly Workers		Salaried Workers	
	No.	Per Cent	No.	Per Cent
Yes	58	64.4	90	72.0
No	26	28.9	29	23.2
Don't Know	6	6.7	6	4.8
Total	90	100.0	125	100.0

About seven out of ten thought the trip was, indeed, "absolutely necessary." (The six who had not made a trip are included in the "No" category.) Apparently there was a bit more of a tendency for the salaried group to believe the trip had been necessary. Of those who thought the trip had not been necessary in order for them to make a decision about moving, about four out of five had decided to go before they made their first trip to Dover. The trip was useful for these people, as indeed it was for all of the respondents, in that it allowed them to canvass the Dover housing market and perhaps make preliminary arrangements for the purchase of a home.

A perspective on the importance of the pre-move Dover trip can be obtained when the experience of the typical migrant is considered.

The Survey Research Center discovered that only 25 per cent of the migrants in the 1958-62 period "made a special trip to look the situation over in the new area."[1] It must be assumed that these trips were not financed by employers. One-third of those who did make such trips obtained no "specific information" from the trip.[2] General Foods made certain that all who visited Dover received very specific information on the Dover area. Here again the General Foods transfers constitute an unusual group of migrants. The pre-move trips provided them with information which the typical migrant normally does not obtain. That this was important information can be seen by the number of GF transfers who indicated that the trip was "absolutely necessary." A smoothly functioning labor market requires that workers have an adequate amount of information so that rational choices can be made. Most migrants have limited sources of information. The amount of information supplied to the General Foods worker and the amount he was able to obtain for himself on the pre-move trip allowed him the opportunity to make a more rational choice than would otherwise have been possible.

As we saw in Chapter IV, all regular employees with one year of service at the shut-down plants were eligible for severance pay.

---

[1]John B. Lansing, _et al._, _The Geographic Mobility of Labor: A First Report_ (Ann Arbor, Mich.: Survey Research Center, 1963), p. 137.

[2]_Ibid._

In making their decision to move, were the relocated workers fully aware of the options available to them? Did they all realize that by electing termination they would be eligible for severance pay, which, depending on their age and length of service, might amount to a considerable sum? A relocated worker who failed to take account of the corporation's severance pay policy hypothetically might have elected termination, had he been more aware of the precise options before him.

Relocated workers were asked:

> Would you have been eligible for a termination allowance or severance pay if you had chosen to terminate instead of moving to Dover?

Since all relocated workers had at least one year of service, it follows that all should have answered "yes" to this question. This is especially true, since the corporation carried on a vigorous counseling program to inform the workers before the move of their "rights." In fact, 86 per cent of the relocated workers did answer "yes." Yet it is significant that the remaining 14 per cent (thirty workers) answered "no" or indicated that they did not know whether they had been eligible for severance pay. However, of this group of thirty, nineteen had three or fewer years of service. The one or two-week benefit which they would have received evidently made very little impression on them. The remaining eleven workers had from five to twenty-eight years of service. They were all certainly informed that they would be eligible for a benefit upon termination, although it is conceivable that some of them simply did not realize that this benefit was called a "termination allowance" or "severance pay."

One should probably concentrate on the finding that more than eight out of ten of the relocated workers were aware of their eligibility for a termination allowance, and so were able to take adequate account of it in making their decision to relocate.

Impact of the Move on the Household

What was the impact of the relocation on the household of the relocated worker? Here, two facets of the impact are examined: (1) the composition of, and change, if any, in the size of the household, and (2) the effect of the move on the working behavior of the wife of the relocated worker.

It was shown in Chapter VI that the size of the relocated worker's household in terms of the number of dependents was, on the average, greater than the size of the displaced worker's. This in itself is somewhat surprising. By contrasting the composition of the relocated worker's household with the composition of the household of migrants in the 1958-62 period (interviewed by the Survey Research Center), one sees some significant differences. This comparison is shown in Table 7.3.

TABLE 7.3

COMPOSITION OF HOUSEHOLD OF GENERAL FOODS RELOCATED WORKERS
COMPARED TO MIGRANTS IN 1958-62
(Percentage Distribution)

	GF Hourly Workers	GF Salaried Workers	Migrants 1958-62[1]
Head only	7.8	4.0	21
Married couple	24.4	16.8	20
Married couple plus children	58.9	64.0	47
Head plus children	0.0	0.8	4
Head or married couple plus other relatives	8.9	14.4	3
Not ascertained	0.0	0.0	5
Total	100.0	100.0	100

[1]John B. Lansing. et al., The Geographic Mobility of Labor: A First Report. (Ann Arbor, Mich.: Survey Research Center, 1963), p. 147.

The table shows, first, that the salaried workers' households were even larger than the households of the hourly workers. Eight out of ten of the salaried workers' households consisted of three or more members (primarily married couples with one or more children). Less than seven out of ten of the hourly workers' households consisted of three or more members. But it can be seen from Table 7.3 that both groups of General Foods workers had larger households than migrants in general.

As noted earlier, the Survey Research Center interviewed only heads of households. It is known from other studies that most of the geographic movement in the country is carried on by unattached individuals, who are not necessarily (or were not prior to their move) the heads of households. Considering just the migrants interviewed in the SRC survey, one finds that 21 per cent were the single person in their household. The contrast with the relocated GF workers is striking: only 7.8 per cent of the hourly workers and 4.0 per cent of the salaried workers lived alone in the sample of relocated workers.

Proportionately more of the GF workers lived with their wives and children than migrants in general. A significant proportion of the GF workers lived in households which included other relatives, such as parents, in-laws, brothers and sisters. Only three per cent of all migrants lived in such households.

The relocated workers were also asked to list the persons who had been living in their households who did not make the move. The Survey Research Center asked a similar question of the migrants it interviewed. The results are compared in Table 7.4. About 20 per cent of the General Foods respondents indicated that one or more persons living in their former households had not made the move. For migrants in the SRC survey "about 12 per cent of all moves involve a division in a family group."[3] For hourly GF workers, about 18 per cent of the households were divided by the move; for salaried workers, about 22 per cent of the households were divided.

Table 7.4 shows that these divisions occurred with relatively less frequency among the General Foods workers, compared to all migrants, when a single (*i.e.*, unattached) person moved. For migrants in general, it was more likely that a division in a household would occur if one person moved than if more than one person moved at a time. For General Foods workers just the opposite was true: it was *less* likely that a division in a household would occur when the move was made by one person.

In sum, the relocated GF workers had larger households than both migrants in general and other GF displaced workers. In addition, the

---

[3]*Ibid.*, p. 149.

TABLE 7.4

OF THE FAMILY LIVING TOGETHER BEFORE THE MOVE, DID ANYONE NOT MAKE THE MOVE? A COMPARISON OF GENERAL FOODS RELOCATED WORKERS WITH MIGRANTS IN THE 1958-62 PERIOD (Percentage Distribution)

Who Made the Move	GF Hourly Workers	GF Salaried Workers	Migrants 1958-62[1]
Head of family only	7.8	4.0	21
Everyone moved	6.7	1.6	15
Someone did not move	1.1	2.4	6
Married couple	24.4	16.8	20
Everyone moved	18.8	11.2	19
Someone did not move	5.6	5.6	1
Married couple plus children	58.9	64.0	47
Everyone moved	50.0	58.4	44
Someone did not move	8.9	5.6	3
Other combinations	8.9	15.2	7
Everyone moved	6.7	8.0	5
Someone did not move	2.2	7.8	2
Not ascertained	0.0	0.0	5
Total	100.0	100.0	100

[1]John B. Lansing, *et al.*, *The Geographic Mobility of Labor: A First Report* (Ann Arbor, Mich.: Survey Research Center, 1963), p. 148.

relocation meant a division in a greater percentage of the relocated workers' households than the households of migrants in general. One subsidiary finding is worth noting. The interviews with relocated GF workers were held, on the average, about one year after the workers had moved. Only four of those interviewed indicated that anyone in their household had moved back to the old area.

As noted in Chapter VI, a working wife was most likely not a barrier to the relocation of a male General Foods worker. Yet it was also seen that about the same percentage of the relocated workers' wives were in the labor force before the move as after it. A few working wives were also General Foods workers and transferred to the new plant in Dover with their husbands. It is also possible that the nature of a wife's work did not require her to give up her job in order to move to Dover with her husband. For example, one wife did free-lance typing at home, and hence could continue to do the same work in Dover. In most cases, however, a wife who worked in the old location necessarily had to give up her job in order to move to Dover with her husband. Were the wives who entered the labor force in Dover the same as those who had worked in the old location?

This question can be answered by using Table 7.5. First, let us examine how the labor force status of a GF worker's wife (at the time of the interview) differed for the hourly and salaried employee

TABLE 7.5

IN ORDER TO MOVE TO DOVER, DID YOUR WIFE HAVE TO GIVE UP A JOB IN YOUR OLD LOCATION? A COMPARISON OF GENERAL FOODS HOURLY AND SALARIED RELOCATED WORKERS BY CURRENT LABOR FORCE STATUS OF WIFE (Percentage Distribution)

Labor Force Status of Wife	GF Hourly Workers	GF Salaried Workers
Working full-time	17.9	10.6
Gave up job	7.5	7.7
Did not give up job	10.4	2.9
Working part-time	7.5	6.7
Gave up job	7.5	4.8
Did not give up job	0.0	1.9
Looking for work	6.0	4.8
Gave up job	4.5	3.8
Did not give up job	1.5	1.0
Withdrawn from labor force	68.6	77.9
Gave up job	11.9	8.7
Did not give up job	56.7	69.2
Total	100.0	100.0

groups. The table shows that proportionately more of the hourly workers' wives were in the labor force. For the married male hourly group, 31.4 per cent had wives in the labor force, compared to 22.1 per cent of the married salaried workers. About 18 per cent of the hourly workers' wives were working full-time, compared to about 11 per cent of the salaried workers' wives. Prior to the Dover move, 31.4 per cent of the hourly workers' wives had been working, compared to 25 per cent of the salaried workers' wives. These percentages do not include wives who might have been looking for work in the old area prior to the move. However, it is not likely that <u>any</u> wives were looking for work in the old area just prior to the move, unless the search was for extremely short-term employment. Therefore, it appears that about the same proportion of wives were in the labor force before the move as after. But were they the same wives?

Table 7.5 shows us that they were not, and that in fact there was a good deal of change with regard to a wife's labor force status before and after the move. Curiously, these changes tended to offset one another. For example, among hourly workers, about 12 per cent of the wives who had been working before the move were no longer in the labor force. However, this was offset by about 12 per cent now being in the labor force who had <u>not</u> been at work just prior to the move. For salaried workers, about nine per cent who had been working before the move were no longer in the labor force, whereas about six per cent who had not been working prior to the move had entered the labor force in Dover. The net change is about three per cent for the salaried group (but under two per cent for all relocated workers).

Our findings illustrate the volatile nature of the female secondary earner, who is prone to change her labor force status easily and often. Of those wives in the labor force in Dover, fully one-third had not been at work prior to their husbands' relocation. The proportion is slightly higher among the wives of hourly workers: about 38 per cent had not been at work before the move.

Relocated workers were also asked:

> When your wife is not employed, has she usually actively sought work?

Responses to this question perhaps give a better indication of the size of the proportion of wives who are more or less permanent members of the labor force. About 30 per cent of the married male hourly group and 18 per cent of the comparable salaried group answered this question affirmatively. About one in four of the wives who were reported by their husbands to have "usually actively sought work" were not currently in the labor force. While most of these had had jobs before moving to Dover, a handful, not currently in the labor force, had not had a job before the move either. It is possible that these women had typically sought work in the old area, but had given it up after moving to Dover. In any event, most wives who usually sought work constituted about 65 per cent of all wives who were either currently in the labor force or who had had jobs before the Dover move and were now out of the labor force. Therefore, it appears that about two-thirds of all wives who had labor-force experience, past or present, were more or less permanent labor-force participants.

Boldly summarizing our findings, we find that of the wives of the General Foods workers, about six-ninths are never in the labor force, about two-ninths are always in the labor force, and about one-ninth constitute the volatile element, changing their labor-force status with relative frequency. For hourly workers, the proportion out of the labor force is smaller, and the "volatile element" larger than for salaried workers.

To gain insight into the dynamics of the labor force, it would be helpful if an explanation could be found for the labor-force participation of the General Foods workers' wives. It would be particularly interesting to discover what factors were responsible for the changes in the labor-force status of the wives resulting from the move. Many studies have explored the question of the determinants of the labor-force participation of wives.[4] In the broadest sense, two factors appear to account for the labor-force participation of the wife: (1) the stage of the life-cycle of the household, and (2) the income of her husband.[5] Although we have seen that some divisions of households were brought about as a result of the Dover move, obviously the life-cycle of the household itself did not change as a result of the move. That is to say, the life-cycle of the household would have been the same whether the household moved or not. Life-cycle changes are necessarily long-term changes related to the aging process, not to short-term changes in the location of the household.

On the other hand, the relocation did bring about some significant changes in the income of the household and of the primary breadwinner. One might hypothesize that an increase in income for the General Foods worker, brought about by the move, might have led to a decrease in the labor-force participation of the wife. Alternatively, a decrease in the GF worker's income might have led to

---

[4]See, e.g., Clarence D. Long, The Labor Force under Changing Income and Employment, pp. 7-9, 82-143; Jacob Mincer, "Labor Force Participation of Married Women," Aspects of Labor Economics, a conference of the Universities--National Bureau Committee for Economic Research (Princeton, N. J.: Princeton University Press, 1962), pp. 63-97.

[5]Neil W. Chamberlain, The Labor Sector (New York: McGraw-Hill, 1965), pp. 4-10.

an increase in the labor force participation of the wife. That is, those wives who were not working in the old location might have entered the labor force in Dover because of a decrease in their husbands' income. Such hypotheses are not borne out by the data. There is no apparent relation between changes in the husband's and/or household's income and changes in the labor-force participation of the wife. In fact, there is no single factor which seems capable of explaining the changes in the labor-force status of wives brought about as a result of the move.

Pre-Move Job-Searching Activity

The relocated workers were asked a series of questions designed to elicit the extent to which they had sought out alternative job opportunities in their former locations before electing to transfer to Dover. If a significant proportion of the relocated workers had sought another job before moving, it might indicate that a significant amount of doubt had existed among the workers about the efficacy of the move. Why look for another job if one is convinced that the relocation represents one's best opportunity? On the other hand, the worker who engaged in a pre-move job search might be considered the model of the rational decision-maker, canvassing all opportunities open to him before making an important decision. Why uproot one's family for such a move, no matter how attractive the opportunity may seem, without first making sure that equally attractive opportunities are not right at one's doorstep? There is no way of telling for sure whether the pre-move job searcher was a "reluctant mover," unconvinced of the desirability of relocation, or whether he was simply insuring the "optimality" of his decision, whatever it might be.

In any event, 31 per cent of the sample of relocated workers indicated that they had looked for other work before moving. However, of this number, two-thirds noted that they had searched for work, "but not very actively." Only 11 per cent reported making an "active" search for work before relocating. Three out of four who looked for work reported having at least one job interview. All but one of those reporting not having had job interviews also counted themselves as "inactive" job searchers. The respondents were consistent on this point, and apparently used their number of job interviews as an index to classify themselves as either active or inactive job searchers. In other words, active job searchers reported having preponderantly more job interviews than inactive job searchers.

Twenty-three per cent of the total sample and 75 per cent of those who searched for work reported receiving at least one job offer before moving to Dover. (No one who had <u>not</u> searched for work reported receiving a job offer.) The respondents were also consistent on relating the number of job offers they had received to their self-classification as an active or inactive job searcher. That is, all but one of the active searchers reported receiving at least one job offer, whereas only six out of ten of the inactive job searchers reported receiving at least one job offer.

One must take the fact of the relocation itself as *prima facie* evidence that the job offers received by the respondents were not as attractive as the relocation opportunity. A worker can be defined as acting irrationally if he perceived a job offer to be more attractive than transferring to Dover, and yet elected to transfer. It must be assumed that the workers acted rationally in the sense of their behavior being consistent with their perceptions. There is a difficulty, however, in that one cannot be sure how the respondents chose to define a "job interview" and a "job offer." Were the job offers reported *bona fide* offers? There is no way of estimating the authenticity of the responses, and it may be that the amount of pre-move job searching activity was inflated intentionally or inadvertently by the workers.

There were differences in the extent of pre-move job search activity reported by hourly and salaried employees. Table 7.6 shows

TABLE 7.6

PRE-MOVE JOB SEARCH ACTIVITY, JOB INTERVIEWS, AND JOB OFFERS FOR GENERAL FOODS RELOCATED WORKERS (Percentage Distribution)

	GF Hourly Workers	GF Salaried Workers
Looked for work actively	10.0	12.0
no job interviews	1.1	0.0
one or two job offers	1.1	0.0
one or two job interviews	3.3	3.2
one or two job offers	3.3	3.2
several job interviews	4.4	7.2
no job offers	1.1	0.0
one or two job offers	3.3	5.6
several job offers	0.0	1.6
many job interviews	1.1	1.6
one or two job offers	0.0	0.8
several job offers	1.1	0.8
Looked for work, but not very actively	12.2	24.8
no job interviews	4.4	8.8
no job offers	3.3	7.2
one or two job offers	0.0	1.6
several job offers	1.1	0.0
one or two job interviews	5.6	12.8
no job offers	1.1	1.6
one or two job offers	4.5	10.4
several job offers	0.0	0.8
several job interviews	2.2	3.2
no job offers	1.1	0.0
one or two job offers	1.1	2.4
several job offers	0.0	0.8
Did not look for work	77.8	63.2
Total	100.0	100.0

that a greater proportion of salaried workers than hourly workers engaged in a pre-move job search. Twelve per cent of the salaried workers reported actively seeking work, compared to 10 per cent of the hourly, while about 25 per cent of the salaried employees reported having looked for work, "but not very actively," whereas about 12 per cent of the hourly workers placed themselves in that category.

Although relatively more salaried than hourly workers had engaged in either an active or inactive pre-move job search, for both groups the proportion of the searchers reporting at least one job interview was 75 per cent. That is, about 17 per cent of the hourly workers and 28 per cent of the salaried workers indicated having had at least one job interview. About eight per cent of the hourly and 12 per cent of the salaried workers reported having "several" or "many" job interviews. This difference perhaps accounts for the fact that the salaried workers reported slightly greater success in receiving job offers than the hourly group. Twenty-eight per cent of the salaried workers reported receiving at lease one job offer; this represents 76 per cent of all salaried job seekers. About 16 per cent of the hourly workers reported receiving at least one job offer, and this represents 70 per cent of all hourly job seekers.

In sum, comparison of GF hourly and salaried employees shows that the salaried group was much more active in its pre-move job-searching activity, searched for a job a bit more intensively (in terms of reported job interviews), and succeeded in receiving slightly more job offers than the hourly group.

Studies of the methods of job search used by workers have been almost completely confined to the study of methods used by unemployed workers or young workers seeking their first job. These studies have shown that young workers and unemployed workers use "informal" methods of job search (direct application at place of employment; information supplied by friends and relatives) as opposed to "formal" methods (use of public or private employment services; use of want ads; sending résumés).[6] Little research has been

---

[6]William Haber, _et al._, _The Impact of Technological Change: The American Experience_ (Kalamazoo, Mich.: The W. E. Upjohn Institute for Employment Research, 1963), pp. 29-30. See also Charles A. Myers and George P. Shultz, _The Dynamics of a Labor Market_ (New York: Prentice-Hall, 1951), pp. 45-73; Lloyd G. Reynolds and Joseph Shister, _Job Horizons_ (New York: Harper and Bros., 1949), pp. 35-51; Richard C. Wilcock and Walter H. Franke, _Unwanted Workers_ (Glencoe, Ill.: The Free Press, 1963), pp. 114-116; Leonard T. Adams and Robert L. Aronson, _Workers and Industrial Change_ (Ithaca, N. Y.: Cornell University, 1957), pp. 68-81; Irvin Sobel and Hugh Folk, "Labor Market Adjustments by Unemployed Older Workers," _Employment Policy and the Labor Market_, Arthur M. Ross, ed. (Berkeley and Los Angeles: University of California Press, 1965), pp. 343-345.

centered on the question of the methods of job search used by workers who are currently employed but who are canvassing the market for different job opportunities. Do workers who are currently employed differ in their job-seeking procedures from workers who are unemployed or seeking their first job? One reason why this question has never been tested is because it is obviously difficult to find in one place a sample of workers looking for jobs who are also currently holding a job. The General Foods relocated workers who engaged in a pre-move job search constitute such a sample. No pretense is made that any definitive answers can be found in the experience of sixty-six individuals -- but perhaps there will be clues.

Table 7.7 lists a variety of methods of job search and shows the number of pre-move job seekers who indicated that the method had been used. The most popular method of job search, used by twenty-nine workers, or 44 per cent of all job seekers, is the use of want ads in newspapers. Hence, a method generally listed in the "formal" category[7] is shown to have been the most frequently used by our sample. Although other studies have shown want ads to be a frequently used method,[8] none show it as leading the list. Aside from

---

[7]Myers and Shultz, op. cit., p. 71

[8]Sobel and Folk, op. cit., note that it was used by 38 per cent of their sample.

TABLE 7.7

METHODS OF JOB SEARCH USED BY RELOCATED GENERAL FOODS WORKERS WHO LOOKED FOR WORK PRIOR TO MOVING

Method of Search	Number of Workers Using Method	Per Cent of Job-Seekers Using Method[1]
Direct application at place of employment	23	35
Used friends or relatives	20	30
Used public employment service	2	3
Used private employment agency	17	26
Used want ads in newspapers	29	44
Sent out résumés	14	21
Other	8	12
Number of job-seekers	(66)	
Mean methods used per job-seeker	1.7	

[1]Column adds to more than 100, since multiple answers are possible.

want ads, however, the most frequently used methods were of the informal variety. Direct application and use of friends and relatives were reported as used by 35 and 30 per cent, respectively, of the sample of job seekers. Only two workers reported using the public employment service, demonstrating once again how infrequently workers make use of this method.

Table 7.8 breaks down the data on the basis of whether the worker actively or inactively sought work and occupational status. As one would expect, those who reported actively seeking work also reported using more methods to seek work than those who reported an inactive job search. Salaried workers also tended to use more methods than hourly workers (salaried workers who actively sought work reported an average of 2.7 methods used). It also appears from Table 7.8 that salaried workers had a greater tendency to use formal methods than hourly workers. There are too few workers in each category, however, to be able to draw hard conclusions.

The Decision to Relocate

In this section the questions of *who* in the worker's household participated in the relocation decision and *when* that decision was made are examined.

TABLE 7.8

METHODS OF JOB SEARCH BY TYPE OF JOB SEARCH FOR GENERAL FOODS HOURLY AND SALARIED WORKERS (Percentage of job-seekers in a given category using method)[1]

Method of Search	GF Hourly Workers: Actively Sought Work	GF Hourly Workers: Inactively Sought Work	GF Salaried Workers: Actively Sought Work	GF Salaried Workers: Inactively Sought Work
Direct application at place of employment	56	64	27	23
Used friends or relatives	44	28	33	26
Used public employment service	11	0	7	0
Used private employment agency	11	0	73	16
Used want ads in newspapers	33	28	73	39
Sent out résumés	11	0	53	16
Other	22	0	0	19
Number of job-seekers	(9)	(11)	(15)	(31)
Mean methods used per job-seeker	1.9	1.2	2.7	1.4

[1]Columns add to more than 100 since multiple answers are possible.

Table 7.9 shows the relocated workers' responses to the question, "Would you say in deciding to come to Dover that the decision was primarily your own, or did it involve others?" About half the sample indicated that the decision had been made by the worker and his spouse. When hourly and salaried workers are compared, one discovers that a greater proportion of the salaried workers had made the relocation decision by themselves. On the other hand, proportionately twice as many of the hourly workers as salaried workers reported that the decision was a "family decision."

The somewhat larger participation of the family in the hourly worker's decision to relocate might reflect the gravity of the decision for the hourly workers. It is clear that hourly workers are not likely to transfer even under the best of circumstances; when the necessity to transfer in order to hold one's job arises, it is an occurrrence which is not likely to have been anticipated by the hourly workers, and one which, in many cases apparently, demands family consultation. The salaried worker, on the other hand, often anticipates transfer as a standard part of the career he has chosen for himself. The transfer decision becomes a routine decision which does not need family participation. Such explanations seem consistent with the tendencies exhibited in Table 7.9.

TABLE 7.9

WHO MADE THE DECISION TO MOVE TO DOVER?
A COMPARISON OF HOURLY AND SALARIED WORKERS

	GF Hourly Workers		GF Salaried Workers	
	No.	Per Cent	No.	Per Cent
Primarily respondent's own decision	22	24.4	39	31.7
Primarily a decision made by respondent and spouse	45	50.0	66	53.7
Primarily a family decision	21	23.3	15	12.2
Decision made by others in addition to the respondent's family	2	2.3	3	2.4
Total	90	100.0	123	100.0

Table 7.10 examines the timing of the relocated worker's decision to move. The responses tabulated here must be interpreted cautiously. It must be remembered that the workers were asked as long as three years after the fact to specify the period in which their decision had been made.

Nearly one in four of the relocated workers indicated that they had decided to move "just after the initial announcement of the old plant's closing." This is significant because these "early deciders" could not know in the Spring of 1962 where the new plant would be located, what specific policies would be used to transfer them to the new location, or what specific job assignment they would have in the new plant. If this finding is close to the truth, these workers may be considered the company's "ultra-loyalists," willing to move anywhere with the company under any conditions. Additional findings, to be discussed below, suggest that perhaps more workers indicated an early decision than in fact was the case.

About one in three workers in the sample noted that they had decided to move only when they received a definite job offer from the company. Now it is true that all workers were guaranteed a job at the new plant at the time the shutdown announcement was made. However, individual job offers, detailing the nature of the job assignment, wages, and other conditions of employment were not issued

TABLE 7.10

WHEN DID THE RESPONDENT DECIDE TO TRANSFER TO DOVER?
A COMPARISON OF HOURLY AND SALARIED WORKERS

	GF Hourly Workers		GF Salaried Workers	
	No.	Per Cent	No.	Per Cent
Decided just after the initial announcement of the old plant's closing; *i.e.*, about 3/62	20	22.2	29	23.2
Decided after hearing that Dover would be the site of the new plant; i.e., about 9/62	1	1.1	4	3.2
Decided after it was clear what policies the company would use to transfer people to Dover; Fall, 1962	14	15.6	10	8.0
Decided when definite Dover job offer was received; Winter and Spring, 1963	31	34.4	37	29.6
DEcided after making a "pre-move" trip to Dover	9	10.0	16	12.8
Decided late in 1963 or 1964 to move to Dover	13	14.5	23	18.4
Other	2	2.2	6	4.8
Total	90	100.0	125	100.0

until nearly a year after the initial announcement had been made. To make individual job offers, the company had to wait for the precise manning requirements of the new facility to be developed. In some cases the specific job offer involved a wage or salary reduction. There is some tendency for the higher wage or salaried workers to have decided to move at an earlier period. But there is an even clearer relation between the timing of a worker's decision and his seniority. There was a pronounced tendency for "early deciders" to be the most senior workers at the old plants.

When hourly and salaried workers are compared, as in Table 7.10, it appears that proportionately more hourly workers (15.6 per cent of the hourly worker sample) than salaried workers (8.0 per cent of the salaried worker sample) hinged their decision on the nature of the transfer policies implemented by the company. This finding is another small indication of the influence of the "interplant transfer system" on the relocation of the blue-collar worker. The nature of the company's transfer policies apparently weighed less heavily in the white-collar worker's decision-making, possibly because he assumed from the first that some such transfer system would be developed.

In analyzing relations between the various questions asked of the sample of relocated workers, it was discovered that those workers who expressed the most satisfaction with the move, the new plant, and the new community also tended to report having made an early decision to move. In fact, when certain attitudinal questions were cross-tabulated with the responses to the question as to when the transfer decision had been made, chi-square tests revealed significance at the ten and even five per cent level. It may be that those most satisfied with the move were in fact those who had made an early decision to move. For the employee who finds his work and his attachment to the company highly rewarding, it might have been natural to decide to transfer early, and to find an equal satisfaction with his job, and even a preference for Dover over his old location, after the move. It may be that those most anxious to move -- *i.e.*, those who decided early -- might have been the easiest to satisfy. On the other hand, it may also be that those who found the move to their liking, who were generally satisfied with the new plant and community, were, by indicating that an early decision to transfer had been made, granting themselves a degree of foresight which they might not have actually possessed. The worker generally satisfied with his relocation might convince himself that he had known from the start that the move would be efficacious, and therefore note that he decided early. It is often extremely difficult for an individual to pinpoint a moment in time when a certain personal decision had been made, and current circumstances may have a strong influence on that kind of remembrance. Therefore, it is probably wise to discount the strong, positive relations between the alleged timing of the worker's decision and his present satisfactions. Moreover, all of the responses listed in Table 7.10 must be taken with the proverbial grain of salt.

The Process of Moving

Of the 215 relocated workers interviewed for this study, about 90 per cent had used an automobile to move to Dover, which they either owned, borrowed (one case), rented (four cases), or drove in with friends (three cases). This figure is not very much higher than the comparable 84 per cent figure reported for all migrants in the 1958-62 period.[9] Most households moved all at one time. However, 34 per cent of the salaried workers moved to Dover ahead of their household, which followed later, while 17 per cent of the hourly workers moved ahead of their household. A number of salaried employees were needed in Dover in the earliest stages of the plant's construction, while other families stayed behind for a period to clear up certain personal affairs, such as the sale of a home.

---

[9]Lansing *et al.*, *op. cit.*, p. 162.

The Survey Research Center discovered that 40 per cent of the migrants in the 1958-62 period had received help from friends or relatives living in the place to which the move took place. One-third of the migrants had no friends or relatives living in the place to which the move took place, and so received no help.[10] About one-quarter of the SRC migrants had received help from friends or relatives *not* living in the place to which the move was made.[11] As Lansing, *et al.*, conclude, the availability of assistance from friends or relatives "is an important factor in people's moves to new geographical areas."[12]

Most General Foods transfers, on the other hand, were not familiar with the Dover area, and had no friends or relatives living in the area. Only twenty-two respondents (about 10 per cent of the sample) had friends or relatives living in the Dover area before they had moved. Some of these respondents were undoubtedly referring to friends or relatives who were also General Foods employees and had moved earlier than the respondent. Therefore, the General Foods migrant had to depend almost entirely upon the company for information and assistance in moving to the Dover area.

---

[10] *Ibid.*, pp. 141-143.

[11] *Ibid.*, pp. 145-146.

[12] *Ibid.*, p. 145.

When the relocated worker received assistance from friends or relatives in moving, it was from persons living in his old area. About 37 per cent of the sample reported receiving help in moving from friends or relatives who were not members of the worker's household. Friends or relatives aided the relocated workers by helping to sell or lease his home, by helping to cart and move the worker's possessions, by supplying information on the trip to Dover, and in a variety of other ways. Most workers, however, received no help at all from persons outside their households, and this is not untypical of migrants in general.

General Foods workers were asked three questions relating to the costs of relocation:

> Even though most of your moving cost was paid by General Foods, did you find there were expenses connected with moving <u>not</u> covered by General Foods?
>
> Can you give us an idea of the things you had to pay for yourself?
>
> What is your best estimate of the <u>actual cost</u> of your moving, including all expenses directly or indirectly involved?

Unfortunately, the third question proved to be ambiguous. Workers were not certain whether to estimate the total cost of their move, including the portion paid by General Foods, or to estimate just that portion of the total costs which they personally incurred. It was noted in Chapter IV that the average cost per relocated worker to the company was $3,880 for salaried workers and $1,432 for hourly workers. The median cost estimate reported by the respondents was $1,250 for the hourly workers and $1,750 for the salaried workers; averages, if they could be computed, would undoubtedly be higher for both groups. It appears that most workers had a fairly good notion of the costs of relocation, even though a good portion was paid directly by the company.

The General Foods inter-plant transfer system has been characterized in this study as a very liberal system. Yet, about half the sample indicated that there were moving costs not covered by the company. Moreover, proportionately more salaried workers (53 per cent) than hourly workers (43 per cent) reported incurring expenses not paid for by General Foods, even though the range of compensated costs was greater for the salaried worker than for the hourly worker. Of course, salaried people, being generally more affluent, and likely to have more furniture and personal effects, have greater transfer costs in any event. But since the company paid nearly $4,000 per transferred salaried worker, it is perhaps surprising that so many salaried workers reported incurring additional costs.

The Survey Research Center investigated the expenses incurred by transferring workers and discovered that about 40 per cent had incurred expenses.[13] Most of these transfers were white-collar personnel, and hence comparable to our salaried group. Of these SRC transfers, about 40 per cent reported that their employer did not pay _any_ of the moving expenses of transfer.[14] The median cost per employee to the employer of moving this sample of workers was closer to $400 than to $4,000.[15] Therefore, the transfers in the Survey Research Center sample were less likely than General Foods workers to have additional moving expenses, even though many were not compensated at all for their transfer, and the average cost per transfer was from one-tenth to one-fifth the average cost of a General Foods transfer.

It must be added that the additional costs incurred by the GF salaried worker were typically marginal and incidental. While it was less likely that additional costs of any sort would be incurred by the hourly worker, it was more likely that if they _were_ incurred, they would be more substantial than those of the salaried worker. A few hourly workers with large families found that the company's upper limit of $1,000 on moving and traveling expenses was not high enough.

---

[13] _Ibid._, p. 153. There were 74 transfers in the Survey Research Center's sample of migrants in the 1958-62 period.

[14] _Ibid._, p. 156.

[15] _Ibid._, p. 151.

Relocated workers were asked whether their moving experience had been more or less trouble than they had anticipated. Table 7.11 shows that answers to this question are more varied for the hourly workers than for salaried workers. For a relatively larger number of hourly workers, their expectations about the "trouble" of moving were not fulfilled. For some the move was more trouble, and for others, less trouble than had been anticipated. This is perhaps a reflection of the hourly worker's relatively limited experience in moving, compared to that of the salaried worker.

Consequences of the Move: Changes in Home Ownership

In Chapter VI it was shown that for the General Foods relocated worker there was, surprisingly, a positive relationship between homw ownership and mobility. The explanation for this result was found in the company transfer policies, which, as explained in Chapter IV, were generous with respect to home owners, and also in the nature of the Dover housing market, which was limited in terms of rental opportunities.

Table 7.12 shows what changes took place in the home ownership of the relocated worker as a result of his move. The table shows clearly that on the whole those who had owned homes in their old locations bought, or were in the process of buying, homes in the Dover

TABLE 7.11

"ALL IN ALL, WOULD YOU SAY THAT MOVING TO DOVER WAS MORE TROUBLE THAN YOU EXPECTED OR LESS?"

	GF Hourly Workers		GF Salaried Workers	
	No.	Per Cent	No.	Per Cent
More trouble than expected	24	26.7	24	19.2
About as much as expected	48	53.3	81	64.8
Less trouble than expected	18	20.0	19	15.2
Not ascertained	0	0.0	1	0.8
Total	90	100.0	125	100.0

TABLE 7.12

CHANGES IN HOME OWNERSHIP AS A RESULT OF RELOCATION
(Percentage Distribution)

Home Ownership in Dover	GF Hourly Workers	GF Salaried Workers
Own a home or buying one	66.7	75.2
Owned a home or was buying one in old location	53.3	57.6
Rented home in old location	6.7	10.4
Rented apt. in old location	6.7	5.6
Lived with relatives in old location	0.0	1.6
Rent a home		
Owned a home or was buying one in old location	2.2	3.2
Rented home in old location	4.4	2.4
Rented apt. in old location	12.3	2.4
Lived with relatives in old location	1.1	0.0
Rent an apartment	6.6	13.6
Owned a home or was buying one in old location	1.1	3.2
Rented home in old location	2.2	0.0
Rented apt. in old location	2.2	6.4
Lived with relatives in old location	1.1	4.0
Live with relatives	2.2	1.6
Owned a home or was buying one in old location	0.0	0.8
Rented apt. in old location	1.1	0.0
Lived with relatives in old location	1.1	0.8
Live in trailer	5.5	1.6
Owned a home or was buying one in old location	2.2	0.0
Rented home in old location	1.1	0.0
Rented apt. in old location	1.1	0.8
Lived with relatives in old location	1.1	0.8
Total	100.0	100.0

area. Moreover, there was a net increase of home ownership among both the hourly and salaried groups. A greater proportion of both groups owned or were buying homes after the move than before. About 16 per cent of the entire sample changed from renters to home-owners as a result of the move, and this represented a net gain in the home-owner proportion of the sample of about nine per cent.

Among hourly workers there was an increase of from 14 to 19 per cent in the proportion of the sample renting homes. Most of the hourly workers renting homes in Dover had been apartment dwellers in their former communities. On the basis of some impressionistic evidence, there is reason to believe that a good number of those renting homes were doing so with the option to purchase at a later date. About half of the hourly home-renters in the old areas became home-owners in the Dover area. In addition, whereas no one in the entire sample had lived in a trailer in the old location, seven families in the sample moved into trailers in Dover. About one in four of the hourly workers had been apartment dwellers in their old communities; but less than seven per cent rented apartments in Dover.

About 65 per cent of the salaried workers had been home-owners before the move, and this increased to 75 per cent in Dover. The proportion of the salaried workers renting apartments stayed about the same after the relocation; but, in contrast to the hourly workers, the proportion renting homes declined. Like the hourly workers, there was a tendency for past home-renters to become hone-owners in Dover.

In sum, the bulk of the relocated workers had been and remained home-owners. The proportion who had been home-owners in the sample before the move was somewhat greater than the proportion of home-owners among all families (which, as pointed out in Chapter VI, is about 60 per cent) and <u>increased</u> as a result of the move. The relocation was accompanied by a good deal of movement from one of the categories of Table 7.12 to another: about one in three of the relocated workers changed categories. In terms of Table 7.12, this movement tended to be in an upward direction: from living with relatives to renting an apartment; from renting an apartment to renting a home; and from renting a home to buying a home.

If the relocated worker owned a home before moving, did he try to sell his home; and, if he did, did he make any money? The experience of the GF workers is contrasted with all migrants in Table 7.13. The effect of General Foods' policies of providing aid to the home-owner can be seen in the table. It is quite obvious from the Survey Research Center data reproduced in the table that migrants are not usually home-owners. However, of those that are, about one-third do not sell their homes after moving. One in ten try, but do not succeed. In contrast, about 90 per cent of the General Foods home

TABLE 7.13

WHETHER TRIED TO SELL HOME BEFORE MOVE AND WHETHER TOOK A LOSS ON THE SALE: A COMPARISON OF GENERAL FOODS RELOCATED WORKERS WITH MIGRANTS IN 1958-62 (Percentage Distribution)

	GF Hourly Workers	GF Salaried Workers	Migrants 1958-62[1]
Tried to sell and sold	53.3	57.6	19
Made money on the sale	6.7	24.0	7
Broke even on the sale	24.4	24.8	6
Lost money on the sale	22.2	8.8	6
Tried to sell but did not sell	1.1	1.6	3
Did not try to sell	4.4	5.6	7
Did not own a home	41.2	35.2	71
Total	100.0	100.0	100.0

[1] John B. Lansing, *et al.*, *The Geographic Mobility of Labor: A First Report* (Ann Arbor, Mich.: Survey Research Center, 1963), p. 82.

owners succeeded in selling their homes. Only about two per cent tried to sell but did not succeed. It is quite probable that a much larger proportion of GF workers than migrants in general tried and succeeded in selling their homes because of the assistance they received from the company.

It is quite apparent from Table 7.13 that salaried workers made out better on the sale of their homes than hourly workers. In relative terms, almost four times as many salaried workers as hourly workers reported making money on the sale of their old homes. By contrast, a far smaller proportion reported losing money. Many factors might be responsible for the difference: among them, the fact that the corporation offered to buy unsold homes from salaried workers, but not from hourly workers, may be considered significant. In Chapter IV it was shown that the corporation absorbed a loss of more than $127,000 on the purchase and re-sale of thirty-nine relocated salaried workers' homes.

The relocated workers were asked three additional questions on the availability of rental opportunities in Dover, the relative price of houses in Dover, and on the quality of their Dover living quarters. About 60 per cent of the respondents thought that rentals were "not as good" in Dover as in the old locations. Only eight per cent thought rentals were better in the sense of either more rentals available or lower rents charged. On the other hand, opinion was rather evenly divided on the question of the price of Dover houses between those who thought Dover prices were higher, those who thought they were lower, and those who thought they were about the same as prices in the old areas. These responses help to explain, first, the greater attractiveness of the Dover area to a home-owner compared to a renter, and, second, the necessity for former renters to become home-owners.

Finally, whether home-owner or renter, the relocated worker was generally satisfied with his Dover living quarters. More than four in ten reported that their present living quarters were better than their former, while less than one in five considered their present living quarters not as good as their former. This latter group consisted primarily of those who were forced to change from either a renter or owner status to the opposite.

Consequences of the Move: Changes in Household Income and Financial Adjustments

In this chapter the impact of the move on the workers and their families has been examined in several dimensions. In this section we will explore two additional effects of the move: changes in household income and certain financial adjustments necessitated by the move.

Table 7.14 shows how the income of the households of the relocated workers changed as a result of the move. The separate experiences of former Walter Baker and Jell-O workers is shown because of the markedly different impact of the move on the household incomes of the Walter Baker hourly workers. For this group, about 46 per cent of the workers suffered a decrease in household income because of the move. The simple explanation for this is that downward wage adjustments implemented by General Foods in the Dover plant primarily affected hourly workers from the Walter Baker plant. Moreover, as previously noted, the incentive system used at the Dorchester plant was abolished at Dover. These changes adversely affected the incomes of a significant proportion of Walter Baker hourly transfers.

With the exception of the Walter Baker hourly group, the move resulted in a decrease in household incomes for only a small proportion -- about 11 per cent -- of the other groups of the relocated workers, and more than half indicated that their incomes had increased. Some of these workers received a wage or salary increase, in some cases because of a straight promotion to a higher paying job, because of the move. Others were earning more by working longer hours in the Dover plant.

Changes in the household incomes of the relocated workers resulted almost entirely from changes in the wage or salary of the worker

TABLE 7.14

HOW HOUSEHOLD INCOME CHANGED AS A RESULT OF THE MOVE:
A COMPARISON OF HOURLY AND SALARY WORKERS BY PLANT OF ORIGIN
(Percentage Distribution)

How household income changed as a result of the move	GF Hourly Workers			GF Salaried Workers		
	Walter Baker	Jell-O	Total[1]	Walter Baker	Jell-O	Total[L]
Raised	17.3	58.6	37.8	55.3	50.0	53.6
No change	36.5	24.1	28.9	34.1	38.2	35.2
Lowered	46.2	10.3	31.1	10.6	11.8	11.2
Not ascertained	0.0	7.0	2.2	0.0	0.0	0.0
Total	100.0	100.0	100.0	100.0	100.0	100.0
Cases	52	29	90	85	34	125

[1]Totals include workers in the sample from all four shut-down plants.

himself. There is no evidence, for example, that changes in household income were the result of movement into or out of the labor force by the wife of the relocated worker. Moreover, changes in household income appear unrelated to worker satisfactions with the new plant and community (to be discussed in the next section).

Workers were also questioned about certain financial adjustments that might have been made as a result of the relocation. Their responses are tabulated in Table 7.15. More than 40 per cent of the hourly workers and almost one-half of the salaried workers reported having to use some of their savings as a result of their transfer to Dover. It is likely that savings had to be drawn down in a number of cases in order to provide for the down-payment on a home and to cover moving expenses not covered by General Foods.

About one-third of the total sample also indicated that they had to "economize" as a result of the move. There is a clear, positive relation between the number reporting the need to economize and the number reporting a decrease in household income as a result of the move. Most of the 38 per cent of the hourly workers who reported the need to economize were Walter Baker hourly workers who reported a decrease in their household income.

Few workers reported the need to cancel, cash, surrender or borrow on an insurance policy, and fewer still needed to sell any per-

TABLE 7.15

"AS A RESULT OF TRANSFERRING TO DOVER, HAVE YOU HAD TO DO ANY OF THE FOLLOWING?" (Percentages)

	GF Hourly Workers[1]	GF Salaried Workers[1]
"Use any savings you had before the transfer"	41	48
"Cancel, cash, surrender or borrow on any insurance policy"	9	8
"Economize, *i.e.*, generally cut down on over-all expenses or postpone anticipated purchases"	38	26
"Sell any of your personal property to meet family expenses (for example, for moving)"	3	4
None of the above indicated	32	39

[1]Column totals add to more than 100, since multiple answers were possible.

sonal property. About one-third of the total sample reported that they did not have to resort to any of the measures listed in Table 7.15. Proportionately more salaried workers (39 per cent) than hourly workers (32 per cent) reported no need to resort to the measures listed in the table.

Consequences of the Move: Worker Satisfactions and Evaluations

In this section the matter of the satisfactions of the relocated workers is examined. Were the relocated workers satisfied with the move? Were they happy in their new community? Did they like the new plant? If they had it to do over again, would they still make the same decision to move? It seems obvious that these are important questions and, in one form or another, they were put to the relocated workers. Yet this is an exceedingly difficult area. At all times the limitations of the study must be kept in mind when interpreting the workers' answers.

We have no way of determining whether the "attitudes" we have discovered have endured or will endure. Because the relocated workers were interviewed on just one occasion, there is no way of telling to what extent their responses indicate a fixed sentiment about their work and community environment or to what extent their responses were prompted by the whim of the moment. For the same methodological reason, there is no way of telling to what extent the relocated workers subsequently exhibited behavior consistent with their expressed attitudes. For example, did dissatisfied workers tend to quit? While we could ask the workers about their intentions, without further checking and interviewing we have no way of knowing whether their actual behavior was consistent with their interview responses.

It would have been preferable to have interviewed the workers both before and after their relocation. Only in this manner would it have been possible to check on the stability of the workers' satisfactions. There is no way of telling from our study to what extent the workers' satisfactions underwent change as a result of their move. It may very well be that those workers who expressed some dissatisfaction at the time of their interview had always been dissatisfied workers. While it may be safe to assume that truly dissatisfied workers would probably have terminated rather than transfer, we really have no way of verifying this assumption. To a very limited extent the displaced workers serve as a kind of control group for cross-checking the attitudes and sentiments of the relocated workers. However, on those questions on which comparison is possible, it turns out that there is very little difference between the relocated and the displaced worker. Both, for example, expressed a high degree of satisfaction with their General Foods jobs. What significance can be drawn from this result? Probably very little. There is no way of really standardizing the responses of the two groups of workers.

The reader should be reminded of the circumstances under which the relocated worker was interviewed. The atmosphere of the company's personnel office probably had an inhibiting effect on the workers' expression of opinion, above and beyond the usual tendency to dissemble, despite the repeated assurances that the questionnaire information would be kept in strictest confidence. Another possibility is that an unfavorable response to a given question may reflect an unfavorable response to the interview itself, to the interviewer or result in being taken off the job.

More important than any methodological limitation, however, is the question of the true and precise significance of worker satisfactions. The significance of these expressions depends on one's perspective. From the viewpoint of the company, a satisfied group of workers is probably to be considered an asset. General Foods on many occasions expressed concern for the welfare of its workers; we have no reason to doubt the legitimacy of this concern. However, if the company's major objective is economic performance, there is no compelling reason for assuming a necessary relationship between the workers' productivity and their expressions of satisfaction or dissatisfaction with their work and community environment. Berelson and

Steiner, in reviewing the literature, found that "the relationship between satisfaction with the job and performance on it is complicated and conditional: at any rate, there is no direct, positive correlation. Actually, the over-all finding is still in some dispute."[16] While the exact relationship may be in doubt, the management of General Foods assumed a positive correlation, and at all times took pains to keep worker morale high.

The satisfactions and adjustment problems of the General Foods workers were of concern to the community of Dover. The influx of relocated workers and their families, totaling some 1,500 people, represented an increment in the Dover population of more than 10 per cent. Dover inhabitants rightfully expected that their community would be substantially changed by the settlement of a large number of new people. Aside from the obvious physical changes, such as the building of large, new housing developments and the provision of utilities, schools, and other public services for the newcomers, the social character of the community was likely to be affected by the integration (or lack of integration) of the migrants into community affairs. The management of General Foods, fully aware of the possible disruptive effects on local organizations and institutions caused by

---

[16]Bernard Berelson and Gary A. Steiner, Human Behavior (New York: Harcourt, Brace and World, 1964), p. 41.

the relocated workers, cautioned plant officials not to exert too quick an influence on local organizations and thereby threaten the community social structure with a "take-over" by new General Foods people. The problems created by the inflow of a substantial group of new people into a small community are many and varied. Suffice it to say here, from the standpoint of the community, that the satisfactions and adjustment problems of the relocated workers were of prime importance.

Finally, of course, job and community satisfactions are important to the workers themselves. It is probably reasonable to assume that the General Foods workers would not have elected to transfer had they expected the new location to be unsatisfactory in one way or another. The methodological constraint of "one interview only" prevents a complete testing of this assumption. It may well be that workers expressing an unfavorable attitude to their new job or location were <u>less</u> dissatisfied after the relocation than they had been before. By the same token, it may be that "satisfied" workers after the move were <u>less</u> satisfied than <u>before</u> the move. Again, there is no way of accounting for improvement or deterioration -- <u>i.e.</u>, change -- in the attitudes of the workers.

General Foods relocated workers were asked about their feelings concerning staying in the Dover area. A similar question was put to family heads interviewed by the Survey Research Center. The responses are contrasted in Table 7.16.

According to the SRC study, about three-quarters of all family heads would prefer to stay in their present area. About one in five would prefer to move. For General Foods relocated workers, about half preferred to stay in the Dover area; but, like family heads in general, about one in five preferred to move away. About 28 per cent of the relocated workers were indifferent to moving or staying, compared to only three per cent of all family heads. Table 7.16 shows a greater diversity of answers among General Foods workers, compared to family heads in general, with more GF workers holding extreme positions. This is particularly true of hourly workers: about one-quarter strongly preferred to move or stay, compared to five per cent of all family heads. Almost 20 per cent of the hourly workers strongly preferred to stay in Dover, which, by any comparison, indicates a high degree of satisfaction with the area on the part of a significant proportion of the hourly workers.

A related question asked the workers whether they preferred to live in Dover or in their old location. Table 7.17 shows remarkable similarity in the answers of hourly and salaried workers. About 40 per cent of the sample preferred living in their old location, compared to about 29 per cent who preferred Dover. Approximately three in ten workers indicated no preference between the two areas.

TABLE 7.16

PREFERENCES REGARDING PRESENT AREA OF RESIDENCE:
A COMPARISON OF GF RELOCATED WORKERS AND FAMILY HEADS
INTERVIEWED BY THE SURVEY RESEARCH CENTER

	GF Salaried Workers		GF Hourly Workers		SRC Sample of Family Heads[1]
	No.	Per Cent	No.	Per Cent	Per Cent
Strongly prefer to stay	16	12.8	17	18.9	4
Prefer to stay	47	37.6	31	34.4	70
Indifferent: no opinion one way or the other	37	29.6	24	26.7	3
Prefer to move away	20	16.0	13	14.4	18
Strongly prefer to move away	5	4.0	5	5.6	1
Not ascertained	0	0.0	0	0.0	4
Total	125	100.0	90	100.0	100

TABLE 7.17

DOVER AND OLD LOCATION COMPARED: DO YOU PREFER TO LIVE HERE, IN DOVER, OR AT YOUR OLD LOCATION?

	GF Salaried Workers		GF Hourly Workers	
	No.	Per Cent	No.	Per Cent
Prefer to live in Dover	36	28.8	26	28.9
Prefer to live in old location	51	40.8	36	40.0
No preference: like each location about equally	38	30.4	28	31.1
Total	125	100.0	90	100.0

On this question there were some differences in attitude between workers who had transferred from Dorchester (Boston) and those who had transferred from LeRoy. For both hourly and salaried groups, former LeRoy workers were more satisfied with Dover than former Dorchester workers were. Apparently the Dorchester workers missed the urban characteristics of their former location. The Dover area is more similar to the LeRoy area than it is to the Dorchester or Boston area. In written comments, former Dorchester workers were prone to complain about the lack of shopping facilities, recreational opportunities, and other "small town" characteristics of Dover.

Workers were also asked to "compare the general 'standard of living' in Dover against the standard of living in your old location." No definition was provided for "standard of living." Nevertheless, again there was marked similarity between the responses of the hourly and salaried workers. More than half the sample indicated that "the standard of living is about the same," while 40 per cent noted that "the standard of living is not as good in Dover." Less than 10 per cent thought that the standard in Dover was better than in the old location.

Several questions were asked of the relocated workers about their jobs in the new Dover plant. A question similar to one used by the Survey Research Center read:

> How do you like your work in Dover compared to the work you did before?

Responses to this question and the Survey Research Center question are contrasted in Table 7.18. It is clear that relocated GF workers were less satisfied with their Dover jobs than migrants in the national survey who had moved to an area to work for a new employer. Furthermore, hourly GF workers were more dissatisfied than salaried workers. About one-third of the hourly workers did not like their present work as well as their former work, compared to 20 per cent of the salaried workers and 13 per cent of the workers in the SRC survey. This result is all the more significant since, in most cases, General Foods relocated workers were performing exactly the same kind of work in Dover as they had in their old locations. Therefore, it seems reasonable to assume that this expression of dissatisfaction is a reflection _not_ of the job _itself_, but of other factors.

Relocated workers were also asked whether their present hours and shifts were "more convenient" or "less convenient" than those they had had at the shut-down plants. Table 7.19 shows that more hourly workers than salaried workers favored their present hours and shifts. This may be a reflection of the fact that some hourly workers were able to exercise their seniority rights in the Dover plant to choose

TABLE 7.18

HOW DOES WORKER (OR HEAD) LIKE HIS WORK IN THE NEW AREA COMPARED TO THE WORK HE DID BEFORE?

	GF Salaried Workers		GF Hourly Workers		SRC Sample[1]
	No.	Per Cent	No.	Per Cent	Per Cent
Much better now	19	15.2	6	6.7	18
Better now	28	22.4	7	7.8	29
About the same	53	42.4	47	52.2	21
Not as good now (worse now)	16	12.8	23	25.6	12
Much worse now	9	7.2	7	7.8	1
Not ascertained; don't know	0	0.0	0	0.0	19
Total	125	100.0	90	100.1	100

[1]Includes only heads of families in SRC sample who moved to a new area to work for a new employer. John B. Lansing, *et al.*, *The Geographic Mobility of Labor: A First Report* (Ann Arbor, Mich.: Survey Research Center, 1963), p. 170.

TABLE 7.19

OPINION ON HOURS AND SHIFTS:
DO YOU FIND YOUR PRESENT HOURS AND SHIFTS MORE CONVENIENT OR LESS CONVENIENT THAN THEY WERE AT YOUR OLD LOCATION?

	GF Salaried Workers		GF Hourly Workers	
	No.	Per Cent	No.	Per Cent
More convenient now	14	11.2	29	32.2
Less convenient now	23	18.4	14	15.5
About the same	88	70.4	46	51.2
No answer	0	0.0	1	1.1
Total	125	100.0	90	100.0

a shift more to their liking. Also, much overtime was available to hourly workers in the first year or so of the operation of the Dover plant. On the other hand, there was little change in the hours worked by salaried employees, which explains why 70 per cent of the salaried group indicated their hours in Dover were about as convenient as their hours in the old location.

Perhaps an indication of the degree of satisfaction with the new plant and community found by the relocated workers is the number of times they had returned "home," i.e., to their old locations, since making the transfer. As Table 7.20 shows, the number of return trips reported by the workers varied greatly; however, the average appears to be about three return trips per worker. There are any number of reasons why a worker might have returned to his old location: to visit relatives; to complete the sale of a home; to bring back his family with him, if they had not moved in the first instance. But it is also true that those who preferred Dover to their old location made fewer trips home than those who did not. Similarly, those who preferred to move away from Dover also tended to have made more trips back to their old location. Finally, Walter Baker workers, apparently less satisfied with the Dover area than other transfers, tended to have made more return trips than other relocated workers.

TABLE 7.20

NUMBER OF TIMES RETURNED TO OLD LOCATION SINCE MOVING TO DOVER

	GF Salaried Workers		GF Hourly Workers	
	No.	Per Cent	No.	Per Cent
Not at all	17	13.6	10	11.1
Once or twice	45	36.0	35	38.9
Three to five times	35	28.0	28	31.1
Six to nine times	16	12.8	7	7.8
Ten or more times	12	9.6	10	11.1
Total	125	100.0	90	100.0

When asked about whether they planned to stay on in Dover after retirement, about 35 per cent of the relocated workers noted that it was "too early to tell." Another 15 per cent did not know where they would spend their retirement years. About 12 per cent indicated that they did plan on living in Dover after retirement; while about 38 per cent said that they did not plan on retiring in Dover. There was no relation between the workers' retirement plans and their age or seniority. Older workers were just as unsure about what they intended to do as younger workers. On the other hand, there was a clear relation between retirement plans and expressed attitudes about the Dover area. There was a tendency for those who preferred the Dover area to plan on retiring in Dover, while those who preferred the old location did not plan on retiring in Dover. Those who had no location preference tended not to be sure about where they would spend their retirement years.

Whatever their attitudes and preferences about the Dover area and the new plant were, few workers were trying to find another job. Only three workers in the entire sample indicated that they were "actively" trying to find another job. Another fourteen respondents indicated that they were carrying on an "inactive" job search. Nine out of ten of the relocated workers were not seeking another job. It appears, then, that a number of relocated workers were dissatisfied with their current situation but were not so dissatisfied that they intended to change jobs. In addition, most workers thought that alternative job opportunities were very limited in the Dover area, and this feeling probably constrained some dissatisfied workers from making an active job search. However, the methodological limits of this study, mentioned earlier in this section, must be kept in mind in interpreting the results. There is no way of knowing how satisfactions changed as a result of the move, and hence whether the level of dissatisfaction in Dover was greater than it had been before the move.

Relocated workers were asked whether, if they had to do it all over again, they would make the same decision to move to Dover. About seven in ten of the respondents said that they would make the same decision. About 11 per cent said that they would not make the same decision again. Close to one-fifth of the workers did not know what their decision would be, if they had to make it again.

Finally, the relocated workers were asked for a general evaluation of the move: "All things considered, was the move a good idea?" This question matched one put to migrants of the 1958-62 period interviewed by the Survey Research Center. The contrasting results are tabulated in Table 7.21. The table shows that only a small proportion of either the GF workers or migrants in general were disposed

TABLE 7.21

GENERAL EVALUATION OF THE MOVE: ALL THINGS CONSIDERED, WAS IT A GOOD IDEA?

	GF Salaried Workers		GF Hourly Workers		Migrants 1958-62[1]
	No.	Per Cent	No.	Per Cent	Per Cent
Very good idea	17	13.6	8	8.9	12
Good idea	29	23.2	11	12.2	69
Good in some ways, not in others	75	60.0	61	67.8	4
Poor idea	1	0.8	6	6.7	7
Very poor idea	3	2.4	4	4.4	1
Not ascertained	0	0.0	0	0.0	7
Total	125	100.0	90	100.0	100

[1]John B. Lansing, *et al.*, *The Geographic Mobility of Labor: A First Report* (Ann Arbor, Mich.: Survey Research Center, 1963), p. 172.

to think their move had been a mistake. However, while very few migrants expressed uncertainty about their most recent move, most of the GF relocated workers fell in the uncertain or ambivalent category, thinking their relocation to be "good in some ways, not in others." Eighty-one per cent of the SRC migrants thought that their move had been a good or very good idea, compared to 36.8 per cent of the GF salaried workers and 21.1 per cent of the GF hourly workers.

In sum, based on the questions discussed in this section, it appears that the majority of relocated workers were well satisfied with their move, their new job, and their new community. However, a rather significant proportion registered doubt or dissatisfaction with one or more aspects of the relocation. What ramifications this kind of dissatisfaction had for the company or the community cannot be assessed with any accuracy on the basis of a questionnaire interview. It is probable that truly dissatisfied workers would tend to leave the company, possibly to return to their former locations. (At the time of the interviews, about seventy-five who had transferred had moved back.) It is also likely that a number of relocated workers were going through an extended adjustment period. One might speculate that in time these workers would adapt themselves to their new work and community environment.

Chapter Summary

In this chapter the impact of the move on the relocated workers has been examined. Our major findings are summarized below:

1. The great majority of the relocated workers thought that at least a one-year notice was needed before a plant shutdown, with most of the hourly group believing a two-year notice was needed. At the same time, the hourly group was much more likely to indicate that a shorter notice would have affected their decision to move than the salaried group, for whom the advance notice was a less important consideration.

2. All but six of the sample of relocated workers had made a pre-move trip to Dover at company expense. About seven in ten of the sample felt that the trip was "absolutely necessary" in order for them to make up their minds about moving. By comparison, only about 25 per cent of the migrants in general made such pre-move trips to the area of movement, and many of these trips yield no useful information.

3. General Foods relocated workers had larger households, on the average, than migrants in general or displaced GF workers. Salaried relocated workers had larger households than hourly relocated workers. Moreover, about 20 per cent of the relocated workers indicated that one or more persons living in their former households had not made the move to Dover. The comparable figure for migrants in general is 12 per cent.

4. The move to Dover caused a good deal of movement into and out of the labor force by the wives of General Foods workers. Curiously, these moves tended to offset one another, so that about the same proportion of wives was in the labor force after the move as before. About 31 per cent of the wives of hourly workers and 22 per cent of the wives of salaried workers were either working or looking for work in the Dover labor market.

5. More than 30 per cent of the relocated workers had looked for other jobs before moving to Dover. However, two-thirds of this group indicated that their

search had not been very active. About three quarters of the job seekers (23 per cent of the total sample) reported receiving at least one job offer. In comparison to displaced workers, there was a greater tendency among these job seekers, particularly the salaried job seekers, to use formal as opposed to informal methods of job search.

6. Proportionately twice as many hourly workers as salaried workers reported that the decision to relocate had been a "family" decision. Although nearly 25 per cent of the relocated workers reported deciding to move "just after the initial announcement of the old plant's closing," most workers waited for at least a year before making a decision to transfer.

7. Despite the extent to which General Foods covered the expense of relocation, about half the sample indicated that there were moving costs not covered by the company. Many of these non-covered expenses were marginal, however. Most workers found the move itself to be about as much "trouble" as they had

expected. A relatively larger number of hourly workers found their expectations not fulfilled: more than one-quarter found moving more trouble than they had expected.

8. In contrast to migrants in general, home ownership was not a barrier to relocation for General Foods workers. Moreover, the proportion of the GF workers owning homes increased from 62 per cent to 70 per cent as a result of the move. Whereas only about two-thirds of migrant home owners sell their homes, about 90 per cent of the relocated GF workers sold their homes. Hourly workers did not make out as well on the sale of their old homes as salaried workers. Nearly one-quarter reported losing money on the sale. However, General Foods purchased homes directly from salaried employees, a policy not offered to the blue-collar workers.

9. With the exception of the Walter Baker hourly transfers, the move resulted in a decrease in household income for only a small proportion --

about 11 per cent -- of the other relocated workers, and more than half indicated that their incomes had increased. Nevertheless, more than 40 per cent of the hourly workers and almost half of the salaried workers reported having to use some of their savings as a result of their transfer to Dover.

10. The workers expressed general -- but not complete -- satisfaction with their new jobs, the new plant, and the new community. For example, 40 per cent of the relocated workers preferred living in their old locations to Dover, and 30 per cent were indifferent. About 20 per cent would prefer to move away from Dover. One in three hourly workers did not like the work in Dover as well as the work in the old plant. Most workers had returned to their old locations at least once, and 20 per cent had returned six or more times, in the year or so that they had lived in Dover.

On the other hand, only a handful of workers were looking for other work and 70 per cent said they would make the same decision to transfer all over again. More than 80 per cent of all migrants think their most recent move to have been a good or very good idea, compared to 30 per cent of the relocated General Foods workers. It is likely that many GF workers were going through an extended adjustment period and would in time adapt themselves to their new work and community environment.

CHAPTER VIII

THE EXPERIENCE OF THE DISPLACED WORKERS

This chapter explores in depth three dimensions of the experience of the sample of Walter Baker displaced workers. First, what was the reaction of the displaced workers to the announcement that their place of employment was to be shut down? Second, what reasons did the displaced workers give for not moving with the company to the new plant? And third, what factors were important in the re-employment of the displaced workers? The first two questions are answered by making use of the workers' own reactions, elicited in the give-and-take atmosphere of a fairly unstructured interview. The third question is analyzed quantitatively through tables and statistical regression methods.

There are other aspects of the displaced workers' experience which are not touched upon in this chapter. For example, no extensive analysis of the jobs found by the displaced workers is made here. It should be noted, however, that those workers who found new jobs usually suffered a loss of wages and often were forced to move into less skilled lines of employment. The exceptions were the skilled maintenance men, who were not only able to maintain their previous occupation, but often moved into higher-paying jobs. Industrial mobility for the sample was very high: less than ten per cent found new jobs in the food processing industry. With the exception of the skilled maintenance men, wage or salary reductions were most often related to age and duration of unemployment. Older workers were much more likely than younger workers to take a lower-paying job, if they were able to find new employment at all. And it also appears that the longer a man had been unemployed, the more likely it was that he would be forced to take a lower wage and/or lower skilled job.

It should also be noted that, with the exception of those workers who found new jobs immediately and a few who were, for a variety of reasons, ineligible, the entire sample received unemployment compensation from the State for the period they were without work. The standard allowance in Massachusetts in 1964 and 1965 was $45 a week for thirty weeks, with $6 added for each dependent. The degree to which the unemployed worker was afforded financial protection during his period of unemployment is explored in the final section of this chapter.

Workers' Reactions to the Shutdown Announcement

Because interviews held with the displaced workers were verbal and largely unstructured, much information of a non-quantitative nature was obtained. Workers had an opportunity freely to express their attitudes, opinions, and reactions to the shutdown and relocation of the Walter Baker plant's operations. This information provides us with a side of the relocation story not previously touched upon in this study. The interviewer attempted to record faithfully the workers' answers to certain questions, and these responses, interesting for what they reveal about worker attitudes and motivations, at the same time reveal much about the "human side" of a plant shutdown.

For example, displaced workers were asked, "Briefly, what was your reaction when you first heard the news of the shutdown?" The workers' responses revealed a range of sentiment from anger and resentment to acceptance and understanding. About as many workers seemed to have expected the imminent shutdown as were surprised by it.

Typical comments from those who expected an eventual plant shutdown include the following:

> "Ever since General Foods took over Walter Baker there have been rumors they were going to move. I wasn't phased when the word finally came."

> "There had been a lot of scuttlebutt before the announcement, so I wasn't too surprised. We had heard rumblings for years."
>
> "They had made 'soundings' and I suspected something. I thought they might build in Dorchester, but I told my boss five years ago, 'I bet you $5 this plant is shut down within five years,' but he wouldn't take it."
>
> "My brother told me three years before the shutdown what was going to happen. He must have had some inside information. There were rumors for years. None of us were very surprised."
>
> "Ten years ago when we heard they had bought Northern Dairy, we thought they'd move to Chicago to be near that milk supply -- they had all the figures. So we old-timers figured they would shut down sooner or later. We just didn't know when. I had a friend who was approaching retirement, and he used to say, 'I just hope I get out of here before they shut this place down.'"

There were those who had heard "rumors" for years, but nevertheless believed their jobs to be secure:

> "There had been rumors. Still, I thought Baker's was a secure job. Even after the announcement I thought some operations would remain in Dorchester."
>
> "We saw these men walking around the plant just before the announcement. We knew they weren't rating the jobs, so we thought something was up. Still I was surprised when the news came. Usually these things get on the grapevine, but we had no word."

There were those who were surprised, and a few who were angry:

> "I was mad. They shouldn't have pulled out, leaving workers in a bad way. They gave us a raw deal. I could tell you a lot. . . They could have remodeled here. Now I hope they lose money down in Dover."

Others were surprised but understood the company's position:

> "The stockholders got a right to make a buck. I don't blame them. Every blessed plant I ever worked for shut down. I worked for _____ Company, and they shut down and went to Maine. Then Baker. I'm working at the paper mill and who knows what? That's the thing about industry. You don't know from day to day whether the company is going to stay one day or fifty million."

Among those who were surprised were those who considered the Baker plant a permanent community institution:

> "Boy, we thought we were set down there. Good pay, good benefits. Then, boom! Everything blows up! My father worked there forty years, and I thought I would too."

> "It was a real shock! It knocked us on our cans. We couldn't believe they'd shut down. It's like them closing down John Adams' birthplace."

Even while there was much surprise and some dismay about the shutdown of the Walter Baker plant, most workers seemed to accept the shutdown as an eventuality one must face in working life. There was a good deal of stoicism and, all things considered, very little misunderstanding of General Foods' reasons for shutting down the plant. Although some workers chose to believe that "politics," "unions," or "taxes" played a large role in the shutdown decision, most workers recognized that the age and obsolescence of the plant itself was the major reason for the closure.

The Choice of Termination

An examination of a variety of factors, such as age, sex, occupation, income, etc., has revealed *who* among the General Foods workers was likely to terminate. Our interviews with the displaced workers allowed us to hear in the workers' own words *why* they terminated.

The following comment is typical:

> "It was the most difficult decision of our lives. We talked about it for months. Finally I decided to leave General Foods and start a new life. Many things made us decide. We didn't like Dover. Nothing to do there. General Foods would be the only company there. We didn't like giving up our friends in the Boston area. I'd have known no one in Dover but General Foods people. Who wants to work all day with someone and then see them at night too?"

Many expressed dissatisfaction with the job they *thought* they would hold in the new plant:

> "The job was only common labor. If they would have offered me a *position*, I would have gone. As it was I would have had to take a pay cut, plus no overtime and no incentive. I talked to a lot of men who were down and didn't like it. I hear a lot of them are coming back."

> "There was no certainty in Dover. I didn't want to take a job that paid only $2.00 an hour. I would have had to spend $20,000 on a new home. What would I have done if I'd been laid off? Where could I go? There are only two other industries."

> "I couldn't see it. My kids told me I'd have to go alone if I wanted to go. But I didn't want to go anyway. I couldn't see going for so much less money. And no union! It would take at least a year to get one organized and all that time you wouldn't have no protection."

> "They offered me $92 a week straight. That would have been $30 a week less than I made at Baker's. Then they said I'd have two machines to run. More responsibility, which I don't mind. I mean, I could do it, but at less money, no. They'd have to give me at least the same to get me to do a job with more responsibility. After twenty-five years of service, they reward you with a pay cut."

Despite the best efforts of the corporation to carry on an effective communication program with the workers, there are, in the above quotations, certain misconceptions. It is not true that _all_ production workers received a pay cut on transferring to Dover. Some of the Walter Baker production workers did receive an hourly wage reduction. All Walter Baker production workers suffered a loss by transferring because of the elimination of the incentive system. However, it is clear that some workers were exaggerating the pay reduction they would have received because of transfer. It is also not true that no overtime would be available in the Dover plant, although it is true that _less_ overtime would be available than had been typical of the Walter Baker plant in the last year of its operation. Over that last year there was, virtually, unlimited overtime available to Walter Baker workers, so that when a few workers spoke of a pay cut at the new plant they were not necessarily speaking of an hourly wage reduction, but of a pay cut resulting from a reduction in overtime available below the abnormal levels that had existed in the Walter Baker plant over the last year or so of its operation.

A good proportion of the workers mentioned a lack of "security" in the Dover plant as the reason they terminated. One worker's comment is typical: "I hadn't much seniority. I was afraid of being laid off in Dover and having no place to turn." It is clear that the workers who made this kind of comment were misconstruing the position they would hold after transfer to Dover. Even though a union would not be representing the workers in the early stages of the Dover plant's operation, the corporation would still be using seniority to govern layoffs, recalls, etc. In that event, any worker who transferred to Dover with any seniority _at all_, even one month, would have more seniority than the 1,300 new hires taken on by the new plant. The relocated production worker with the _least_ seniority among all transfers would still have 85 per cent of the workers at the new plant below him on the seniority list. All transfers, then, were relatively immune to the risk of layoff.

If General Foods had realized that the fear of layoff prevented a number of workers from electing transfer, and had provided counseling and information on the relative position of transfers in the new plant to alleviate those fears, it is possible that an increased number would have elected transfer.

Many workers who chose termination were not attracted by the Dover area:

> "I wouldn't move to Dover if they paid me $50 an hour. New York, yes. Michigan, yes. Even California. But not Delaware. That's a farmer state! They have different customs."

> "I talked to guys who had been down and they said there was nothing down there. I wouldn't go because I got responsibilities to the kids. What would they do down there? Like they go to one theatre and one bowling alley, and a couple of bars, and that's it. For the wife and me it wouldn't be so bad. But for the kids it would be awful!"

For different reasons, a few people objected to the "southern" location:

> "We didn't know what would happen in Dover. We could go down there and they could throw you out on your ear. . . What are these people like down there? They're southerners, aren't they? What if we didn't like them or they didn't like us?"

> "It was primarily the area. I could have gotten $125 for going, so it wasn't the money. They've got nothing down there unless you're an alcoholic. They've got plenty of bars. . . Not that I have anything against them, but there are a lot of Negroes down there and they keep wages low. . ."

One man came to the following conclusion:

> "I went down to Dover, but I couldn't see it. I couldn't see any future for my kids down there. I looked into it and found that thirty years ago the population of Dover was 7,500, and that's what it is now. To me that meant that all the children left the town, and I found out I was right. They've got to go to Baltimore, Philadelphia or some other big town."

These comments contain misconceptions and misinformation about the Dover area. In fairness to Dover, it must be remembered that of those who did transfer to the area, nearly 30 per cent actually preferred it to their old location, and another 30 per cent liked it just as well. It is perfectly true, however, that Dover represented a different kind of community for the Boston area residents. Dover had all the disadvantages of a small, fairly rural community -- and all the advantages, which were perhaps not so apparent to the metropolitan Boston workers.

The displaced workers also cited family and community ties as reasons for not transferring. For example, one worker commented:

> "I had this happen to me before, when the Ford plant shut down in Somerville. I could have gone to Ohio then, but my family didn't want to move. My mother-in-law is next door. My wife's been with her all her life and she doesn't want to leave her. My daughter is diabetic and is treated at Children's Hos-

> pital. . . You can't get better care than that. I would have gone. I told my wife, 'My future's with General Foods', especially at my age, but we just couldn't swing it."

There is also the sad story recounted by a middle-aged couple who had both been employed by Walter Baker:

> "We had decided to go to Dover. Both of us would have had jobs in the new plant, so we had even purchased land to build a home. At the last minute we decided to stay in Boston. You see, our children were against the move -- they felt there was nothing to do in Dover. No dances, only one show in town. The only other thing was a bowling alley. Also my wife's parents were both ill. Well, over the past year our daughter has gotten married and moved away, our son has gone into the service, and my wife's parents have died. My wife is still without work, and I hate my new job."

One worker frankly admitted that he overestimated his ability to find another job in the Boston area:

> "I was too cocky. I thought I could easily get a good job in Boston. I overrated myself."

The interviewer was left with the strong impression that the shutdown experience had deflated the egos of many of the displaced workers. For a few it apparently had caused severe depression. This was particularly true of the older worker. Several workers noted that they had only a short time to go before retirement, and that it would have been foolish to transfer to Dover. For some of these workers the termination worked no hardship:

> "I could have gone down for nine months and worked. I had nine months before retirement. But what with my pension and severance pay, I made more money by staying here. . . . If I would have been fifty, I would have stuck with them and gone."

Others, of course, were not by any means in so fortunate a position. One sixty-two year-old gentleman, unemployed for more than a year, with family responsibilities, cried for most of the interview.

In sum, displaced Walter Baker workers gave a variety of reasons for not relocating to Dover. Principally they included: dissatisfaction with the Dover job, particularly because of anticipated pay reductions, but also because of a somewhat illogical anxiety about security of employment in Dover; dislike of the Dover area as a place to live; family and community ties in the Boston area; and age, for those nearing retirement.

Unemployment Experience of the Displaced Workers

Every major study on displaced workers has been concerned with specifying personal factors that are important in the re-employment of displaced workers. In this section the displaced Walter Baker workers will be analyzed with the same aim in mind. In fact, roughly the same factors revealed by previous studies to have been important in the re-employment of displaced workers are found to have been critical for the Walter Baker workers. One or two factors, such as alternative sources of income and severance pay, not extensively analyzed in other studies, are considered here. Also, an attempt has been made to carry the analysis farther than previous studies have done. Linear regression analysis has been applied in an effort to weigh more precisely the factors important in the re-employment of displaced workers. The results, while not highly encouraging from an analytical point of view, are given later. First, the more traditional tabular approach is presented.

It must be kept in mind that a pre-condition for the successful re-employment of any individual is an adequate level of demand for labor in the market in which job search takes place. In 1964 and 1965 the Boston labor market area was classified by the Bureau of Employment Security as an area of "moderate unemployment," *i.e.*, unemployment was in the 3.0 per cent to 5.9 per cent range.[1] The actual unemployment rate for the Boston area was estimated to be 4.1 per cent in November, 1964; 5.1 per cent in January, 1965; and 4.7 per cent in March, 1965.[2] It was in the November to March period that interviews with the Walter Baker workers were obtained during 1965.

1. Duration of Unemployment and Re-entry into the Labor Market

Table 8.1 shows the frequency and cumulative distributions of the weeks of "unemployment" of our sample of displaced workers. A word of explanation is needed concerning the use of the term "unemployment." What is actually being measured is the number of weeks without work between the date of the worker's displacement and the date of his first job, or the date of his interview, if no new job was found. "Weeks without work" would be a more accurate title, but we will use "unemployment," provided the reader keeps in mind our definition of the term.

---

[1]U. S. Department of Labor, Bureau of Employment Security, *Area Trends in Employment and Unemployment*, January, 1965, p. 8; February, 1965, p. 11; and March, 1965, p. 8.

[2]*Ibid.*, January, 1965, p. 32; March, 1965, p. 40; and May, 1965, p. 42.

TABLE 8.1

WEEKS OF UNEMPLOYMENT: FREQUENCY AND CUMULATIVE DISTRIBUTIONS

Weeks	Number	Per Cent	Cumulative Per Cent
0	11	9.5	9.5
1-5	12	10.3	19.8
6-10	14	12.1	31.9
11-15	12	10.3	42.2
16-20	12	10.3	52.5
21-25	26	22.4	74.9
26-30	10	8.6	83.5
31 or more	19	16.5	100.0
Total	116	100.0	
Average Weeks per Worker	18.6		

In most cases, weeks without work and weeks of unemployment are synonymous. However, there were a number of workers who reported not looking for work after being terminated. Table 8.2 shows that twenty workers reported not looking for work at all after termination. These workers were, in a sense, not unemployed, if one defines unemployment to mean making an active search for work. These workers have not been eliminated from the succeeding analysis, however, for a number of reasons.

First, it is reasonable to assume that all the workers would have been at work, had Walter Baker _not_ shut down. Not to consider these workers unemployed is not to take account of the product they would have produced in the interim after the shutdown, but did not.

Second, the definition of unemployment used by the Census Bureau and the Department of Labor rests on the twin criteria of "ability" and "willingness" to work.[3] These workers were able to work; the question is whether they were willing to work. While an active search for work is the usual standard by which "willingness" to work is judged, it is not the only standard. For example, workers are considered unemployed even if they are not actively seeking work,

---

[3]Seymour L. Wolfbein, _Employment and Unemployment in the United States_ (Chicago: Science Research Associates, 1964), pp. 13-39.

TABLE 8.2

RE-ENTRY OF THE DISPLACED WORKERS INTO THE LABOR MARKET:
"WHEN DID YOU BEGIN TO LOOK FOR WORK WHEN YOU DISCOVERED YOU WOULD BE LAID OFF BY BAKER?"

Began to look for work:	Sample		Weeks of Unemployment: 15 or Less		Weeks of Unemployment: 16 or More	
	No.	Per Cent	No.	Per Cent	No.	Per Cent
Before the layoff	20	17.2	18	36.7	2	3.0
Immediately after the layoff	44	37.9	18	36.7	26	38.8
1-2 weeks after the layoff	17	14.8	5	10.3	12	17.9
One month after the layoff	10	8.6	4	8.2	6	9.0
More than one month after the layoff	5	4.3	1	2.0	4	6.0
Did not look for work	20	17.2	3	6.1	17	25.3
Total	116	100.0	49	100.0	67	100.0

if they are waiting to be called back to a job from which they had been laid off or if they would have been actively seeking except that there was no work in their line available in their community. Although it is clear that the Walter Baker workers were permanently severed, many considered themselves merely laif off and waiting for re-call. That this hope was not entirely in vain is testified to by the fact that a few actually were called back, either in the closing days of the operation of the plant, or after the plant re-opened for a four-month period in April, 1965. Other terminated workers considered themselves chocolate workers and felt that no work was available in the Boston area in the production of chocolate.

Third, the line between labor-market activity and inactivity is a thin one. Testing labor-market attachment is tricky business at best, and, as Haber and Murray point out, in the end judgment must rest upon an evaluation of the subjective attitudes of the worker.[4] It seemed preferable to err on the side of overstatement of the size of the unemployment problem among the displaced workers. There is only overstatement, however, if the most rigid definition of unemployment is adhered to.

---

[4]William Haber and Merrill G. Murray, Unemployment Insurance in the American Economy (Homewood, Ill.: Richard D. Irwin, 1966), p. 265.

Table 8.2 does show that active re-entry into the labor market and unemployment duration are related. Eighteen of the twenty workers who began a search for work <u>before</u> being laid off found work within fifteen weeks of termination, while seventeen of the twenty workers who did not search for work had more than fifteen weeks of unemployment. However, it is obvious that an immediate active search was no guarantee of success. Of the forty-four workers who indicated entering the labor market immediately after lay-off, 60 per cent had been unemployed for more than fifteen weeks.

One other note: a number of workers included in Table 8.1 had not had any work up to the date of their interview. While most of these workers are included in the "31 or more" category, a number appear in the "21-25" category. In other words, some workers in the 21 to 25-week category were interviewed within six months of their displacement and had not yet found any work. The results in this table and succeeding tables are biased to the extent that the <u>true</u> period of unemployment has not been recorded for some workers, but rather the period recorded has been partly the result of the more or less random timing of the interview. This bias is not a particularly serious one, especially since most of the analysis divides the workers into those with "15 or less" weeks of unemployment and those with "16 or more."

We now turn to an examination of the relation between duration of unemployment and a variety of factors, such as sex, occupational status, age, education, seniority, etc.

2. Sex and Occupational Status

The displaced workers averaged 18.6 weeks of unemployment. In contrast, the average duration for all unemployed in the United States in 1963 was 14 weeks; in 1964 the average was 13.3 weeks.[5] Allowance must be made for our definition of unemployment in making direct comparisons, however.

In analyzing differences in unemployment experience by occupation, we go no further than to separate our sample into its white-collar (salaried) and blue-collar (hourly-rated) components. The displaced salaried worker averaged 16.8 weeks of unemployment, and the displaced hourly worker averaged 19.2 weeks. Female displaced workers averaged 24.8 weeks of unemployment, while males averaged only 16.5 weeks. When the sample is broken down by both occupational status and sex, the following averages are obtained:

Male salaried (14)	16.3 weeks
Male hourly (71)	16.6 weeks
Female salaried (16)	17.2 weeks
Female hourly (15)	32.9 weeks

---

[5] U. S. Bureau of the Census, Statistical Abstract of the United States, 87th ed. (Washington: Government Printing Office, 1966), p. 220.

The numbers in parentheses indicate the number in the sample in each sub-category. While there were only fifteen in the female hourly category, their unemployment experience is so markedly different from the other groups that one can probably safely conclude that the female hourly group clearly had the most difficult time finding re-employment. It is true that a number of these women were not actively seeking work, but all would have accepted suitable jobs, if offered.

The importance of this factor is also shown when the distribution of unemployment is broken down by sex, as in Table 8.3.

TABLE 8.3

DISTRIBUTION OF WEEKS OF UNEMPLOYMENT BY SEX

	Weeks of Unemployment							
	1-5		6-15		16-25		26 or More	
	No.	Per Cent	No.	Per Cent	No.	Per Cent	No.	Per Cent
Male	19	82.6	22	84.6	29	76.3	15	51.7
Female	4	17.4	4	15.4	9	23.7	14	48.3
	23	100.0	26	100.0	38	100.0	29	100.0

Only four of the women had five or fewer weeks of unemployment. About 45 per cent of the women had twenty-six weeks or more of unemployment. Less than 18 per cent of the men had twenty-six weeks or more of unemployment, while about 22 per cent of the men had less than five weeks of unemployment. Nationally, in 1963 and 1964, about 13 per cent of the unemployed had more than twenty-six weeks of unemployment; about 45 per cent had less than five weeks of unemployment.[6]

3. Age

Studies have shown that age is a critical determinant of the re-employment prospects of a displaced worker. Haber, Ferman, and Hudson, in their summary of eighteen studies of displaced workers, concluded:

> "Of all the status characteristics, age appears to have the greatest effect on re-employment opportunities. Many of the studies reported that the older workers have a more difficult time than the younger workers in finding new jobs. The emphasis is on youth in our changing technological system, and the aged are at a disadvantage."[7]

---

[6] Ibid.

[7] William Haber, et al., The Impact of Technological Change (Kalamazoo, Mich.: The W. E. Upjohn Institute for Employment Research, 1965), p. 124.

It is clear from Tables 8.4 and 8.5 that age is strongly related to unemployment experience. Table 8.4 shows the mean weeks of unemployment suffered by workers in various age groups. While the relation is strong, particularly for females, it will be noted that those males aged thirty-five to forty-four averaged fewer weeks of unemployment (10.6) than those males aged twenty-five to thirty-four (15.8 weeks or unemployment). Those males aged forty-five to fifty-four averaged about one-half a week more of unemployment than those aged twenty-five to thirty-four, which is hardly significant. It is really the strong positive relationship between age and unemployment for the females that lends significance to the age-unemployment relation for the entire sample.

Table 8.5 presents the evidence in a somewhat different fashion. It shows that up to age forty-five, relatively more workers had fifteen weeks or less of unemployment, but that after age forty-five, relatively more workers had sixteen weeks or more of unemployment experience. Those who had fifteen or less weeks of unemployment were, on the average, forty-one years old. Those with sixteen or more weeks of unemployment were, on the average, fifty-one years old. Those with thirty-one or more weeks of unemployment were, on the average, fifty-four years old. Clearly age is as significant as sex as a factor related to the re-employment of displaced workers.

TABLE 8.4

MEAN WEEKS OF UNEMPLOYMENT BY AGE GROUP

Age	Total, Mean	Males, Mean	Females, Mean
24 or under	6.0	7.0	5.0
25-34	14.9	15.8	10.8
35-44	11.8	10.6	20.3
45-54	20.3	16.2	28.1
55-65	23.6	20.8	29.1

TABLE 8.5

AGE DISTRIBUTION AND UNEMPLOYMENT

	Weeks of Unemployment			
	15 Weeks or Less		16 Weeks or More	
Age	No.	Per Cent	No.	Per Cent
24 or under	2	4.1	0	0.0
25-34	13	26.5	9	13.3
35-44	17	34.7	7	10.5
45-54	12	24.5	17	25.4
55-65	5	10.2	34	50.8
Total	49	100.0	67	100.0

4. Dependents

Tables 8.6 and 8.7 show that there was a slight inverse relation between number of dependents and duration of unemployment for our sample of displaced workers. Using the same definition for number of dependents introduced in Chapter VI (number of dependents equals the respondent plus all those living in the worker's household who were not active in the labor force) it is shown in Table 8.6 that those with larger households tended to have fewer weeks of unemployment than those with smaller households. Those who had no unemployment at all averaged 4.2 dependents. Those with fifteen or less weeks of unemployment had, on the average, 3.4 dependents. Those with sixteen or more weeks of unemployment had, on the average, 2.2 dependents. The average number of dependents for all workers in the sample was 2.7, and it will be recalled that relocated workers averaged 3.4 dependents apiece.

Table 8.7 shows that about 42 per cent of the sample had only one dependent, the respondent himself. About half in this category lived alone and the other half lived with a working spouse. (By comparison, only about six per cent of the relocated workers lived alone.) As Table 8.7 shows, up to about three dependents, it is more likely that a displaced worker had sixteen or more weeks of unemployment rather than less. Those with four or more dependents were more likely

TABLE 8.6

MEAN NUMBER OF DEPENDENTS AND WEEKS OF UNEMPLOYMENT

Weeks of Unemployment	Mean Number of Dependents	
0	4.2	3.4
1-5	3.0	
6-10	3.2	
11-15	3.3	
16-20	3.0	2.2
21-25	1.8	
26-30	2.9	
31 or more	1.9	

TABLE 8.7

DISTRIBUTION OF DEPENDENTS FOR THE SAMPLE AND FOR THOSE UNEMPLOYED 15 OR LESS AND 16 OR MORE WEEKS

	Sample		Weeks of Unemployment			
Number of			15 or Less		16 or More	
Dependents	No.	Per Cent	No.	Per Cent	No.	Per Cent
1	49	42.2	17	34.7	32	47.8
2	15	12.9	2	4.1	13	19.4
3	15	12.9	4	8.2	11	16.4
4	16	13.8	10	20.4	6	9.0
5	6	5.2	6	12.2	0	0.0
6	9	7.8	7	14.3	2	3.0
7	4	3.5	2	4.1	2	3.0
8	2	1.7	1	2.0	1	1.4
Total	116	100.0	49	100.0	67	100.0

to have less than sixteen weeks of unemployment. About 71 per cent of those with three or fewer dependents had sixteen or more weeks of unemployment; about 70 per cent of those with four or more dependents had fifteen or less weeks of unemployment. Clearly, there is an inverse relation between number of dependents and duration of unemployment.

5. Education

Education is also related to unemployment. As Haber, Ferman, and Hudson discovered, "The less educated displaced workers find reemployment more difficult than the displaced workers with a higher level of education."[8] For Walter Baker displaced workers, those with less than twelve years of education averaged 21.2 weeks of unemployment experience. Those with twelve or more years of education averaged 15.8 weeks. Table 8.8 shows the unemployment experience of the workers at different educational levels. Clearly, completion of a high-school education made it less likely that a displaced worker would have sixteen or more weeks of unemployment. About two out of three workers with less than twelve years of schooling had sixteen or more weeks of unemployment. For those with twelve or more years of education, less than half had sixteen or more weeks of unemployment.

[8] *Ibid.*, p. 19.

TABLE 8.8

EDUCATION AND UNEMPLOYMENT

Years of School	Sample No.	Sample Per Cent	Weeks of Unemployment: 15 or Less No.	15 or Less Per Cent	16 or More No.	16 or More Per Cent
0-8	28	24.1	10	20.4	18	26.9
9-11	33	28.4	10	20.4	23	34.3
12	39	33.6	20	40.8	19	28.4
13-15	12	10.4	7	14.3	5	7.5
16 and up	4	3.5	2	4.1	2	2.9
Total	116	100.0	49	100.0	67	100.0

Those with no unemployment experience at all averaged 11.6 years of school. Those with from zero to fifteen weeks of unemployment averaged eleven years of school. Those with sixteen or more weeks of unemployment averaged 10.4 years of school; and those with thirty-one or more weeks of unemployment averaged 10.1 years of school.

The relation between education and unemployment is clearly, if not strongly, inverse. Within each broad educational group there were differences in duration of unemployment based on age and sex. Therefore, it appears that while education is a determinant of re-employment, it ranks below age and sex in terms of the strength of the relationship. Multi-variate analysis, which showed the combined effect of education, age, and sex, did not reveal education to be significantly related to length of unemployment.

6. Severance Pay

As previously noted, displaced workers in the sample received an average of $1,500 each in severance pay. The relation between severance pay and unemployment experience has not been well explored in studies of displaced workers. Haber and his associates, in surveying the literature, concluded that, "severance pay does not play a major role in re-employment."[9] Most studies of displaced workers have found

---

[9] *Ibid.*, p. 24.

that workers do not tend to use severance pay to help directly in their job search, for example, by using it to undertake retraining. The majority of studies have found, as did Wilcock and Franke, that "the primary effect of severance pay seem(s) to be an easing of the financial burden in the period immediately following the plant closing."[10]

This study confirms the earlier findings. About half the sample of displaced workers had used their severance pay, at least in part, to pay off accumulated debts. About 40 per cent indicated that at least some of the severance pay had been used to meet living expenses in the period following termination. About 60 per cent noted that they had added all or a portion of their severance allowance to their savings. This figure is deceptive, however, because many workers had received large lump-sum amounts, had deposited the amounts in their savings accounts, and then had drawn down the accounts over a period of time to meet living expenses. The 60 per cent figure overstates the amount of real saving done as a result of the receipt of severance pay. Also, the larger the amount of severance pay, the higher the likelihood that the worker had added it to previous savings.

A number of workers, nearly 20 per cent of the sample, in fact, had used at least a part of their severance allowance to take a

---

[10]Richard C. Wilcock and Walter H. Franke, Unwanted Workers (Glencoe, Ill.: The Free Press, 1963), p. 124.

vacation. Very few indicated that their severance pay had gone to pay off a mortgage, or even to make a mortgage payment. Finally, only six workers had used any part of their severance pay to aid them in finding new work. These few workers had used some of their severance pay either to send out a résumé, to pay a private employment agency or, in one case, to pay for the cost of a job-training program. In sum, the Walter Baker workers tended to use their severance allowances to pay off debts and meet short-term living expenses.

Was the receipt of severance pay a help or hindrance in the displaced workers' search for new work? One of the earliest studies of displaced workers, by Clague, Couper and Bakke, found that when displaced workers who had received severance pay were compared to those who did not, "month by month, dismissal wage workers were finding jobs about as quickly as the others. There is no ground whatever for thinking that the dismissal wage operated in any way as a drag on the workers' initiative."[11] Other investigators have not been so sanguine about the effect of "dismissal wages" on job search.[12]

Tables 8.9 and 8.10 explore the relation between duration of unemployment and level of severance pay for the sample of displaced

---

[11]Ewan Clague, _et al._, _After the Shutdown_ (New Haven, Conn.: Institute of Human Relations, Yale University, 1934), p. 38.

[12]Haber, _et al._, _op. cit._, p. 24.

TABLE 8.9

MEAN AMOUNT OF SEVERANCE PAY BY WEEKS OF UNEMPLOYMENT

Weeks of Unemployment	Mean Severance Pay	
0	$1,250	$1,116
1-5	1,139	
6-10	1,119	
11-15	967	
16-20	2,305	$1,800
21-25	1,772	
26-30	2,124	
31 or more	1,350	

TABLE 8.10

SEVERANCE PAY DISTRIBUTION AND UNEMPLOYMENT

	Weeks of Unemployment			
	15 or Less		16 or More	
Severance Pay	No.	Per Cent	No.	Per Cent
$ 0 - 500	20	40.8	17	35.3
501 - 1,000	10	20.4	10	14.9
1,001 - 2,000	10	20.4	18	26.9
2,001 - 4,000	8	16.4	15	22.4
More than $4,000	1	2.0	7	10.5
Total	49	100.0	67	100.0

Walter Baker employees. There is a tendency for the number of weeks of unemployment to be positively correlated with level of severance pay. A relevant break appears to occur at fifteen weeks of unemployment. In fact, in terms of Table 8.9, up to fifteen weeks of unemployment, average severance pay is decreasing. There is a sudden jump from an average of $967 per worker for those with eleven to fifteen weeks of unemployment to $2,305 for those with sixteen to twenty weeks of unemployment. Those with thirty-one or more weeks of unemployment averaged only $1,350 (less than the average for the entire sample). Nevertheless, as the table shows, all those with less than sixteen weeks of unemployment averaged $1,116 in severance pay, while those with sixteen or more weeks of unemployment averaged $1,800.

Table 8.10 also tends to support the proposition that severance pay acted somewhat as a hindrance on the re-employment of the displaced workers. The relevant break occurs somewhere in the neighborhood of $1,000 of severance pay, with those receiving less than $1,000 tending to fall into the fifteen weeks or less category, and those receiving more than $1,000 tending to fall into the sixteen weeks or more category. Two-thirds of the workers who received more than $1,000 of severance pay had more than sixteen weeks of unemployment, compared to about 45 per cent of those workers who received less than $1,000. The evidence is far from conclusive, however, and regression analysis did not reveal a significant relation between level of severance pay and duration of unemployment.

7. <u>Other Weekly Income</u>

In addition to the receipt of severance pay, many workers reported other sources of income for their period of unemployment. The primary source of other weekly income was that received by a working spouse. As pointed out in Chapter VI, 28 per cent of the displaced married male workers had a working wife. In addition, however, workers reported receiving income from such diverse sources as interest and dividends on savings and investments, rental income from owned property, and money received from relatives not in the worker's household. An attempt was made to develop an amount which represented the weekly "income" of each worker, exclusive of his own earnings from work or any unemployment compensation he might have received. The figures developed can certainly be considered no more than estimates.

Table 8.11 shows that 61 per cent of the sample received some weekly income in addition to what they might have earned or received in unemployment compensation. This figure includes workers who might have been receiving as little as a few dollars a week and as much as $200 a week. There is a surprisingly clear relation

TABLE 8.11

OTHER WEEKLY INCOME AND WEEKS OF UNEMPLOYMENT

Weeks of Unemployment	Per Cent Indicating Receipt of Other Income	Mean Other Weekly Income
0	27	$ 6
1-5	33	30
6-10	57	47
11-15	50	25
16-20	67	32
21-25	69	64
26-30	70	41
31 or more	89	79
Sample	61	46

between weeks of unemployment and the percentage in each category indicating receipt of other weekly income. About 27 per cent of those workers who had no weeks of unemployment had alternative sources of income, and the percentage increases rather steadily to 89 per cent (seventeen workers out of nineteen in the category) of those who had thirty-one or more weeks of unemployment. The table also shows that the average amount of other weekly income received by workers in the sample was $46. Excluding workers in the sample who indicated no source of other weekly income increases the average to $75. Those with fifteen or less weeks of unemployment averaged $29 a week in other income, while those with sixteen or more weeks of unemployment averaged $59 a week. When those who received no other weekly income are omitted in the computation of the averages, the result is that workers with less than sixteen weeks of unemployment averaged $68 a week in other income, while those with sixteen or more average $79.

Table 8.12 shows the relationship in a slightly different form. Again it is clear that other weekly income and duration of unemployment are positively related. More than 62 per cent of those not indicating alternative sources of weekly income had fifteen or less weeks of unemployment. Thereafter, the likelihood of having sixteen or more weeks of unemployment increases with the amount of other weekly income received. About 70 per cent of those with any other weekly income had sixteen or more weeks of unemployment.

8. Seniority

The more senior worker is often the more experienced worker. His years of service indicate that he is, in a sense, a loyal worker. These attributes may make him attractive to a prospective employer. On the other hand, the more senior worker is also likely to be an older worker, and this study, as well as other studies, has shown that age is a handicap in gaining re-employment. Moreover, long service might work against a worker if an employer feels that

TABLE 8.12

DISTRIBUTION OF OTHER WEEKLY INCOME FOR THE SAMPLE AND FOR THOSE UNEMPLOYED 15 OR LESS AND 16 OR MORE WEEKS

Other Weekly Income	Sample		Weeks of Unemployment			
			15 or Less		16 or More	
	No.	Per Cent	No.	Per Cent	No.	Per Cent
$ 0	45	38.7	28	57.1	17	25.4
1-49	24	20.7	10	20.4	14	20.9
50-99	27	23.3	6	12.2	21	31.3
100-149	9	7.8	2	4.1	7	10.4
150-199	9	7.8	3	6.2	6	9.0
200 or more	2	1.7	0	0.0	2	3.0
Total	116	100.0	49	100.0	67	100.0

it makes a worker less adaptable to a new environment and more difficult to retrain.[13]

Tables 8.13 and 8.14 explore the relation between seniority and weeks of unemployment. Those workers with less than sixteen weeks of unemployment had, on the average, 11.2 years of seniority. Those with sixteen or more years of seniority averaged 14.8 years of seniority. However, an examination of Table 8.13 reveals that the relation between seniority and unemployment is inverse for those with between zero and fifteen weeks of unemployment, and also inverse

[13] *Ibid.*, pp. 19-20.

TABLE 8.13

MEAN SENIORITY AND WEEKS OF UNEMPLOYMENT

Weeks of Unemployment	Mean Years of Seniority	
0	12.3	
1-5	11.0	
6-10	11.4	11.2
11-15	10.2	
16-20	17.9	
21-25	15.4	
26-30	13.7	14.8
31 or more	12.7	
Sample	13.3	

TABLE 8.14

SENIORITY DISTRIBUTION AND WEEKS OF UNEMPLOYMENT

Years of Seniority	Weeks of Unemployment: 15 or Less No.	Per Cent	16 or More No.	Per Cent
0-4	4	8.2	1	1.5
5-9	21	42.8	27	40.3
10-14	14	28.6	13	19.4
15-19	3	6.1	8	11.9
20-24	3	6.1	5	7.5
25 or more	4	8.2	13	19.4
Total	49	100.0	67	100.0

for those with more than sixteen weeks of unemployment. A sharp break occurs at the fifteen-week mark: those with eleven to fifteen weeks of unemployment averaged 10.2 years of seniority, while those with sixteen to twenty weeks of unemployment averaged 17.9 years of seniority. Those with thirty-one or more weeks of unemployment averaged only 12.7 years of seniority, compared to the sample average of 13.3 years. Moreover, the range of responses was great within each unemployment category. The range was no lower than sixteen years (for those with one to five weeks of unemployment) and as high as forty years for those with thirty-one or more years of seniority.

Table 8.14 shows that most workers, regardless of whether they had more or less than sixteen weeks of unemployment, fell into the five to fourteen-year range of seniority. Sixty-five per cent of the sample fell in this range, 71 per cent of those with less than sixteen weeks of unemployment and about 60 per cent of those with sixteen or more weeks of unemployment. A relatively small proportion of the sample had more than fifteen years of seniority. Of those who did, however, 72 per cent had more than fifteen weeks of unemployment.

Note that the relation between seniority and unemployment is very similar to the relation between severance pay and unemployment. This follows from the fact that the amount of severance pay received was largely a function of seniority. Hence, the two variables are very much intercorrelated (R^2 = .88). However, neither variable was a significant explanatory factor of unemployment duration when linear regression analysis was applied to the data.

The findings on seniority are in line with the highly qualified conclusion reached by Haber, Ferman and Hudson, in their summary of the literature: "(D)isplaced workers with high seniority fare no better in the job market than displaced workers with low seniority."[14]

9. Home Ownership

There was a slight tendency for home-owners to have more unemployment than renters. Of those with less than sixteen weeks of unemployment, about 45 per cent were home-owners. Of those with sixteen or more weeks of unemployment, about 60 per cent were home-owners. Apparently, home ownership was positively but not strongly related with weeks of unemployment. It may be that home ownership is a proxy for a worker's wealth or net equity position. More affluent workers could afford to take their time about finding new employment. In any event, a home-owner may need to pay his property taxes and possibly mortgage charges but is not forced to meet a monthly rental payment, and therefore is probably in a slightly better position than the renter in terms of the need to find new work.

---

[14] *Ibid.*, p. 20.

10. A Regression Model

The author knows of only one other study of displaced workers that attempts to explain the length of unemployment of the workers by using multi-variate analysis. That is a study of displaced engineers by Joseph Mooney.[15] As Mooney points out, the use of regression analysis to explain the unemployment experience of displaced workers is "fraught with difficulties."[16] Primarily this stems from the fact that there is a "large and changing variance in the dependent variable when it is plotted against a particular independent variable such as age."[17]

For our study the following variables were used in the analysis:

X_1 = weeks of unemployment

X_2 = age

X_3 = number of dependents

X_4 = other weekly income

X_5 = $\begin{cases} 0 - \text{male} \\ 1 - \text{female} \end{cases}$

X_6 = years of seniority

X_7 = years of school

X_8 = weekly wage before termination

X_9 = severance pay

---

[15]Joseph Mooney, "Displaced Engineers and Scientists: An Analysis of the Labor Market Adjustment of Professional Personnel" (Ph.D. dissertation, Department of Economics, Massachusetts Institute of Technology, 1965), pp. 110-114.

[16]*Ibid.*, p. 110.

[17]*Ibid.*

Weeks of unemployment were used as the dependent variable, and the next eight variables as the independent variables.

Each of the independent variables was run against X_1, weeks of unemployment. The results indicated that age provided the best single explanation of length of unemployment. The regression equation which resulted when age was run against unemployment was as follows:

$$(1) \qquad X_1 = 1.4194 + .364X_2$$

$$(4.4282) \quad (.0919)$$

$$R_2 = .1207$$

The coefficient of determination, R^2, indicates that 12 per cent of the total observed variance in length of unemployment is linearly associated with the age of the displaced worker. More importantly, perhaps, applying the t-test to the coefficient of the independent variable reveals that the regression is significant at better than the .01 level. Age is shown to be positively and significantly correlated with length of unemployment.

When number of dependents, X_3, is added to the regression equation, the result is as follows:

$$(2) \qquad X_1 = 8.2451 + .3112X_2 - 1.6018X_3$$

$$(4.9012) \quad (.0910) \quad (.5551)$$

$$R^2 = .1811$$

Two variables, age and number of dependents, are able to explain 18 per cent of the variation in length of unemployment. The equation shows that, while age and unemployment are positively related, number of dependents and unemployment are inversely related. The larger the number of dependents, the shorter the period of unemployment for workers in our sample. The coefficients of both independent variables are significant as better than the .01 level.

With the addition of other independent variables to the regression equation, a greater percentage of the observed variance in unemployment is explained. However, tests of significance reveal that the coefficients of the additional independent variables are not as powerfully related to length of unemployment as age and number of dependents. For example, when "other weekly income," X_4, is added to the equation, the result is the following:

$$\text{(3)} \qquad X_1 = \underset{(4.8925)}{7.2470} + \underset{(.0927)}{.2736X_2} - \underset{(.5908)}{1.2296X_3} + \underset{(.0217)}{.0376X_4}$$

$$R^2 = .2024$$

Now 20 per cent of the variation in unemployment can be explained, using the three variables in the equation. The coefficient of age is still significant at better than the .01 level, while the coefficient of number of dependents becomes significant at the .05 level and the coefficient of the added variable, X_4, is significant only at the .10 level.

The addition of the sex variable allows more of the variation in unemployment to be explained, but washes away a high level of significance for all but the coefficient of X_2, age:

$$(4) \quad X_1 = \underset{(4.9960)}{5.1956} + \underset{(.0920)}{.2792X_2} - \underset{(.6223)}{.8691X_3} + \underset{(.0222)}{.0277X_4} + \underset{(2.6757)}{4.5884X_5}$$

$$R^2 = .232$$

The coefficient of X_2 continues to be significant at better than the .01 level. However, now the coefficients of X_3 and X_4 are not significant and the coefficient of X_5 is significant only at the .10 level. The addition of other variables only serves to dilute the significance of the regression. Yet equation (4) does show that 23 per cent of the observed variation in length of unemployment can be explained by use of just four variables.

On the one hand, the fact that a fairly meaningful regression can be obtained with R^2 no higher than .23 indicates that a large number of factors possibly important in explaining the re-employment experience of the displaced workers have not been uncovered. Any individual's success in gaining new employment is undoubtedly the result of a complex set of economic, environmental, and behavioral factors. In this sense, the application of regression analysis yields disappointing results.

On the other hand, the fact that out of the complex of factors responsible for the duration of unemployment of the displaced worker, we have been able to find four that explain as much as 23 per cent of the variation is a result not to be completely discounted. For cross-sectional data obtained from a rather small sample, an R^2 of .23 can be considered quite meaningful. It may be that a curvilinear equation would provide a better fit, although scatter diagrams between each of the independent variables and weeks of unemployment did not reveal any obvious patterns.

In summary, regression analysis reveals age to be the most significant explanatory variable of the duration of unemployment among the sample of displaced workers. Number of dependents, negatively related to length of unemployment, was also found to be significantly related to weeks of unemployment. Other weekly income and sex were also useful: those with higher levels of alternative income had longer periods of unemployment, and women clearly had more weeks of unemployment than men. Other factors, such as education, seniority, and severance pay, were not found to have a very significant relation with weeks of unemployment when analyzed by use of regression methods.

Financial Protection for the Unemployed

It is obvious that for many of the individuals displaced by the plant shutdown, serious problems related to an extended period of unemployment resulted. On the other hand, the plant shutdowns resulted in no net loss of employment opportunity at the corporate level. In March, 1962, General Foods had 1,800 jobs available at four different plants; by the summer of 1965 the corporation had shut down the four plants, but still had 1,800 jobs available at the new plant in Dover. On net, no jobs were destroyed by the plant relocation. In the long run, it is likely that the plant relocation would increase the number of employment opportunities available through the corporation.

However, that fact is little solace to the workers who elected termination. Several factors ought to be considered in estimating the dimension of the problem created by the termination of workers because of the plant shutdowns. First, the corporation did offer to relocate <u>all</u> workers, and termination was not forced on any worker. Second, about one-quarter of the terminated workers were secondary earners in their households. The fact that average "other weekly income" was estimated to be about $46 for workers in the sample indicates the significance of the degree to which protection was offered by the employment of other household members. Third, unemployment compensation and severance pay provided significant protection for the displaced workers over the period of their unemployment. Fourth, the weekly income of workers in the sample was abnormally high in the year or so prior to their displacement. The primary reason for this was the unusual amount of overtime available to workers in the period preceding the plant closing. Also, union negotiations in the summer of 1963 had resulted in a large wage increase for the workers, as pointed out in an earlier chapter. The corporation granted the union demands in large part to insure labor peace over the period of the plant closing and to prevent attrition from rising to undesired levels. It is likely that the Walter Baker workers were overpaid, in the marginal productivity sense, in the year or so prior to their termination. Averaging the income of the displaced workers over a three-year period, say 1963 to 1965, including their unemployment compensation and severance pay, would probably still put them in a high earnings position relative to other comparable groups of workers.

The financial protection offered the displaced workers was substantial by any criteria. The average wage of the terminated worker in 1963 (prior to the increase in earnings opportunities brought about in the final year of the plant's operation) was about $100 a week. We have seen that the average severance pay received by the displaced workers was $1,500. If the average worker was without work for about nineteen weeks, about $80 in severance pay could be used by the work in each week of his unemployment, and $1,500 would be exhausted in the nineteenth week. The average worker had about two dependents, and so would receive $57 a week in unemployment compensation for thirty weeks. The average worker, unemployed for nineteen weeks, could count on $137 a week in income solely from unemployment compensation and severance pay. Adding the $46 figure received by the worker from other sources, one finds that, on the average, a worker unemployed for nineteen weeks had at his disposal $183 a week!

Of course, the above calculations are based on averages, and cannot take account of the hardship which occurred in individual cases. At the same time, the waste of productive resources which resulted from real unemployment among the displaced, from the movement out of the labor market by discouraged job seekers, and from movement into inferior positions which did not tap the full productive potential of a few workers, should not be neglected in estimating the extent of the social problem resulting from the plant shutdowns. In many cases the short-run problems which the displaced workers faced in the period following their termination were probably not as great as the long-run problems they would face after their severance pay and unemployment benefits were exhausted and they found themselves holding down a lower-paying job than they had before the shutdown of the plant.

Chapter Summary

In this chapter several aspects of the experience of the displaced workers have been examined. Particular attention was devoted to an analysis of factors related to the duration of unemployment of the displaced workers. Our major findings are summarized below:

1. Even while there was much surprise and some dismay about the shutdown of the Walter Baker plant, most of the displaced workers seemed to accept the plant closing as an eventuality one must face in working life. Most workers recognized that the age and obsolescence of the plant itself was the major reason for the closure.

2. Displaced Walter Baker workers gave a variety of reasons for not relocating to Dover. Principally they included: dissatisfaction with the Dover job offered to them, particularly when the offer involved a reduction in pay; a somewhat illogical anxiety about security of employment in Dover; dislike of the Dover area stemming from the workers' attitudes concerning the nature of amenities and living conditions in Dover; family and community ties in the Boston area; and age, when the respondent was nearing retirement.

3. The displaced workers averaged 18.6 weeks without work following termination. Male salaried workers had the shortest average period without work: 16.3 weeks. Female hourly workers had the longest average period without work: 32.9 weeks.

4. Aside from sex and occupational status, age was found to be an important determinant of re-employment among the displaced workers. Those under age thirty-five averaged about 14.5 weeks of unemployment, while those over age fifty-four averaged 23.6

weeks of unemployment. Regression analysis showed that age provided the single most powerful explanation of unemployment duration.

5. Number of dependents and other sources of weekly income, primarily that earned by a working spouse, were also found to be significantly related to length of unemployment. The greater the number of dependents and the smaller the amount of other weekly income, the shorter the period of unemployment was likely to be for the displaced worker. Age, sex, other weekly income, and number of dependents were found, through regression analysis, to be capable of explaining 23 per cent of the observed variation in unemployment experience of the displaced workers.

6. Some relation was found to exist between unemployment and seniority, education, severance pay, and home ownership, but these variables did not prove to be statistically significant when tested by use of regression methods.

7. The displaced workers were found, on the average, to have a considerable degree of financial protection for the period of their unemployment. The average worker was protected in the amount of $157 a week from unemployment compensation and severance pay (prorated over the average period of unemployment), and had other income averaging $46 a week. Individual cases varied greatly, however, so that some workers endured a considerable period of hardship following their termination.

CHAPTER IX

CONCLUSION

Summaries at the end of each of the preceding five chapters make it unnecessary to review the major findings of the General Foods study at this point. It remains only for us to make some concluding observations on the significance of the General Foods experience.

One of the major purposes of a case study of this sort is to provide a practical guide to others who find themselves in a similar situation. For employers and workers who face imminent large-scale labor displacements, what are the significant lessons to be learned from the General Foods experience?

Out of the experience of handling problems of labor-market adjustment arising from plant shutdowns has come the belief that the problems are extremely complex and must be attacked using a variety of weapons. For example, Shultz and Weber, in their study of the Armour experience, conclude that it is important to think in terms of a "package" of policies to meet the needs of large-scale labor displacement:

> Essentially any remedial program must consist of a "package" of possible measures helping particular individuals or groups. . . It is critically important to avoid over-commitment to any one means of attacking the problem of large-scale labor displacement, and to include in any remedial program as diverse and broad a package of policy tools as possible. . .[1]

Of course, the same package may not be appropriate for every situation:

> What must be recognized is that big programs mean something only when they fit the needs of particular situations and are helpful to particular individuals. . . (The) program most likely to succeed is the one that remains flexible enough to deal with the individual within the framework of his problems.[2]

Shultz and Weber, therefore, see two criteria as necessary to the success of any program designed to facilitate the labor-market adjustment of displaced workers: diversity and flexibility. However, there is obviously no simple formula which can be translated into effective policy. In fact, the employer seeking to design a policy which is, at the same time, both flexible and diverse may find himself in a dilemma. It may be that the needs of a particular situation dictate that all resources be concentrated on one specific kind of policy approach, that the notion of a "package"

---

[1]George P. Shultz and Arnold R. Weber, Strategies for the Displaced Worker (New York: Harper and Row, 1966), p. 201.

[2]Ibid., p. 202.

is inappropriate under the circumstances of a particular case. At the same time, implementing an elaborate set of policies, which may be useful to both the employer and his workers in a specific situation, may place the employer in a position of having to meet his own standard at some future time when the earlier package is not so useful to the employer and possibly to his workers as well. The employer must determine whether the special needs of workers at the time of a plant shutdown are serious enough to warrant deviation from standard administrative policies. If an extraordinary situation calls forth extraordinary policies, what is the likelihood of these policies becoming part of the standard "web of rules" in the plant?

The point is that every employer will have only limited resources, and will want to apply them for maximum effect both at any given moment and over the lifetime of his enterprise. Most observers will find it praiseworthy that a large corporation decided to allocate a considerable sum of money to the protection of its employees in a period of disruption and dislocation in the life of the company and its workers. On the other hand, this decision was not made wholly in the interests of the welfare of the workers. As the Senior Public Relations Specialist for General Foods and his collaborator put it:

> The decision to offer a job at the new plant -- plus generous moving allowances -- to everyone was motivated by the need for experienced employees and by management's desire for fair and equitable treatment of all. Additionally, the policy was, in part, responsible for maintaining good employee morale at the four old plants and continuing high production efficiencies which prevailed until the three plants were closed.[3]

By implementing a rather unique set of personnel policies, the company felt it was serving not only the interests of its workers, but also those of the corporation, its stockholders, and its customers. In this sense, the outlay of several million dollars on severance pay, interplant transfers, and other personnel policies connected with the plant shutdowns can be considered an investment on which the corporation expected a positive return. Some of the return consisted of greater efficiencies at the four old plants and at the new Dover plant. But a large part of the "return" involved such intangible factors as higher employee morale and increased goodwill for the company, which can only be indirectly translated into higher sales and profits. Whether the General Foods case can serve as a useful model for other companies facing a similar situation depends largely on how much value other companies place on the intangible returns from a set of liberal personnel policies. A company like General Foods, which operates primarily in con-

---

[3]Edmund S. Whitman and W. James Schmidt, Plant Relocation (New York: American Management Association, 1966), p. 154.

sumer markets, probably has more reason to be concerned with the intangible aspects of a set of personnel policies than does one which is not so consumer-oriented.

The corporation was undoubtedly pleased with the results of its "experiment." General Foods workers, past and present, were also disposed to look with favor upon the company's efforts. Nevertheless, an objective evaluation of the General Foods experience must entail a consideration of the following factors.

1. Despite the elaborate transfer opportunity offered by the company, only about 17 per cent of the male blue-collar workers transferred to Dover. Of course, there are few reported cases of a greater proportion of blue-collar workers relocating under similar circumstances. And, it is also true that more than 40 per cent of the <u>white</u>-collar workers relocated to Dover. However, it is quite clear that no company can expect a significant proportion of its production personnel to relocate a significant distance to another facility, even when the relocation opportunity is well delineated and quite substantial, as it was in the General Foods case. One might well ask: Is it worth while promoting the development and elaboration of interplant transfer opportunities in private industry, if the likely

result is that only a handful of workers will take advantage of them? Shultz and Weber conclude that, while a transfer plan is "no panacea for the problems associated with employee displacement," still, "the opportunity to transfer, where the plan is structured with care, will be seized by a substantial margin of workers."[4]

2. If the aim of the corporation was to prevent labor displacement because of the plant shutdowns, then additional policies might have been implemented that would have been of help in achieving that aim. Transfer opportunities were almost entirely limited to the Dover plant. About fifty Hoboken workers were reassigned to the Maxwell House plant in that city. General Foods might have expanded the scope of transfer opportunities available to its employees by permitting them to exercise some type of transfer right to certain other General Foods units. For example, displaced workers might have been offered preferential hiring rights at a selection of General Foods facilities across the country. Probably few affected employees would have exercised such an option, but the company would have had little to lose, and could not be faulted for not making

---

[4]Shultz and Weber, _op. cit._, p. 74.

the opportunity available. However, the company's major objective was not to limit labor displacement, but to staff a new plant. The extension of transfer rights beyond the Dover plant would not have served that objective.

3. Another policy which might have been used to induce an additional number of workers to relocate to Dover is the policy of "flow-back" rights, whereby workers are permitted to transfer with the option of returning to their former location within a stipulated period of time and terminating with no loss of severance pay. Shultz and Weber found the provision of flow-back rights to be a significant feature of the Armour transfer plans.[5] Flow-back rights were added to the General Foods plan, but only at the Walter Baker plant in late summer, 1963. At that point they could have little effect.

4. The example of the late introduction of flow-back rights at Walter Baker illustrates a crucial factor in the success of a set of personnel policies. It is important

---

[5] Ibid., pp. 72-74.

that transfer opportunities be well defined and communicated to workers at as early a date as is feasible. As Shultz and Weber put it, a transfer plan must make use of "procedures that reduce the ambiguity of the available choices as rapidly as possible."[6] The effectiveness of management communication also depends on the media used.[7] It may be overstating the case to say in the popular lexicon that "the medium is the message," but certainly there is an irrevocable tie between the form and content of a communication program. General Foods relied primarily on written forms of communication. The "On the Move" Bulletins, plus the policy statements passed down to workers, doubtlessly fostered understanding of management's motives and intentions and reduced the workers' "ambiguity of choice." But, as the displaced workers' comments illustrated, misunderstanding and misconceptions were not completely eliminated. Two additional steps might have been taken to increase the effectiveness of the communication program

---

[6] Ibid., p. 72.

[7] Paul Pigors and Charles A. Myers, Personnel Administration, 5th ed. (New York: McGraw-Hill, 1965), pp. 75-82, 96-97.

before the plant shutdowns: (1) more attention might have been paid to face-to-face communication between supervisors and workers; (2) the unions at the two Baker plants might have been more usefully employed as channels of communication to the workers.

5. Interviews with the relocated workers revealed various levels of dissatisfaction with the new plant and community. It appears that at the time of the interviews, relocated workers had not yet been successfully integrated into the new plant and community. These problems were not confined to production personnel, but extended to supervisors as well. According to Whitman and Schmidt, "Some supervisors whose only experience was in small plants undoubtedly had trouble visualizing the complex operation of the consolidated plant before they were put to work and asked to make it run."[8] In addition, supervisors who had been "big frogs in little ponds" apparently suffered a "psychological demotion" at the Dover plant.[9] The authors

---

[8]Whitman and Schmidt, *op. cit.*, p. 155.

[9]*Ibid.*

of the AMA report suggest that these problems might have been overcome if the supervisors had been given responsibility for the Dover relocation at an earlier date. As for the non-supervisory personnel, their integration at Dover might have been facilitated if the communication program which had been carried on in the relocation phase had been extended to the "settlement" phase. Beyond an initial effort at orienting the workers to the new plant, the communication program was abruptly terminated. As Shultz and Weber emphasize, "The importance of company and union efforts to organize a cordial reception at the existing plants cannot be overestimated. The move to a new community and a new work situation can often be difficult. . . Under such circumstances, a systematic effort to integrate the transferees into the receiving plant and community is essential."[10]

6. General Foods workers who elected termination were protected not only by the provision of termination allowances by the company and unemployment compensation by

---

[10]Shultz and Weber, _op. cit._, pp. 69-70.

the state but, perhaps most importantly of all, by a reasonably high level of demand in the local labor markets. The complementarity of General Foods' package of policies also provided the terminating workers with some degree of protection: to the extent that some workers were persuaded to transfer, to that extent displaced workers had fewer competitors for the jobs available in the local labor market. This reduction of competition for available jobs is probably insignificant in a large urban area, but it may represent a critical consideration to workers who are affected by the shutdown of the major employer's facility in a small town such as LeRoy.

7. Compared to policies developed in the Armour case, for example, General Foods did little to help the more than 800 workers who terminated to find new employment. If a company's primary objective is to staff a new plant in an area where needed grades of labor are considered to be in short supply, it may make very good sense to make the transfer opportunity seem relatively more attractive than termination. On the other hand, there were additional services that the company could have

provided to its affected employees without seriously diminishing the proportion of workers who elected relocation. The Jell-O Division Personnel Manager did agree, for example, that added counseling services might have been useful for the displaced workers, particularly at Walter Baker. In addition, energetically enlisting the public employment service in aid of the displaced workers, initially considered but never really carried through, would have been a nearly costless service (to the company) that might have been provided to the workers. At the time of the displacements, retraining programs were being initiated in the local areas by the federal government under the Manpower Development and Training Act. Yet the displaced workers in the sample interviewed had almost total ignorance of these retraining programs. A joint effort by the company and the public employment service to publicize such opportunities would doubtless have been helpful to many of the displaced workers.

8. There are many additional forms of protection that might have been offered the displaced workers. For most workers, the provision of severance pay and unemployment compensation provided adequate financial protection to meet the ordinary expenses of everyday living over their period of unemployment. There is one significant area of risk that was left uncovered by any of the policies, private or public, designed to protect the displaced worker. General Foods workers, who had been adequately protected by the company's medical benefits plan, which included hospitalization, surgical, and major medical coverage for the period of their employment, found themselves with little or no health insurance coverage on the day of their termination. The displaced workers, who had been paying from $1.20 to $3.80 a month toward their medical insurance coverage, had the option of continuing the health plans, provided they converted from group coverage to individual contracts and met the total cost of the premiums themselves. In almost all cases the displaced workers considered the cost of this option prohibitive.

Unsolicited comments from many of the displaced workers indicated that the loss of such coverage was a cause of considerable anxiety. In fact, several of the interviewed workers had incurred sizeable medical bills in the period following their displacement, which they were forced to meet out of their own resources. Extension of the company's regular medical benefits plan for a period following the worker's termination, say three months or until the worker had found new employment with comparable medical care protection, would have added significantly to the sum of the protection offered the displaced worker. In the public policy area, recent consideration has been given to extending the "medicare" provisions of the Social Security Act to the disabled.[11] It might also be useful to examine the feasibility of providing public health care protection to the unemployed. In 1960 approximately 132 million people were covered by hospital insurance.[12] Yet a substantial proportion of

---

[11] See, *e.g.*, Bert Seidman, "The Case for Higher Social Security Benefits," *The American Federationist*, Vol. 74, No. 1, pp. 7-8.

[12] John G. Turnbull, *The Changing Faces of Economic Insecurity* (Minneapolis: University of Minnesota Press, 1966), p. 128.

this coverage was dependent upon the continued employment of the primary household worker. The increasingly routine health insurance coverage of employed persons and their dependents makes the lack of such protection for those unfortunate enough to suffer a period of unemployment an anomaly which ought to be subject to public scrutiny.

As the comments above imply, no private program for the alleviation of problems resulting in the unemployment and economic insecurity of displaced workers can be expected to provide all the remedies needed. Our ideal should be an optimal blending of public and private remedies needed to meet the total problem. Undoubtedly public programs must carry most of the burden of meeting the problems of displacement, unemployment and insecurity. Yet, as the General Foods case demonstrates, private firms can make a positive contribution to the welfare of those affected. On the private level, there is room for experimentation and innovation which would not be possible on the public level. Special programs can be devised to meet the particular needs of a given situation. The progressive employer may find that as he seeks to provide protection and equity for his employees, he may be serving his own needs as well.

APPENDIX

LETTER ACCOMPANYING QUESTIONNAIRE

The Industrial Relations Section of M. I. T. is studying the effects of plant shutdowns on workers. In the next few weeks I will be surveying those workers who have been terminated by the Walter Baker Chocolate Company. By studying cases like the Walter Baker closing, we hope to be able to suggest policies for handling the serious problems faced by the terminated worker. Our final report will be read by economists, businessmen, and government experts.

I understand you are one of those workers terminated by Walter Baker. I would like to request your participation in our survey. In a few days I will contact you to arrange for an interview. I would like to ask you questions concerning your experiences with Walter Baker, your opinion of the handling of the shutdown, your efforts to find a new job, and your over-all work history. The information you give us will help make our survey a success.

The interview will take very little of your time. All answers we receive are strictly CONFIDENTIAL. Readers of our report will not be able to identify any individual who takes part in the survey. Finally, the Walter Baker Company has absolutely nothing to do with this survey -- outside of supplying us with your name. The survey is the sole responsibility of myself and the Industrial Relations Section of M. I. T.

I am looking forward to meeting with you in a few days.

Sincerely yours,

David B. Lipsky

QUESTIONNAIRE

1. Name: ________________ Date of Interview: ______

2. Address: ________________ Telephone: ______

3. Age on last birthday: ________ Sex: ________

4. Marital status: Single ____ Married ____ Separated ______

   Divorced ____ Widowed ____

5. Other members of household: Wife ______ Husband ______

   Children (age and sex): ________________

   Others: ________________

6. Children not in household (age and sex): ________________

7. What were you doing last week?

   ____ Working full time ____ On vacation

   ____ Working part time ____ Ill or otherwise incapacitated

   ____ Looking for work ____ Withdrawn or retired from labor force

   Other: ________________

8. I understand that General Foods offered you the opportunity to work in Dover, Delaware. Is that true? ________________

9. Can you tell me the major reasons for your deciding to stay in the Boston area?

   ____

   ____

10. Exactly what did General Foods offer to do for you in the way of a new job?

Nature of job ______________________________

Wages ______________ Hours ______________

Transportation and moving expenses ______________

____

Other: ______________________________

11. In your opinion, why did the General Foods Corporation decide to shut down the Dorchester Plant and move to Dover?

_____General savings to be made in Dover area (transportation, wages, etc.)

_____Obsolescent plant

_____Lack of business

_____Incompetent management of the Dorchester plant

_____Inadequate work force in the Boston area

Other: ______________________________

12. How many years have you lived in the Boston area? __________

13. For the period that you have lived <u>in</u> the Boston area have you ever sought work <u>outside</u> the Boston area? ______________

14. Have you ever been offered a job outside the Boston area (other than that offered by General Foods)? ______________

(If yes) Did you accept or refuse the offer? ______________

If you refused on a previous occasion, can you tell me why?

____

15. If General Foods were now to offer you the same job opportunity, do you believe you would move or would consider moving?

_____Would move

_____Would consider moving

_____Would not move

16. Had you remained with the General Foods corporation, would you rank your job possibilities on the factors listed below as (1) above average, (2) average, or (3) below average?

	Above Average	Average	Below Average
Promotion	_____	_____	_____
Higher pay	_____	_____	_____
Employment stability	_____	_____	_____
Other "fringe" advantages	_____	_____	_____

17. In your efforts to find work, which of the following methods have you used?

_____Direct application at place of employment

_____Public employment service (MSES)

_____Newspaper advertisement

_____Private employment service

_____Friend or relative

_____Company aid

_____Union aid

Other: ____

18. Which of the above methods do you believe is the best one to use to find a job?

____

19. When did you begin to look for work when you discovered you would be laid off by Baker?

_____Before the lay off

_____Immediately after the lay off

_____1-2 weeks after the lay off

_____One month after the lay off

_____More than one month after the lay off

20. In your search for work since leaving Walter Baker, can you tell me how many job interviews you have had? ____________

How many job offers? _________ How many job offers, if any, have you refused? ___________

21. If you have turned down any job offers, can you tell me why?

____

22. Do you own your own home, or are you in the process of purchasing your own home? ______________________________

23. Do you own any other property? ________________________

Where and of what nature? ______________________________

24. Considering everything the family owns, such as real estate, stocks and bonds, savings, cash, checking accounts and so on, would you say it totaled:

_____Less than $1,000

_____Between $1,000 and $5,000

_____More than $5,000

25. Considering everything the family owes (except for home mortgages), such as car loans, charge accounts, installment payment loans and other debts, would you say the amount is:

_____Less than $1,000

_____Between $1,000 and $5,000

_____Over $5,000

26. As a result of leaving Walter Baker, have you had to:

_____Use any savings at the time you left Baker

_____Cancel, cash, or surrender or borrow on any insurance policy

_____Postpone anticipated purchases

_____Sell any of your personal property to meet family expenses

_____Move as a result of leaving Baker

27. Did you receive a termination allowance or severance pay from Walter Baker when you left? ____________________

If yes, how many weeks of severance pay did you receive? ___

28. Did you receive any other benefits (e.g., early retirement)?

____

29. To what uses have you put these benefits?

_____Living expenses

_____Aid in finding new work (e.g., job training course)

_____Addition to previous savings _____ Paying off debts

_____Vacation _____Mortgage payments

Other: ______________________________________

30. Other than income your household has had from wages, or your unemployment compensation, has anyone in your household including yourself had income from any of the following during the period since you left Walter Baker?

_____Social Security (OASDI)

_____Other pensions (company, military, etc.)

_____Unemployment compensation (others in household than yourself)

_____Interest or dividends

_____Rental income from property

_____Income from a farm operation

_____Income from other business

_____Workmen's compensation

_____Money from relatives not living with you

Other: ______________________________

31. How, *i.e.*, in what manner, did you first hear the news of the shutdown?

____

32. Briefly, what was your reaction when you first heard the news of the shutdown?

____

____

33. Do you believe finding work in the Boston area is:

_____Very difficult _____Fairly easy

_____Fairly difficult _____Very easy

34. Would you say that it was harder or easier for people to find jobs in the Boston area than it was last year?

____Harder ____Don't know

____Easier

than two years ago?

____Harder ____Don't know

____Easier

35. Were you satisfied with your job at Walter Baker? ______

What did you like particularly about your Walter Baker job?

____

Dislike? ________________________________

36. Are you now a member of a labor union? ____________

If so, which one? ____________ If not, have you ever been

a member of a labor union? ________________

37. When the Baker Plant began to shut down, what did the union do to help its members?

____

Do you feel the union did all it could do? __________

What else could it have done? ______________

3 . What did the company do to help those employees who were not moving to Dover?

____

Do you feel the company did all it could do? __________

What else could it have done? ______________

Did you take advantage of the company's services? ______

39. Which of the income categories here best describes the total income of your family last year -- including income from all sources such as wages, salaries, self-employment, government payments, and the like?

0- 999	_____	5000-5999	_____
1000-1999	_____	6000-7499	_____
2000-2999	_____	7500-9999	_____
3000-3999	_____	10,000+	_____
4000-4999	_____		

40. I am interested in finding out exactly what kind of work you did with Walter Baker. Can we trace back for a few years the job assignments you had?

DATES				USUAL OCCUPATIONAL ASSIGNMENT	USUAL HOURS PER WEEK	USUAL GROSS WEEKLY EARNINGS
From		To				
Mo.	Yr.	Mo.	Yr.			

41. I'm also interested in finding out what other jobs you've held with other employers

Dates		Your Family Residence at Time	Employer's Name, City and State	Industry	Occupational Assignment	Usual Hours Worked per Week	Usual Gross Weekly Earnings	Reason for Leaving Employer or Changing Occupation
From Mo. Yr.	To Mo. Yr.							

42. If you have experienced periods in the past when you were not working, can you help me with the following information?

Dates		Were you looking for work?	1 If you were looking for work, record how and where looked 2 If not looking, record reason for not looking	Unemployment Compensation				Approx. weekly amount of income other than UC	What were other sources of income?
From	To			Did you apply for UC?	No. of Weeks of Benefits	Weekly Amount	If you did not apply for UC, why not?		
Mo. Yr.	Mo. Yr.								

43. (If married) What was your wife-husband doing last week?

_____Working full time

_____Working part time

_____Looking for work

_____On vacation

_____Ill or otherwise incapacitated

_____Withdrawn from the labor force

Other: ______________________________

44. (If wife-husband is looking for work) How long has your wife-husband been looking for work? (Approximate date, if possible)

____

45. Can you tell me where your wife-husband is now working and also the kind of work she-he has done in the past?

Dates				Usual Occupational Assignment	Usual Hours per Week	Usual Gross Weekly Earnings	Reason for Leaving
From		To					
Mo.	Yr.	No.	Yr.				

46. When not employed, has your wife-husband usually actively sought work? ____________________

47. Are there any other members of the household who work? ___

(Specify) ____________________

____

48. What part of the income earned by the other household members (other than your wife-husband) has been used for family expenses and maintenance?

____All ____Little

____Most ____None

____Half

49. What was your last complete year of schooling? __________

50. Did you receive all your primary and secondary education in Massachusetts?

____

51. Have you ever served an apprenticeship? __________

If so, in what trade? ____________________

52. Have you ever had any vocational training? __________

Explain ____________________

53. Have you ever taken any correspondence courses, any night school courses or had any other schooling above the high-school level? __________ Specify __________

____

54. Have you ever participated in any other training program?

____

55. Do you believe you have any special skills, not indicated by your education and training? ____________________
If so, what are they? ____________________

QUESTIONS FOR THOSE WHO ARE WORKING

1. Can you recall on what date you began your current job? ______

2. How did you first learn about your current job?

    ____Direct application at place of employment

    ____Public employment service

    ____Newspaper advertisement

    ____Private employment service

    ____Friend or relative

    ____Company aid

    ____Union aid

    Other: ________________________________

3. How many job interviews with companies did you have before you accepted your current job? ________________

4. Do you consider your current job permanent? ____________

    If not, have you another job lined up? ____________

5. Do you consider your present job to be:

    ____Better

    ____About the same

    ____Worse

    than your last job with Baker?

6. Are you satisfied with your current job? ________ What do you particularly like about it? ________________

    Dislike? ________________________________

7. Do you believe if you had to find another job right now that you would have a:

_____Very difficult time

_____Fairly difficult time

_____Fairly easy time

_____Very easy time

8. Do you believe the job would be:

_____Better

_____About the same

_____Worse

than the job you are now holding?

QUESTIONS FOR THOSE WHO ARE NOT WORKING

1. Do you think you will be able to find a job before long? _______

2. Which of the following factors do you think is the major cause of your not being able to find work at this time?

_____Lack of jobs _____Lack of education

_____Age _____Illness

_____Lack of Skill _____Don't want work

Other: ____

3. Can you describe the kind of job you would accept if it were offered to you? (Nature of work, location, hours, wages, etc.)

____

4. Do you believe your next job will be:

_____Better

_____About the same

_____Worse

than your last job with Walter Baker?

CONFIDENTIAL SURVEY

CONDUCTED UNDER THE AUSPICES OF THE MASSACHUSETTS INSTITUTE OF TECHNOLOGY AND THE STATE UNIVERSITY OF NEW YORK AT BUFFALO, JUNE-JULY, 1965

1. The purpose of this survey is to discover why, how, and with what consequences employees transfer from one area to another when their company relocates. All the questions on the following pages are designed with only this basic purpose in mind.

2. Filling in the questionnaire. The questionnaire appears long, but it should be very easy to fill in. Most questions provide a choice of answers and require only that the proper answer be checked in the appropriate space.

3. The importance of this survey. We cannot stress too strongly the importance of this survey. Thousands of workers every year find themselves facing a decision on moving to a new location or staying where they are. Companies on the move must decide whether it is wise to encourage their employees to move with them, or not. Surprisingly, very little is known of the factors governing such decisions, and their consequences. The General Foods relocation in Dover -- a unique case in many ways -- provides us with a wonderful opportunity to study in depth the meaning of relocation for the people involved.

4. Parallel surveys. In order to complete the picture of the General Foods transfer of operations we have been conducting surveys among terminated General Foods workers at the old locations. More than 100 former employees have already been interviewed in the Boston area, and another large group will be contacted this summer in the LeRoy area.

5. An independent study. Finally, we want to emphasize that General Foods has had no role in initiating or conducting this project. We asked General Foods to cooperate, and we have kindly been granted permission to use General Foods' premises to conduct this survey. However, no one from General Foods will ever see any of the questionnaires. Furthermore, the questionnaire is anonymous -- nowhere are you asked to give your name. When the final report is written, no one will be able to identify any participant in the survey or his individual responses.

Be sure to answer all questions!

1. What was the date of your move to Dover?

______ ______
Month Year

2. Will you please list below those people living with you in your present household?

Relationship or connection to you (Wife, son, mother, friend, etc.)	Sex	Age
1		
2		
3		
4		
5		
6		
7		
8		

3. Now will you please list below those in your former household at your old location who did not move, and explain in a word or two why they did not move?

Relationship or connection to you	Sex	Age	Reason for not moving
1			
2			
3			
4			

4. Did anyone in your household move here to Dover with you and then decide to return to your old location?

____Yes ____No

5. Briefly, can you tell me your major reasons for moving to Dover?

____

____

____

____

6. Which of the following best explains <u>when</u> you decided to go with General Foods to the location of its new plant?

____I decided just after the initial announcement of the old plant's closing; that is, about March, 1962.

____I decided after I heard that Dover was going to be the site of the new plant; that is, about September, 1962.

____I decided after it was clear what policies the company was going to use to transfer people to Dover. (Fall, 1962)

____I decided when I finally received a definite offer of a job in Dover. (Winter and Spring, 1963)

____I decided after I made a trip to Dover to see what the town and new plant were like.

____I decided late in 1963 or 1964 to move to Dover

Other ____

7. In your opinion, why did the General Foods Corporation decide to shut down the old plants? (Check one or more)

____There were general savings to be made in the Dover area (for example, on transportation, wages, etc.).

____Obsolescent plants.

Other ____

8. General Foods first announced the shutdown of the old plant in March, 1962, more than two years in advance of most transfers. In your opinion, how far in advance should a company notify its employees when it is going to shut down a plant?

_____At least two years _____At least six months _____At least one month

_____At least one year _____At least three months

9. Would your decision to move have been affected if the company had given notice of the plant closing only six months in advance?

_____Yes _____No _____Don't know

10. Other than the information the company supplied you, did you make any other effort to find out about the Dover area?

_____Yes _____No

11. a. Did you make a trip to Dover at the expense of General Foods before moving?

_____Yes _____No

b. If you made such a trip, do you feel it was absolutely necessary in order for you to make up your mind about moving?

_____Yes _____No _____Don't know

12. Would you say in deciding to come to Dover the decision was primarily your own, or did it involve others?

_____It was primarily my own decision to make

_____It was primarily a decision for my wife and me to make

_____It was primarily a family decision

_____It was a decision which involved others in addition to my family

Other ____

13. Would you say the move to the Dover area was a return to a place already familiar to you?

_____The Dover area was not familiar to me

_____I was born in the Dover area

_____I lived here before 1950

_____I lived here after 1950

_____I visited here as a serviceman

_____I visited here on vacation

14. Did you have any friends or relatives living in this area before you moved here?

_____Had friends living here

_____Had relatives living here

_____Had both friends and relatives living here

_____Had no friends or relatives living here

15. Would you say that most of your friends and relatives are now here, or are most of them in your old location?

_____Most are in my old location

_____Most are here in the Dover area

_____About an equal number of my friends and relatives live in both places

16. Did those in your household who made the move come together or did one person move first and the rest follow?

_____We all moved at one time

_____I moved first, and the rest followed later

_____Someone else in the household moved first and the rest of us moved later

Other ______________________________

17. a. Did any of your friends or relatives not living with you help you in any way with the move?

_____Friends helped

_____Relatives helped

_____Both friends and relatives helped

_____No help received

b. If either friends or relatives helped with the move, what kind of help did they give? (Check one or more if applicable)

_____Helped in selling or leasing my old home or apartment

_____Helped in making living arrangements for me in Dover

_____Helped in moving me from my old home to Dover (for example, by helping me to pack, loaning me a truck, etc.)

_____Helped by supplying me with information about the trip and/or the Dover area

Other ______________________________

____

18. Which of the below methods did you (and your family) use to travel here? (Check more than one if applicable)

____Air ____Auto - own a car

____Rail ____Auto - borrowed a car

____Bus ____Auto - rented a car

Other ______________________________

19. a. Even though most of your moving cost was paid for by General Foods, did you find there were expenses connected with moving <u>not</u> covered by General Foods?

____Yes ____No

b. If you answered yes, can you give us an idea of the things you had to pay for yourself?

____

____

20. What is your best estimate of the <u>actual cost</u> of your moving, including all expenses directly or indirectly involved?

____Less than $100 ____$1,000-1,250

____$100-250 ____$1,250-1,500

____$250-500 ____$1,500-1,750

____$500-750 ____$1,750-2,000

____$750-1,000 ____$2,000 or more

21. All in all, would you say that moving to Dover was <u>more</u> trouble than you expected or <u>less</u>?

____More trouble than I expected

____About as much as I expected

____Less trouble than I expected

22. If General Foods had moved to Dover ten years ago, and, assuming you were working for them at that time and were offered the chance, would you have gone?

_____Yes _____No _____Don't know

23. If General Foods had not moved now, but had waited until 1970 to move, and assuming you were working for them and were offered the chance, would you have moved then?

_____Yes _____No _____Don't know

24. a. Aside from the move to Dover, how many times did you change your place of residence since 1950?

_____None _____Once _____Twice _____Three times

_____Four times _____Five times _____Six or more

b. How many of these changes of residence involved a move from one city to another?

_____None _____One _____Two _____Three

_____Four _____Five _____Six or more

25. In the five years before your move to Dover, how many trips did you take to places 100 miles or more from your old home?

_____None _____Three to five trips _____Ten or more trips

_____One or two _____Six to nine trips

26. Have you ever in your entire life gone away from your home temporarily to work?

_____Followed construction work

_____Followed other work that moved often

_____Took a job at a long distance from my home but on a temporary basis

_____Had a brief assignment in another area for General Foods

_____Had a brief assignment in another area, but for another company

_____Went away for other reasons

_____Never went away temporarily to work

27. How many years did you live in your old area?

____

28. For the period that you lived in your old area, did you ever seek work outside that area?

_____Yes _____No

29. a. Were you ever offered a job outside your old home area by anyone other than General Foods?

_____Yes _____No

b. If you were offered such a job, did you accept or refuse the offer?

_____Accepted _____Refused

30. a. Did you make any effort to look for work in your old area before moving to Dover?

____Yes, actively

____Yes, but not very actively

____No (if you answer no, go on to Question #31)

b. If you did make an effort to look for work before leaving for Dover, can you tell me if you had any job interviews?

_____No _____Yes, one or two _____Yes, several

_____Yes, many

c. If you looked for work, did you receive any job offers?

_____No _____Yes, one or two _____Yes, several

d. If you made any efforts to find work before leaving your old location, which of the following methods did you use?

____Direct application at place of employment

____Used friends or relatives to help seek work

____Used the public employment service (the "unemployment office")

____Used a private employment agency

____Used the want ads in the newspapers

____Sent out résumés

Other____

31. Would you have been eligible for a termination allowance or severance pay if you had chosen to terminate instead of moving here to Dover?

_____Yes _____No _____Don't know

32. Your current job:

a. What is your usual occupational assignment? ____________

b. How many hours do you usually work a week? ____________

c. What are your usual gross weekly earnings?

_____Under $70	_____$110-119	_____$160-169
_____$70-79	_____$120-129	_____$170-179
_____$80-89	_____$130-139	_____$180-189
_____$90-99	_____$140-149	_____$190-199
_____$100-109	_____$150-159	_____Over $200

d. How many years have you worked for General Foods?
(That is to say, how many years seniority do you have?)

____

33. Your former job:

a. What was your usual occupational assignment at your old plant?

____

b. How many hours a week did you usually work at the old plant?

____

c. What were your usual gross weekly earnings at the old plant <u>in 1963</u>?

_____Under $70	_____$110-119	_____$160-169
_____$70-79	_____$120-129	_____$170-179
_____$80-89	_____$130-139	_____$180-189
_____$90-99	_____$140-149	_____$190-199
_____$100-109	_____$150-159	_____Over $200

34. Is your wife now working?

____Working full time

____Working part time

____Looking for work

____On vacation

____Ill or otherwise incapacitated

____Withdrawn from the labor force (That is, not working and not looking for work)

Other ____________

35. In order to move here to Dover, did your wife have to give up a job in your old location?

____Yes ____No

36. When your wife is not employed, has she usually actively sought work?

____Yes ____No

37. If your wife is now employed, can you tell me the following about her job?

a. Her usual occupational assignment ____________

b. Usual hours worked per week ____________

c. Usual gross weekly earnings ____________

d. How long has your wife held this job? ____________

38. Are there any other members of the household who work?

____Yes ____No

39. What part of the income earned by these other household members has been used for family expenses and maintenance?

____All ____Most ____Half

____Some ____None

40. How has the income of your household changed as a result of the move?

____Raised ____No change ____Lowered

41. In your old location -- did you own a home, or rent?

____Owned a home, or was in the process of buying a home

____Paid rent and lived in a house

____Paid rent and lived in an apartment

____Lived with relatives

Other ____

42. Here in the Dover area -- do you own a home, or rent?

____Own a home, or am in the process of buying a home

____Pay rent and live in a house

____Pay rent and live in an apartment

____Live with relatives

____Live in trailer (or "mobile home")

Other ____

43. a. In your old location -- did you sell your home?

____Sold

____Tried to sell, but did not sell

____Did not try to sell

____Did not own a home

b. If you sold your home, did you

_____Make money on the sale

_____Break about even, or

_____Lose money on the sale?

44. Would you say your living quarters here in Dover were:

_____Better than

_____About the same as, or

_____Nor as good as

your living quarters in your old location?

45. Do you think the price of houses in Dover is:

_____Higher than

_____About the same as, or

_____Lower than

houses in your old location?

46. How would you compare <u>rentals</u> (of both apartments and houses) in Dover with rentals in your old location?

_____Better here (more rentals available and/or lower rents)

_____About the same

_____Not as good here (fewer rentals available and/or higher rents)

47. As a result of transferring to Dover, have you had to do any of the following? (Check as many as are applicable)

_____Use any savings you had before the transfer

_____Cancel, cash, surrender, or borrow on any insurance policy

_____"Economize," that is, generally cut down on over-all expenses or postpone anticipated purchases

_____Sell any of your personal property to meet family expenses (for example, for moving)

48. Other than income your household has had from wages, has anyone in your household (including yourself) had income from any of the following since your transfer to Dover?

_____Social Security (OASDI)

_____Pensions (General Foods, military, etc.)

_____Unemployment compensation

_____Interest or dividends (including interest on savings accounts)

_____Rental income from property

_____Income from a farm operation

_____Income from other business

_____Workmen's Compensation

_____Money from relatives not living with you

Other ____

49. Considering everything the family owns, such as real estate, stocks and bonds, savings, cash, checking account, automobiles, and so on, would you say it totaled:

____Less than $1,000

____Between $1,000 and $5,000, or

____More than $5,000?

50. Considering everything the family owes (except home mortgages), such as car loans, charge accounts, installment payment loans and other debts, would you say the amount is:

____Less than $1,000

____Between $1,000 and $5,000, or

____More than $5,000?

51. Which of the income categories here best describes the total income of your family last year -- including income from all sources such as wages, salaries, self-employment, government payments, interest and dividends, rental income, and the like?

____$ 0- 999

____ 1,000-1,999

____ 2,000-2,999

____3,000-3,999

____4,000-4,999

____$ 5,000-5,999

____ 6,000-7,499

____ 7,500-9,999

____ 10,000-14,999

____ 15,000 plus

52. What are your feelings about staying in the Dover area?

____I strongly prefer to stay

____I prefer to stay

____No opinion one way or the other

____I prefer to move away

____I strongly prefer to move away

53. Do you prefer to live here, or at your old location?

_____Prefer to live here in Dover

_____Prefer to live at the old location

_____No preference; like each location about equally

54. Can you briefly say why you do or do not prefer living in Dover?

____

____

____

55. How would you compare the general "standard of living" in Dover against the standard of living in your old location?

_____The standard of living in Dover is better

_____The standard of living is about the same

_____The standard of living is not as good in Dover

56. How do you like your work in Dover compared to the work you did before?

_____Much better now

_____Better now

_____About the same

_____Not as good now

_____Much worse now

57. Do you find your present hours and shifts more convenient or less convenient than they were at your old location?

_____More convenient now

_____Less convenient now

_____About the same

58. How does the distance you must travel each day from your home to your job here in Dover compare with that in your old location?

_____Distance I must travel here is shorter

_____About the same

_____Distance I must travel here is longer

59. Are you now trying to find another job?

_____Yes, actively   _____Yes, inactively   _____No

60. Outside of the jobs here at General Foods, would you say that there is more work available in the Dover area, or in your old home area?

_____More work available here

_____More work available in old location

_____About the same

61. Do you believe finding work in your old location is:

_____Very difficult

_____Fairly difficult

_____Fairly easy

_____Very easy

_____Don't know or no opinion

62. How many times have you returned to your old location since moving here to Dover?

_____Not at all
_____Six to nine times
_____Once or twice
_____Ten or more times
_____Three to five times

63. If you had to make the decision to move over again, do you believe you would have made the same decision?

_____Would have made the same decision
_____Would not have made the same decision
_____Don't know

64. When you retire, do you plan on staying here in the Dover area?

_____Yes
_____Don't know
_____No
_____Too early to tell

65. All things considered, was the move a good idea?

_____Very good idea
_____Good idea
_____Good in some ways, not in others
_____Poor idea
_____Very poor idea

66. a. How many years of schooling have you had? _______________

b. Did you receive any college education?

_____Yes
_____No

67. Age on last birthday ____

68. Marital status:

____Single

____Married

____Separated or divorced

____Widowed

69. Place of birth ______________________________

(City) (State)

70. What was your old location? ______________________

If you have any additional comments you would like to add, please do so below.

Thank you for your cooperation!

BIBLIOGRAPHY

A. Books

Adams, Leonard P. and Robert L. Aronson, *Workers and Industrial Change*, Ithaca, New York: Cornell University, 1957.

Bakke, E. Wight, *A Positive Labor Market Policy*, Columbus, Ohio: Charles E. Merrill, 1963.

____________, *et al.*, eds., *Labor Mobility and Economic Opportunity*, New York: The Technology Press of MIT and John Wiley and Sons, 1954.

Beaumont, Richard A. and Roy B. Helfgott, *Management, Automation, and People*, New York: Industrial Relations Counselors, 1964.

Belcher, David W., *Wage and Salary Administration*, 2nd ed., Englewood Cliffs, N. J.: Prentice-Hall, 1964.

Berelson, Bernard and Gary A. Steiner, *Human Behavior: An Inventory of Scientific Findings*, New York: Harcourt, Brace, and World, 1964.

Chamberlain, Neil W., *Labor*, New York: McGraw-Hill, 1958.

____________, *The Labor Sector*, New York: McGraw-Hill, 1965.

Clague, Ewan, *et al.*, *After the Shutdown*, New Haven, Conn.: Institute of Human Relations, Yale University, 1934.

Dubin, Robert, ed., *Human Relations in Administration*, Englewood Cliffs, N. J.: Prentice-Hall, 1951.

Gordon, Margaret S., *Retraining and Labor Market Adjustment in Western Europe*, Washington: U. S. Department of Labor, Manpower Administration, Monograph No. 4, August, 1965.

Haber, William and Merrill G. Murray, Unemployment Insurance in the American Economy, Homewood, Ill.: Richard D. Irwin, 1966.

Hawkins, Everett D., Dismissal Compensation, Princeton: Princeton University Press, 1940.

Healy, James J., ed., Creative Collective Bargaining, Englewood Cliffs, N. J.: Prentice-Hall, 1965.

Lansing, John B., et al., The Geographic Mobility of Labor: A First Report, Ann Arbor, Michigan: Survey Research Center, 1963.

Long, Clarence D., The Labor Force under Changing Income and Employment, Princeton: Princeton University Press, 1958.

Major, Nettie Leitch, C. W. Post: The Man and the Hour, Washington, D. C.: Judd and Detweiler, 1963.

Morgenstern, Oskar, On the Accuracy of Economic Observations, Princeton: Princeton University Press, 1963.

Myers, Charles A. and George P. Shultz, The Dynamics of a Labor Market, New York: Prentice-Hall, 1951.

Parnes, Herbert S., Research on Labor Mobility, New York: Social Science Research Council, Bulletin 65, 1954.

Pigors, Paul and Charles A. Myers, Personnel Administration, 5th ed., New York: McGraw-Hill, 1965.

Reynolds, Lloyd G., The Structure of Labor Markets, New York: Harper and Brothers, 1951.

Reynolds, Lloyd G. and Joseph Shister, Job Horizons, New York: Harper and Brothers, 1949.

Ross, Arthur M., ed., Employment Policy and the Labor Market, Berkeley and Los Angeles: University of California Press, 1965.

Selltiz, Claire, et al., Research Methods in Social Relations, New York: Holt, Rinehart, and Winston, 1962.

Shostak, Arthur B. and William Gomberg, eds., Blue Collar World, Englewood Cliffs, N. J.: Prentice-Hall, 1964.

Shultz, George P. and Arnold R. Weber, Strategies for the Displaced Worker, New York: Harper and Row, 1966.

Somers, Gerald G., et al., eds., Adjusting to Technological Change, New York: Harper and Row, 1963.

Turnbull, John G., The Changing Faces of Economic Insecurity, Minneapolis: University of Minnesota Press, 1966.

Universities - National Bureau Committee for Economic Research, Aspects of Labor Economics, Princeton: Princeton University Press, 1962.

Whitman, Edmund S. and W. James Schmidt, Plant Relocation: A Case History of a Move, New York: American Management Association, 1966.

Wilcock, Richard C. and Walter H. Franke, Unwanted Workers, Glencoe, Ill.: The Free Press, 1963.

Wolfbein, Seymour, Employment and Unemployment in the United States, Chicago: Science Research Associates, 1964.

B. Periodicals

Rehn, Gosta and Erik Lundberg, "Employment and Welfare: Some Swedish Issues," Industrial Relations, Vol. 2, No. 2, February, 1963, pp. 1014.

Seidman, Bert, "The Case for Higher Social Security Benefits," The American Federationist, Vol. 74, No. 1, pp. 1-8.

Weber, Arnold R. and David P. Taylor, "Procedures for Employee Displacement: Advance Notice of Plant Shutdown," The Journal of Business, Vol. 36, No. 3, July, 1963, pp. 302-315.

"Billions in the Pantry," Time, Vol. 71, June 9, 1958, pp. 86-88.

"General Foods: High Profits in a Low Profit Industry," Forbes, Vol. 90, August 1, 1962, pp. 20-24.

"General Foods Is Five Billion Particulars," Fortune, Vol. 69, March, 1964, pp. 114-117, 158-165.

"Just Heat and Serve," Time, Vol. 74, December 7, 1959, pp. 92-96.

"Obstacles to Labour Mobility and Social Problems of Resettlement: A Survey by the European Coal and Steel Community," International Labour Review, Vol. 76, No. 1, July, 1957, pp. 72-83.

"Ready for Instant Growth," Business Week, April 25, 1965, pp. 69-74.

C. Bulletins and Reports

Armour Automation Fund Committee, Progress Report, Chicago, June 19, 1961.

Bradburn, Norman M., Inter-Plant Transfer: The Sioux City Experience, Chicago: National Opinion Research Center, University of Chicago, May, 1964.

Creamer, Daniel and Charles W. Coulter, Labor and the Shutdown of the Amoskeag Textile Mills, U. S. Works Progress Administration, Report No. L-5, Philadelphia: Works Progress Administration, November, 1939.

Creamer, Daniel and Gladys V. Swackhamer, Cigar Makers -- After the Lay-off, U. S. Works Progress Administration, Report No. L-1, Philadelphia: Works Progress Administration, December, 1937.

General Foods Corporation, Annual Report, various years, 1960-1965.

Haber, William, et al., The Impact of Technological Change, Kalamazoo, Michigan: The W. E. Upjohn Institute for Employment Research, 1963.

Meatcutters and Butcher Workmen, Amalgamated, AFL-CIO, and The Walter Baker Chocolate Company, General Foods Corporation, Agreement between, August 27, 1961.

Meat Cutters and Butcher Workmen of North America, Amalgamated, AFL-CIO, Amalgamated Food and Allied Workers Local 56, and the Jell-O/Dover Operations, General Foods Corporation, Agreement between, October 1, 1964.

National Industrial Conference Board, Severance Pay Patterns in Manufacturing, Studies in Personnel Policy, No. 174, New York: NICB, 1959.

National Industrial Conference Board, Severance Pay Patterns in Manufacturing, Studies in Personnel Policy, No. 178, New York: NICB, 1960.

Palmer, Gladys and Constance Williams, Reemployment of Philadelphia Hosiery Workers after Shutdowns, U. S. Works Progress Administration, January, 1939.

Smith, Luke M. and Irving A. Fowler, Do Workers Move When Their Plant Is Relocated? The Case of the Ford Motor Company Plant Relocation, Buffalo: Department of Sociology, University of Buffalo, 1960.

Steelworkers of America, United, AFL-CIO, and United States Steel Corporation, Agreement between, September 1, 1965.

U. S. Bureau of the Census, 1960 Census of the Population, Supplementary Reports, May 18, 1962, PC (S1)-19, Geographic Mobility of the Population of the United States, April, 1960.

U. S. Bureau of the Census, Statistical Abstract of the United States, 87th ed., Washington: Government Printing Office, 1966.

U. S. Congress, Joint Economic Committee, Programs for Relocating Workers Used by Governments of Selected Countries, Economic Policies and Practices, Paper No. 8, 1966, 89th Congress, 2nd Session.

U. S. Department of Labor, Bureau of Employment Security, Area Trends in Employment and Unemployment, January, February, March and May, 1965.

U. S. Department of Labor, Bureau of Employment Security, Work Force Adjustment to Technological Change: Selected Employer Procedures, Bulletin No. E-215, January, 1963.

U. S. Department of Labor, Bureau of Labor Statistics, Collective Bargaining Clauses: Dismissal Pay, BLS Bulletin 1216, 1957.

U. S. Department of Labor, Bureau of Labor Statistics, Dismissal Pay Provisions in Union Agreements, December, 1944, BLS Bulletin 808, 1945.

U. S. Department of Labor, Bureau of Labor Statistics, Labor-Management Contract Provisions, 1949-50, BLS Bulletin 1022, 1951.

U. S. Department of Labor, Bureau of Labor Statistics, Severance Pay and Lay-off Benefit Plans, BLS Bulletin 1425-2, 1965.

U. S. Department of Labor, Office of Manpower, Automation, and Training, Mobility and Worker Adaptation to Economic Change in the United States, Manpower Research, Bulletin No. 1, July, 1963.

White, K. K., Reimbursing Personnel for Transfer and Relocation Costs, New York: American Management Association, 1964, AMA Research Study 67.

D. Unpublished Materials and Newspapers

Allan, Jerry, "A Shimmering $67 Million from $450 Outlay in Jell-O," Buffalo Evening News, March 14, 1962, p. 27.

Automobile Manufacturers Association, "Technological Change and Employment in the Automotive Industry," A Statement to the National Commission on Technology, Automation and Economic Progress, 1965.

Bedingfield, Robert E. "Personality: Soap Flakes to a Mixed Fare," New York Times, March 7, 1965, Sec. 3, p. 3.

Mooney, Joseph, "Displaced Engineers and Scientists: An Analysis of the Labor Market Adjustment of Professional Personnel," Ph.D. Dissertation, Massachusetts Institute of Technology, 1965.

Richmond, Dean, "Lawless, Container Buys Former Jell-O Factory in LeRoy," Buffalo Evening News, May 4, 1966, p. 18.

BIOGRAPHICAL NOTE

Mr. David B. Lipsky was born in 1939 in Bethlehem, Pennsylvania. He graduated from Liberty High School in Bethlehem in 1957, and attended Lehigh University for one year. In June, 1961, he received a Bachelor of Science degree from the New York State School of Industrial and Labor Relations at Cornell University. He was a graduate student in the Department of Economics at Massachusetts Institute of Technology from September, 1961, through August, 1965. In 1963-64 Mr. Lipsky was a teaching assistant in the Department of Economics at M.I.T. In September, 1965, he became Lecturer in Industrial Relations at the State University of New York at Buffalo. He re-entered M.I.T. in February, 1967, and received a Ph.D. degree in Economics in June, 1967. He is now Assistant Professor of Industrial Relations at the State University of New York at Buffalo. He is married to the former Alexandra Anne Chapko, and is the father of one daughter, Anne Alexandra.